'Technology is at the heart of the contest between the United States and China for global supremacy. This book is notable for combining a sharp understanding of the technological question with the knowledge of its historical and political context. If the contest ends up creating a world divided into two separate spheres, our most cherished beliefs about progress and globalisation will be shattered. Is this inevitable? Nigel Inkster will guide you through this essential question.'

Bruno Macaes, formerly Portugal's Europe minister (2013–15) and author of *Belt and Road: A Chinese World Order and History Has Begun*

'Linking his knowledge of China past and present to fascinating detail of China's achievements and aspirations in advanced technology, Nigel Inkster provides a powerful and compelling narrative of the decoupling of China and the United States. You will learn much of importance from this book.'

Lord Mervyn King, former Governor of the Bank of England

'Former senior official and Mandarin speaker Nigel Inkster proves a sure-footed guide to the consequences of the collision between the US as global superpower with a re-emergent and emboldened China. His book provides a compelling account of how the Chinese now think about themselves, their rediscovery of their technological tradition, and what it is about the Chinese state-directed internet and its use to control their vast population that leaves Western liberal democracy at serious risk from "the great decoupling". Highly recommended.'

Professor Sir David Omand, GCB, former Director of GCHQ

'This is a superbly written, cogently argued, and insightful discussion of China's digital rise. It needs to be read by all concerned about the deepening rivalry between China and the USA.'

Hans van de Ven, Professor of Modern Chinese History, University of Cambridge

'Nigel Inkster has written a timely, sane and compelling account of the techno-strategic contest that will shape the world of the 2020s and beyond. Beyond its insightful analysis, *The Great Decoupling* also traces the policy contours of great-power coexistence as the alternative to a 21st century Great War.'

Professor Rory Medcalf, head of the National Security College, Australian National University, and author of *Indo-Pacific Empire*

'A lucid, pragmatic and succinct overview of where the world's second largest economy currently stands and what it might look like as it moves towards number one status. Inkster draws on his long experience, both in dealing with China and as a diplomatic practitioner, to give authoritative judgements of what this world where China plays an increasingly dominant role might look like, and what the key challenges for the outside will be.'

Kerry Brown, Professor of Chinese Studies and Director of the Lau China Institute, King's College London

THE GREAT DECOUPLING

NIGEL INKSTER

The Great Decoupling

China, America and the Struggle
for Technological Supremacy

HURST & COMPANY, LONDON

First published in the United Kingdom in 2020 by
C. Hurst & Co. (Publishers) Ltd.,
41 Great Russell Street, London, WC1B 3PL
© Nigel Inkster, 2020
All rights reserved.
Printed in Great Britain by Bell and Bain Ltd, Glasgow

Distributed in the United States, Canada and Latin
America by Oxford University Press, 198 Madison Avenue,
New York, NY 10016, United States of America.

A Cataloguing-in-Publication data record for this book is
available from the British Library.

ISBN: 9781787383838

This book is printed using paper from registered
sustainable and managed sources.

www.hurstpublishers.com

CONTENTS

Acknowledgements   ix

Introduction   1

1. China's Intellectual and Scientific Traditions   15
2. China Meets the West   33
3. China Goes Digital   51
4. China's Leadership: Version 3.0   69
5. China, the Techno-Security State   87
6. China, the Intelligence State   109
7. A World Order with Chinese Characteristics   129
8. Projecting Digital Power   151
9. Fighting and Winning Wars: The People's Liberation
   Army   173
10. China as Hi-Tech Superpower   193
11. US–China Relations: Chronicle of a Death Foretold?   217
12. The Great Decoupling   241

Notes   255
Index   275

ACKNOWLEDGMENTS

In my own defence I had never planned to write this book. I hadn't planned to write any book about China and I certainly don't consider myself to be a professional Sinologist. But I have long had a fascination with China and Chinese culture and was lucky enough to receive a solid grounding in Chinese language, literature and culture for three wonderful years at Oxford University. This coincided with a period during which China had become particularly inaccessible which didn't make my task any easier. But I had some inspiring teachers including Mark Elvin, Taotao Liu and the late Glen Dudbridge. They probably didn't realise it then, but between them they managed to light a flame that never quite went out. I owe them a huge debt of gratitude.

My first direct encounter with China was in November 1976, when I arrived for a two-week visit the day after the Gang of Four, Mao Zedong's principal henchmen during the Cultural Revolution, had been overthrown. China had at that point hit an all-time low, its institutions trashed, and its people traumatised and impoverished to a degree scarcely imaginable. But even at its nadir the enormous potential of this attractive, talented and hard-working people was manifest. And in the ensuing years I was able first to live in, then periodically visit, China and what might be termed greater China and was hence able to take snapshots of its remarkable progress towards a modern identity.

During the course of a long career in the British government I benefitted from the collaboration and wisdom of many professional colleagues, all of whom helped me to understand China better than I would have been able to on my own. This included two years in Beijing under the incomparable Percy Cradock as ambassador and colleagues who included Tony Galsworthy, Bob Pierce and William Ehrman, a remarkable concentration of talent and with whom I was privileged to be involved. I also enjoyed three years in Hong Kong prior to the handover when I was privileged to work with the then Governor Chris Patten, an immensely stimulating experience. There were many others from my government career who helped further my understanding of China. They would not thank me for mentioning their names. But they know who they are.

More recently, during my second career at the International Institute for Strategic Studies, I was able to benefit from the scholarship of a remarkable group of colleagues who, between them, greatly expanded my intellectual horizons and with whom it has invariably been a pleasure to work. I can't mention them all but I would want to single out John Chipman who has led the organisation with distinction over many years. I would also single out for special mention Gary Li, who introduced me to the Chinese Internet, Virginia Comolli, Eneken Tikk, Samantha Hoffman and Meia Nouwens. It was at IISS that I first became involved in cyber security and began to appreciate how important a role China would play in this arena. Here I benefitted from the stimulating companionship of Rafal Rohozinski, John Mallery, Alexander Klimburg and many others including all my fellow Commissioners on the Global Commission for the Stability of Cyberspace. One of the highlights of my think-tank career was organising a Track 1.5 Cyber Security Dialogue with

China on behalf of the UK Foreign Office. Through this I got to know many Chinese experts including Professors Cui Liru, Zhang Li and Tang Lan from the Chinese Institutes for Contemporary International Relations (CICIR) all of whom provided me with an important appreciation of how China viewed these issues. I was also privileged to attend the World Internet Forum in Wuzhen on several occasions. And to speak at a number of conferences at the National Defence Technical University in Changsha, organised by Professor Zhu Qichao who invariably chose challenging themes and brought together an impressive array of young Chinese scholars and practitioners to address them.

I received a lot of indirect help and encouragement from Lik Suen of SOAS who gave me many important insights into contemporary Chinese culture and language. I also benefitted from collaboration with Diana Choyleva, founder of Enodo Economics, with whom I have enjoyed some stimulating discussions and from whom I shamelessly purloined the title of this book.

Two other people deserve special mention. One is Mr John Brookes of Moorfields Hospital whose expertise in glaucoma and skill as a surgeon gave me the means to continue reading reams of Chinese Communist Party documentation, a task which the late Simon Leys likened to swallowing buckets of sawdust but which is a prerequisite for anyone wanting to understand how modern China operates.

The other is my wife Chui Fun who combines traditional Confucian wifely virtues with a modern-minded iconoclasm and has put up with me for more years than anyone would have a right to expect.

INTRODUCTION

China is a topic that invites hyperbole. Its sheer size exercises a gravitational distortion that is impossible to resist. And now that China has emerged on the international stage as a peer competitor to the USA and with claims to global leadership, this is attracting a great deal of hyperbolic commentary, not all of it informed by a detailed understanding. China has been on a long and dramatic journey during which it has gone from being one of the greatest nations on the planet to becoming—practically overnight—the object of international derision as the result of its perceived backwardness and weakness before re-emerging as a global economic and technological behemoth. This book is about China's search for a modern identity and the role that technologies have played in that. It is a story about the nature of China's interaction with a West that was until recently secure in its technology dominance but now faces a challenge from a China that has become a global technology power. And it is a story about what is almost certainly the most consequential geo-political development of the twenty-first century, namely a parting of the ways between China and the USA which forms the title of this book, *The Great Decoupling*, and the possible emergence of a bifurcated world. But to get from here to there it is necessary to look at the evolution of the

1

technologies that have brought us to where we are now and explain why they have had such a dramatic impact.

The early days of the Internet now seem like an age of pre-lapsarian innocence. The leading proponents of the Internet and the information era it ushered in imagined a world where unfettered communication and the free exchange of information would make physical borders redundant and rebalance the dynamic between citizens and the state to the benefit of the former. That vision was most dramatically articulated in John Perry Barlow's "Declaration of the Independence of Cyberspace," published in Davos in 1996. "Governments of the Industrial World, you weary giants of flesh and steel, I come from Cyberspace, the new home of Mind. On behalf of the future, I ask you of the past to leave us alone. You are not welcome among us. You have no sovereignty where we gather."[1]

The USA, which had given birth to the Internet, was predictably less dismissive of the role of the nation state but no less imbued with optimism. The Internet had come into being at a particularly heady moment in history. In 1989 the Berlin Wall had fallen. In 1992 the Soviet Union had collapsed under the weight of its internal contradictions. China had at long last begun to open up and reform its chronically underperforming economy. The threat of apocalyptic nuclear conflict had ebbed away. The values of liberal democracy and free markets appeared to have carried the day and the world seemed poised to enter an era of unparalleled freedom and prosperity.

Speaking at the 1994 World Telecommunications Development Conference in Buenos Aires, then-US vice-president Al Gore exemplified this mood of optimism in a speech extolling the virtues of the Clinton administration's Global Information Infrastructure (GII) initiative. This initiative, designed to create a global network of "information superhighways" would, in Gore's words, allow us to share information, to connect and to communicate as a global community. From these connections, we will derive robust and sustainable economic progress, strong democracies, better solutions to global and local economic challenges, improved healthcare and—ultimately—a greater sense of shared stewardship of our small planet [...] The GII will not only be a metaphor for a functioning democracy, it will in fact promote the functioning of democracy by greatly enhancing the participation of citizens in decision-making [...] I see a new Athenian Age of democracy forged in the fora the GII will create.[2]

In many ways US optimism was justified as the impact of this new disruptive technology began to make itself felt, unleashing innovation in science, technology, commerce and finance and in a growing range of applications that offered convenience for consumers. In the developed world the growth of the digital economy amounts to 10% of total economic activity and this figure continues to grow. In the developing world Information and Communications Technologies (ICTs) offer the possibility of overcoming severe deficits in physical infrastructure and access to hitherto unattainable financial, medical and other services. A combination of growing computing power and the generation of ever greater volumes of online data give new impetus to the discipline of Artificial Intelligence (AI). This enables a growing range of functions previously performed by humans to be performed faster and more reliably by machines, and makes feasible the development of autonomous vehicles, autonomous manufacturing and intelligent functionality in areas such as energy use.

But there turned out to be quite a few serpents in this Garden of Eden. Firstly, the Internet had evolved from ARPANET, a computer network linking US scientists working primarily in the defence sector. This was a network characterised by high levels of trust and driven by the desire to share information. Online security was never a priority. This approach informed the architecture of what was to become the Internet with the result that a combination of hardware and software vulnerabilities created an endemically insecure environment vulnerable to malign exploitation. Hacking emerged as a problem in the 1980s even before the Internet proper became established. Many early hackers were driven by either intellectual curiosity or a vaguely anarchist agenda. But online criminality was quick to follow as a Gadarene rush by both private sector organisations and government departments to network their operations with little regard for security provided opportunities for ever richer pickings. In an industry with annual sales of US$ 4 trillion a year based on a rush-to-market approach to pre-empt potential competition, security by design has remained an elusive concept.

The second problem was that the free exchange of information and the freedom of expression guaranteed by the First Amendment to the US Constitution and baked into an Internet that was essentially a US construct had perverse consequences. These included a tidal wave of pornography including child pornography, a phenomenon that had largely been driven underground by the 1990s as paedophiles in the pre-Internet era found it ever harder to communicate securely or share images. And as social media took hold, an equally large tide of vituperation, conspiracy theorising and misleading or downright mendacious content such as anti-vaccination propaganda emerged. These latter phenomena were greatly exacerbated by a business model characterised by the US scholar Shoshana Zuboff as "surveillance capitalism." This model, which emerged following the 2000 "dot-com boom," sought to monetise online behaviour by selling "behavioural surplus"—the infinite variety of online activity providing insights into the behaviour and proclivities of users but which service providers could not use to improve their own products—to enable targeted advertising aimed at selling goods and services that the purveyors could be confident customers would be predisposed to buy.[3] In effect, Silicon Valley's "surveillance capitalists" sought to make manifest the workings of Adam Smith's hidden hand to ensure the market always operated in their favour. This business model incentivised the providers of services that were nominally provided free of charge to keep users online as long as possible; they quickly learnt that content which generated outrage or fear was by far the most effective way of getting and keeping users' attention.

Thirdly, by no means all states subscribed to the vision of the Internet promoted by the US government. For authoritarian regimes, the prospect of untrammelled and uncurated information flows was anything but attractive. In 1999 Russia, the successor state to a Soviet Union that had only made limited strides in computing during the Cold War, demanded concerted international action to curb the threat of "information weapons"— the use by states of information to undermine the official narratives of other states and to subvert or undermine the will of their populations. China, which had adopted the Internet in 1994 believing it to be essential for delivering economic reform but concerned about the challenge it posed to the Chinese Communist Party narrative, promoted the concept of Internet sovereignty by which it meant the internationally acknowledged right of states to determine what information transited their "information space." In pursuit of this objective China set up the Golden Shield project, commonly referred to as the Great Firewall of China, to monitor and censor externally-generated content. In the year 2000, then-US president Bill Clinton famously remarked that trying to control the Internet was like "nailing jello to the wall."[4] A decade later Chinese walls were covered in jello.

In short, the nation state set out to demonstrate that reports of its demise as envisaged by cyber-utopians such as Barlow had been greatly exaggerated. And in doing so states did not confine themselves to erecting digital defences to hide behind. Russia, with a long tradition of information warfare and "active measures," led the way in demonstrating how states could use the cyber domain to project power and pursue national advantage with a 2007 distributed denial of service (DDoS) attack on Estonia—essentially an exercise in overwhelming a target network with an unmanageable flood of messaging. Estonia's offence had been to relocate a Soviet World War II memorial from the centre of the capital, Tallinn, to a less prominent location. This was followed in 2008 by cyberattacks against Georgia that accompanied a Russian military incursion to "liberate" the breakaway region of Abkhazia. Though it had largely failed to match the USA in computing and was ideologically resistant to the idea of computer networking, the Soviet Union had an education system that was strong in what are now called STEM subjects (science, technology, engineering and mathematics). In the economic chaos that followed the collapse of the Soviet Union many young Russians quickly mastered information technologies and, in the absence of opportunities for licit employment, formed cyber criminal groups tolerated by the state as long as they focused their criminal exploits outside of Russia—and put their skills at the disposal of the Russian state.

This kind of activity was not just confined to Russia—though much of the malicious code (malware) that enabled it originated there—by some estimates, as much as 80%. Before the advent of the Internet, covert communications interception at a global level had been the province of a few major intelligence powers: the USA and its "Five-Eyes" intelligence partners, and the Soviet Union. Such activity required geographical proximity to target communications and expensive infrastructure such as satellites and supercomputers to capture, process and store the resulting intelligence product. By contrast, in the information era any state with a national telecommunications agency could in principle establish a signals intelligence agency with global reach. And while the major players in this arena continued to be the established intelligence powers with China now added to their ranks, this led to the emergence of some on the face of it unlikely second-tier cyber actors such as Iran and North Korea. These states used the Internet to launch asymmetric attacks against the financial and energy production systems of more powerful adversaries such as the United States and Saudi Arabia and, in the case of North Korea, to engage in state-sponsored cyber criminality to compensate for the losses caused by international sanctions.

The cyber domain has become a zone of contestation between states with significantly different agendas, interests, ideologies and capabilities. Much of this contestation is taking place in the form of cyberattacks either for the purposes of espionage or sabotage—the difference between the two amounts to no more than intent and a few additional lines of code—in what has been termed "operations short of war" or "grey zone operations." Espionage is itself a grey zone in terms of international law, being neither explicitly permitted nor prohibited. But espionage is not considered to be something that justifies an armed response. Sabotage on the other hand potentially does provide such a justification if it results in human casualties or physical destruction. To date nobody has demonstrably died as a direct result of activities undertaken in the cyber domain (the word "direct" is important here since international law does not take account of second-order effects such as deaths arising from interruptions in the provision of utilities). But the day when that happens may not be far off.

Because the disruptive effect of cyber activities is growing. Such activity is troubling both because of its intrinsic impact but also because it acts as a catalyst to wider global instability by encouraging states to engage in behaviour that seems to be low cost and low risk but may turn out not to be and which is inherently destabilising. The danger is that such behaviour may lead states inadvertently to overstep the mark and invite retaliation, leading to an escalatory cycle, a particular concern if the states in question are nuclear-armed. The United States has for example reserved the right to respond to a cyberattack by whatever means it judges appropriate, including the use of armed force. Thus far the USA has responded to the multiple cyberattacks it has experienced with restraint—not least because, as the world's most network-dependent country, it is uniquely vulnerable to digital disruption—but a new strategy of persistent engagement on the part of US Cyber Command may be raising the ante in an arena where to date there have been few internationally agreed ground rules.

Russia tends to be regarded as a major disruptor in the cyber domain precisely because it has engaged in so many high-profile cyber exploits including in support of military action. But while Russia is a disruptive actor which seeks to use force or the threat of it to justify its status as a major power—it is by no stretch of the imagination a superpower—and defines its security as a function of others' insecurity, it is far from being the most consequential actor within the cyber domain. Russia has thus far failed to commercialise its considerable cyber capabilities with the result that its economy remains heavily dependent on energy revenues. Nobody outside Russia would ever buy a Russian computer, operating system or network and there are no Russian equivalents of the major US technology giants such as Google, Amazon or Facebook. Russia is still struggling to secure its own information space in the way that China has succeeded in doing for over a decade. And while Russian diplomats have been at the forefront of moves to shape the international landscape in the areas of cyber governance and cyber security in ways that favour the interests of authoritarian states at the expense of liberal democracies, the Russian state has limited ability to create facts on the ground in support of their objectives other than through the malign actions outlined above.

The contrast with China could not be more stark. For millennia, China was the world's largest economy and a global technology power accounting for roughly half the world's inventions. But having missed the Industrial Revolution China made itself vulnerable to Western incursions that reduced it to a semi-colonial state. Since the mid-nineteenth century, therefore, China has been engaged in a struggle to define for itself a modern identity consistent with its historical sense of self. For much of the twentieth century its economy consistently underperformed and it was only in the 1980s that this began to change as the country began to experiment with a range of different economic strategies. Since then China has undergone a dramatic transformation to become the world's largest economy in absolute terms; mastery of ICTs and other advanced technologies has been key to this growth.

China now has the world's largest online user community and digital economy. Its main service providers Baidu, Alibaba and Tencent are on the way to becoming international household names on a par with Facebook, Amazon, Google and Microsoft. Its national telecommunications champion Huawei is providing network services to a growing range of countries including the UK and twelve states in the USA. On the back of this initial success China now has declared ambitions to become a world leader and standard setter in fifth-generation telecommunications (5G) which if successful would effectively give it the keys to the future of global communications with all the economic and geo-political advantages that would confer. It is in the process of developing and promoting an entire alternative architecture for the Internet that would be state-directed: in effect an Internet with border controls and health checks, with a view to eliminating much of the creative anarchy of the current model.

These ambitions have however set China on what looks increasingly like a collision course with the USA, which since the end of the Cold War has occupied the position of the world's only superpower. Despite having undergone extensive liberalisation since the early days of the People's Republic when the state controlled all aspects of people's lives and allowed them no access to the outside world, China remains a Marxist–Leninist state with an ideology and values at odds with those of the USA and other liberal democracies. It also has a carefully nurtured sense of grievance in relation to the humiliations it suffered at the hands of the West during the nineteenth and early twentieth centuries together with a strong sense of its political and cultural superiority. China's ambitions include building modern military forces that, in the words of President Xi Jinping, can fight and win wars. It is already a space power of consequence.

In pursuit of its long-term ambitions China has done what every emerging power throughout history has done, namely acquire the technologies of the rivals it aspires to supplant by whatever means. And China itself has been the victim of such actions in former times such as when British adventurers in the nineteenth century smuggled tea cuttings to India, or when the Byzantine empire, tired of seeing so much of its wealth being spent on Chinese silks, covertly acquired the secrets of sericulture. Over the past decade China has become associated with pervasive state-sponsored cyber espionage for both economic and, increasingly, political purposes. It has begun to use its growing economic and technological clout to shape the global telecommunications environment through engagement in international negotiations on cyber governance and cyber security. This has formed part of a wider Chinese agenda to reshape the instruments of a global governance agenda set up by the USA and its allies in the aftermath of World War II and which China argues is no longer fit for purpose. This Chinese agenda holds considerable appeal to developing states in the Global South— many of whom did not exist in their present form when the post-World War II order was established and believe it does not adequately represent their interests.

Technology is now at the heart of a contest between the United States and China for global pre-eminence which is likely to shape the global geo-political landscape for at least the first half of the twenty-first century. The USA feels threatened by China's emergence as a peer competitor in areas it had become accustomed to dominating and is now engaged in a broad push-back as manifested in the trade dispute that broke out in 2018. This dispute is about much more than just technology: it stretches to questions such as whether the early promise of the Internet as a unifier of mankind can still be realised or whether we will see the emergence of a technologically and economically bifurcated world—the "Great Decoupling" that this book takes as its title; whether the USA can remain the dominant naval power in the Western Pacific; whether it can retain its role as security guarantor of last resort for liberal democracies; whether China's ambitions ultimately extend to replacing the USA as global hegemon; whether the current international order will remain rules-based; and, ultimately, whether liberal democracy can remain a viable mode of government in the twenty-first century. Meanwhile other states are increasingly facing the unenviable prospect of navigating a course between the two technology giants as they progressively decouple whilst maintaining their freedom of manoeuvre and remaining true to their values. It is impossible to determine how this contest will play out though some observers such as Graham Allison have argued that competition between an incumbent and a rising power—the Thucydides Trap—have more often than not resulted in conflict. But it is safe to say that no part of the world will remain immune from what happens.

The purpose of this book is to examine what China is doing and why. It seeks to examine the historical and cultural factors that have informed China's political culture and its engagement with the outside world. It looks at how China's traditions of science and engineering have shaped both China and the wider world and traces China's decline from global technology leader to global laggard as the Age of Exploration and the Industrial Revolution reshaped the global geo-political landscape. It uncovers contemporary China's struggle to achieve a modern identity consonant with its historical self-image and the critical role that science and technology have played and are playing in this struggle. And it looks at the political, diplomatic and military implications of this struggle and how the responses of other major powers to China's re-emergence as a great power might shape this dynamic.

It now seems inevitable that the United States and China are facing a parting of the ways. What that might look like is still unclear but the main elements look likely to be a significant economic decoupling with the USA replicating or repatriating a significant quantity of its China-based manufacturing; a sustained effort by the USA to deny China access to advanced technologies such as microchips and prevent China from dominating global technology standards; similar efforts by the USA and other Western countries to constrain China's ability to acquire Western companies or otherwise exploit the freedoms afforded by open societies to obtain unfair advantage; and a reduction in academic exchanges. China meanwhile is unlikely to step back from the contest and will seek to impose economic penalties on the USA whilst redoubling efforts to promote the renminbi as an alternative reserve currency.

It is still far too early to tell whether this decoupling will bring the two parties into direct conflict though the potential for miscalculation and escalation cannot fail to increase. But a broader question that merits consideration is whether the world might in due course see a kind of role reversal in which China's determination to achieve global pre-eminence and the readiness of its people to accommodate technological change put it in pole position with a more conservative West lagging behind. An alternative vision of the future is one in which everyone loses from decoupling as global trade diminishes and technologies stall as a lack of international exchange and collaboration translates into a reduction in innovation. None of these futures is yet clear. But understanding the factors that may shape them has never mattered more.

1

CHINA'S INTELLECTUAL
AND SCIENTIFIC TRADITIONS

Pretty much everybody knows that the Chinese invented paper, printing, the magnetic compass and gunpowder—though Francis Bacon, who described these four inventions as marking the modern world out from antiquity, apparently did not. These discoveries, important as they were, represent only a minuscule proportion of the scientific inventions and engineering feats produced by China in the pre-industrial era. As with other civilisations, such inventions began with the agrarian revolution and the urbanisation and organised warfare that accompanied it. China at that point meant essentially north China. The Chinese Communist Party, in its references to the "great rejuvenation of the Chinese race" (*minzu*) announced in 2013 by Xi Jinping, speaks of China as a unitary civilisation spanning five millennia.[1] That is in the broadest sense true if one takes into account early cultures that evolved in the late Neolithic era and whose existence probably informed some of China's earliest mythology. It rather oversimplifies a complex history that involved extensive colonial expansion that continued into the nineteenth century CE, significant interchange with and borrowings from foreign cultures, expansions and contractions of China's borders, periods of dynastic collapse and civil war and periods when China was ruled by alien dynasties including the Mongols and Manchu. But it is the case that the concept of China as a unitary state enjoying at least regional if not global pre-eminence is deeply rooted in the collective Chinese psyche and explains much about how China sees itself in the world today.

For much of recorded history China, however conceived, was one the wealthiest and most technologically advanced civilisations on earth, accounting at its apogee for some 30% of global economic output. China was at the forefront of an agrarian revolution that transformed Chinese society and which was, over time, responsible for a remodelling of the landscape that was more all-encompassing than was true for any other civilisation. For over two millennia Chinese farmers had been using technologies that included efficient iron ploughshares and hoes, row planting and multi-tube seed drills that maximised agricultural outputs, techniques not adopted in Europe until the eighteenth century. For most of recorded history Western agriculture was entirely dependent on rainfall. In China by contrast agriculture was from an early stage enabled by complex systems of irrigation and hydraulic management that involved redirecting and damming rivers and constructing canals for grain transportation. Techniques such as iron smelting using blast furnace techniques dated back to the fourth century BCE. China was the first country to produce cast iron and from there quickly moved to produce wrought iron and steel that enabled the construction of suspension bridges and bore-holes to extract brine and natural gas, some going down over 4,000 feet. Lacquer had been in production since the thirteenth century BCE and porcelain was in common use by the third century CE.[2]

Urbanisation came early to China although until the modern era it is unlikely that more than 10% of China's population ever lived in cities. The earliest Chinese cities that emerged during the Shang dynasty, as is true for other cultures in the Middle East and the Americas, had predominantly administrative and ritual purposes and were protected by high walls. From the fourth to the second centuries BCE the growing sophistication of China's economy, which involved the development of private commerce, expanded trading routes and a money economy, resulted in a corresponding sophistication in China's urbanisation. Cities were still surrounded by walls with much of the population living in suburban areas but contained amenities such as markets and centres of entertainment, some very lavish. The population of the first Han capital Chang'an (206 BCE–9 CE) is estimated at 250,000 and the second Han capital in Luoyang (25 CE–220 CE) roughly double that. When Chang'an became the capital of the Tang dynasty (seventh to tenth centuries CE) the population rose to 1 million. Cities were complemented by a growing number of market towns that played a prominent role in both commerce and administration.[3]

As in other cultures, warfare provided a stimulus to technical innovation. As cavalry warfare replaced the chariot-borne conflict of early dynasties—a technique likely acquired from Indo-European cultures—China developed the iron stirrup as a means of greatly enhancing the horse-borne warrior's stability in the saddle. Another early game-changing invention was a crossbow with great range and penetration power, the production and possession of which was a state monopoly. From about the fourth century BCE Chinese armies were using various forms of poisoned gas, blown towards enemy forces using bellows. It is widely but incorrectly believed that the use of gunpowder, invented in China around the tenth century CE, was largely restricted to the production of fireworks. In reality gunpowder was used in a range of bombs, grenades and mines and also rockets as a form of artillery. Actual artillery in the form of cannons and mortars arrived in China during the Mongol occupation in the thirteenth century CE. Chinese military forces were for much of recorded history far larger than those of Europe, numbering in the tens and even hundreds of thousands.

China also witnessed early advances in the fields of astronomy, cartography and mathematics. By the second century BCE Chinese mathematicians had developed a decimal system and decimal fractions, the concepts of zero and negative numbers, higher numerical equations and algebraic expressions of geometric shapes. Seismology was another area in which China made early advances with the Astronomer Royal Chang Heng developing a seismograph in the late Han dynasty (second century CE). Early medical advances, contained in texts such as the second century BCE's *Yellow Emperor's Classic of Internal Medicine* (*Huangdi Neijing*), included an understanding of blood circulation, circadian rhythms, diabetes, and diseases caused by dietary deficiencies (it is ironic that in the twenty-first century diabetes has become one of China's most serious and least well-regulated public health issues). Immunology began around the tenth century CE with vaccination against smallpox. Vaccination did not become widespread until the sixteenth century CE—but still significantly earlier than in Europe.

China is thought of, and has tended to think of itself as a predominantly land-based power. And throughout Chinese history the main national security threats have come in the form of land-based attacks on China's northern and western borders by a succession of nomadic peoples including the Xiongnu, Tibetans, Khitan, Jurchen, Mongols and Manchu. But some of China's most significant technical advances took place in the maritime domain. These included the rudder, batten sails that were far easier to control than sheets of canvas, fore-and-aft rigs and lug sails enabling vessels to tack into the wind, leeboards to control drift while tacking, watertight compartments—and of course the magnetic compass to enable accurate navigation. Maritime trade between China and the Arabian Peninsula dates back to the Han dynasty and Chinese communities were spread throughout South-east Asian countries which had a long tradition of sending tributary missions to China.

Traditional Chinese navigation reached its apogee in the early fifteenth century CE with the voyages of the "Thrice Precious" eunuch admiral Zheng He who between 1405 and 1433 led a series of naval expeditions to South-east Asia, India, Arabia, the Horn of Africa and East Africa—and, it has been claimed, the Americas, though there is no convincing physical evidence to substantiate this. According to an inscription carved into a stone pillar that was discovered in Liujia harbour in Fujian in the 1930s, the purpose of these voyages was to demonstrate China's power and collect tribute from barbarian states. As part of that objective Zheng He took military action to secure the sea lanes of communication. In the words of the inscription: "When we reached foreign countries, we captured barbarian kings who were disrespectful and resisted Chinese civilisation. We exterminated bandit soldiers who looted and plundered recklessly. Because of this the sea lanes became clear and peaceful and foreign peoples could pursue their occupations in safety."[4] Scholars have disputed whether the "treasure ships" in which Zheng He sailed were actually as large as the official Ming dynasty records suggest—44 zhang long by 18 zhang wide or 447 by 183 feet. But there can be little doubt that they were markedly superior in almost every respect to the European vessels that were to launch the Age of Exploration just a few decades later. Foreign visitors to China both before and during the Zheng He period, including Marco Polo, Ibn Battuta and Niccolò de' Conti talk of seeing large multi-masted multi-deck vessels capable of carrying between 500 and 1,000 passengers.

It is ironic that China's projection of maritime power came to a halt just as the West's Age of Exploration was about to begin.

The reasons for this are still not fully understood. One obvious driver was a resurgent Mongol threat that coincided with a decision to relocate the Ming capital from Nanjing to Beijing in 1402 CE. The need to launch what became annual military expeditions to contain this threat used up much of the funding that would have been needed to sustain the maritime expeditions. Other relevant factors may have included opposition at the Ming court to what was perceived as excessive influence by the eunuch faction, a common feature of Chinese dynastic politics, and a Confucian desire by the Yongle and Xuande emperors to show respect for their ancestor and founder of the Ming dynasty Hongwu, who had imposed a ban on maritime activity and established a system of coastal defences in order to deal with the problem of Japanese piracy. (This ban led to an explosion of smuggling, in particular of silver, which became the de facto state currency and was always in short supply.) Whatever the reasons, the consequence was that the Chinese state cut itself off from the wider world just at the time when the Age of Exploration was about to begin fundamentally reshaping the globe.

The extent of China's contribution to global science and technology in the pre-industrial era was largely unappreciated in the West and its significance might never have been properly recognised but for the efforts of a single Western scholar. Dr. Joseph Needham, a young microbiologist at the University of Cambridge in the inter-war years, became aware of China when some Chinese scientists arrived at his college. One of them, a young female microbiologist, Lu Gwei-djen, became his long-term lover and muse. With Lu's help, Needham began a serious study of the Chinese language and when the Sino–Japanese war broke out in 1937 he became a forceful opponent of the British government's apathetic response to Japanese atrocities that included the Rape of Nanjing, Lu's home city. In 1942 Needham found himself in the wartime Chinese capital of Chongqing with a remit from the

UK government to help rebuild a Chinese tertiary education system that had been systematically targeted for destruction by the Japanese. Needham travelled throughout those areas of China controlled by the Nationalist government and in the course of his travels began collecting materials that revealed to him exactly how advanced China's pre-industrial society had been. The outcome of this was a history of Chinese science and technology running to twenty-four volumes that took up the rest of his life (in fact the final six volumes are still being completed by his collaborators following his death). It is possible to criticise Needham for presenting an exaggerated picture of Chinese technological achievements and overinterpreting what is sometimes slender evidence. His work was however a valuable corrective to the picture of China as irremediably backward that had emerged during the nineteenth and early twentieth centuries.

Needham was fascinated by what China had been able to achieve in the pre-modern era and puzzled over "why between the 1st century BC and the fifteenth century AD Chinese civilisation was much more efficient than occidental in applying natural human knowledge to practical human needs."[5] But an equal if not more pressing concern for Needham was the question of "why modern science had not developed in Chinese civilization (or Indian) but only in Europe." Indeed, from the fifteenth century onwards, China had seemed to go into reverse and lose sight of some of the knowledge it had pioneered. As the Jesuit missionary Matteo Ricci, who worked in China from 1583 until his death in 1610 put it, "The Chinese have no concept of the rules of logic...though at one point they were quite proficient in arithmetic and geometry, in the study and teaching of these branches of learning they laboured with more or less confusion."[6] The situation was worse even than Ricci appreciated. One of the ways in which the Jesuits sought to win the trust of their Chinese hosts was with the provision of clocks and prisms, both of which were highly sought after. Ricci was however unaware, as were his hosts, of the fact that during the Song and Yuan dynasties (tenth to fourteenth centuries CE) China had experienced what Joseph Needham called a "blaze of horological exuberance" which inter alia had produced such things as striking clocks, by Ricci's time no longer in evidence.[7]

This was not of course the first time human knowledge had stalled then gone into reverse. In the fifth century BCE the Greek philosopher Democritus of Abdera produced works on a wide range of topics including mathematics, cosmology, geography, medicine, physics, natural sciences, art, language and ethics. Only the titles of these works survive in quotations in other works. But Democritus' greatest contribution to scientific thinking was to conceive of the cosmos as a boundless space in which atoms, the smallest indivisible particles of matter, ceaselessly flow, collide and combine in endless variations to make up all the things we conceive of as reality in a process that has no final purpose. This, as we now know broadly correct, depiction of the cosmos was not of course truly scientific in that it was supported neither by mathematics nor empirical experimentation. But had this model become the accepted norm, the evolution of human society might have taken a rather different course. As it was, the finalistic view—the idea that everything in nature had to have a purpose—propagated by Aristotle and Plato prevailed and was eventually co-opted into a Christian model of an anthropocentric cosmos in ways which discouraged scientific inquiry.[8] Something similar happened in the late mediaeval Islamic world, which went from being both a guardian of classical learning and a significant innovator in areas such as mathematics to an intellectual backwater characterised by religious obscurantism.

In both these examples a combination of organised religion and political expediency seems to have acted as a brake on scientific progress. Bertolt Brecht's play *Leben des Galilei—The Life of Galileo*—contains a scene in which Galileo is brought before the Inquisition and required to repudiate the heliocentric model of the universe that he had observed through the latest scientific invention, the telescope. Galileo invites one of his inquisitors to use his own eyes and look through the telescope. The inquisitor replies that he is accustomed to reading the works of the Divine Aristotle and in so doing does indeed use his own eyes. In reality the Catholic Church knew perfectly well that the heliocentric model was correct but to admit this was seen as tantamount to calling into question the Church's entire raison d'être and hold on society.

China's approach to astronomy and cosmology was equally controlling but for different reasons. As the astrophysicist and dissident Fang Lizhi (1936–2012) pointed out, early Chinese writings on cosmology appeared to include an understanding of the concept of the earth as being in a constant state of motion and of the unity of space and time as embodied in the term for the cosmos "*yuzhou*," where "*yu*" refers to physical dimensions and "*zhou*" to time.[9] The Chinese state was not ideologically invested in any particular cosmological model and was happy to draw on the best available expertise, whether provided by Islamic scholars under the Yuan (Mongol) dynasty or Jesuits such as Matteo Ricci under the late Ming and early Qing. (Ironically the latter, though better versed in mathematics than their Chinese counterparts, knew less about astronomy than pre-Christian-era Chinese astronomers, believing as they did in Tycho Brahe's geo-heliocentric model of the universe which amounted to a compromise between the geo-centric and heliocentric models.) But the prevailing ethos of a Confucian system of thought and governance was that the cosmos was a moral construct with mankind's behaviour reflecting the wider functioning of the natural world. As Fang Lizhi observed, this conviction was fundamentally at odds with the idea of a universe operating in accordance with scientific laws that were morally neutral.

In order to demonstrate that they enjoyed the mandate of Heaven, China's rulers needed to be able to produce the most accurate possible calendars to map the seasons and conduct the appropriate rituals to demonstrate that their conduct was aligned with the natural order, and to reliably predict exceptional events such as eclipses for similar reasons. In a system of thought that held mankind to be capable of influencing nature for good or ill, the weather was seen as a reflection of the moral standing of the ruler. The consequence of this was that the study of astrology and cosmology was tightly controlled by the state under the aegis of the Board of Rites and this branch of knowledge effectively became a state secret. Independent study was discouraged for fear that it might lead to discoveries that might be interpreted as presaging the demise of the dynasty or calling its legitimacy into question. And in any case, there was apparently nothing useful to be gained from subjecting a moral order to scientific inquiry.

China's own philosophical traditions began to emerge at roughly the same time as those of classical Athens. This period is known in Chinese history as the Warring States (475– 221 BCE), describing an era in which the Zhou dynasty which had ruled what was then China had broken apart into warring feudal fiefdoms contending for hegemony. The resultant social and economic dislocation demanded solutions. The first thinker to try to provide these was Kong Zhongni, better known to the world as Confucius. Confucius, as was true for most Chinese philosophers, was unconcerned with issues of ontology. Man was what he was and the challenge was to find effective ways to regulate the world in which he found himself. Confucius was equally unconcerned with issues of teleology beyond a general aspiration to see society return to the ideals of the early Zhou state. Nor was he overly preoccupied with religion, declaiming to his disciples, "not yet able to serve the living, how can you serve the spirits?" (*wei neng shi ren, yan neng shi gui*).[10] And while he emphasised the importance of Heaven (*tian*) in human affairs, he appeared to think of it in terms of an organising principle for the universe rather than the physical dwelling of an anthropomorphic deity.

Confucianism looked back to what was perceived to have been the golden age of a Zhou dynasty whose rulers enjoyed the Mandate of Heaven—*tian ming*—and ruled through the exercise of virtuous conduct and the practice of elaborate rites. It emphasised the importance of social hierarchy and respect for and imitation of the ancestors, a combination which gave rise to a social order that demanded a high level of conformity and discouraged heterodox thinking. Confucianism saw man as basically good, and susceptible to improvement through learning, in contrast to the Legalist philosophy that also emerged during the Warring States period. This latter saw mankind as irremediably bad and governable only by keeping people in a state of ignorance and subject to savage punishments for breaking laws the specifics of which they were not allowed to know. Though Legalism never gained traction as a state ideology other than briefly during the reign of the first—and only—Qin emperor, its impact on China's approach to law was and has remained palpable.

The other mainstream philosophy that emerged in this period, Daoism, did address questions of ontology, projecting a view of the cosmos very similar to that of Democritus and depicted in poetic terms in the Daoist classics *Daodejing* and *Zhuangzi* in ways reminiscent of the Epicurean philosopher Lucretius in *De Rerum Natura*. The cosmos was governed by the Way (*dao*), the organising principle of a natural order in a constant state of flux. Man was simply one of the many manifestations of this order which cannot be fully comprehended (the opening words of the *Daodejing* are "the Way that can be spoken of is not the true Way"—*dao ke dao fei zhen dao*). Daoism evolved a cosmological view of the universe based on the concepts of *yin* (negative) and *yang* (positive); the five phases—*wu xing*—of the universe, namely wood, fire, earth, metal and water; *qi*, meaning either vital force or energy-matter; and *li*, the organising principle of matter. This model, which remained the basis of Chinese thinking on these issues until the modern era, was set out most systematically in the Han dynasty text *Huainanzi*.

Daoism remained a significant influence in Chinese thought but moved away from its philosophical origins to become enmeshed with traditional Chinese popular religion—which educated elites viewed with disdain but were obliged to tolerate—becoming coterminous with the concept of withdrawal from the material world. Indeed it has been argued that Daoism may have emerged in response to concern about the development of a material civilisation that was even then starting to have significant ecological implications for China. One enduring aspect of Daoist thought was a focus on the practice of alchemy with the principal aim of achieving immortality. However, where alchemy in the West was a prelude to genuine scientific investigation (Isaac Newton was a practising alchemist), Daoist alchemy failed to undergo a similar evolution.

The final Warring States thinker to merit a mention is Mozi, a name romanised as Micius. Mozi's thinking was in many ways similar to that of Confucius, but rather than subscribing to the Confucian idea of a hierarchy of relationships with some afforded preferential treatment Mozi advocated for universal love—*jian ai*. Mohist doctrines achieved traction with a number of rulers but eventually gave way to Confucianism. Where Mozi is of particular interest and relevance is in his interest in natural science, with a particular focus on optics and mechanics. Joseph Needham drew particular attention to Mozi's observation that "The cessation of motion is due to an opposing force... If there is no opposing force...the motion will never stop," an observation which Needham described as a precursor to Newton's First Law of Motion. In recognition of Mozi's scientific thinking the quantum satellite launched by the Chinese Academy of Sciences in 2016 to perform experiments in quantum key distribution was named Micius.

Confucius achieved little traction during his lifetime but his basic philosophy was developed more systematically by subsequent thinkers, notably Mengzi—Mencius. In the Han dynasty (206 BCE–220 CE) Confucianism became the state ideology and in due course the Confucian Canon, referred to in Chinese as the *Four Books and Five Classics—sishu wujing*—formed the basis for open competitive civil service examinations that were the principal route to high office. Candidates studying for these examinations, who were entitled to state stipends as long as they kept achieving a pass grade in the lowest tier of examinations, had to become sufficiently familiar with the Confucian Canon to be able to recognise and contextualise abstruse classical quotations and use them as a basis to write rigidly structured "eight-legged essays." Some candidates were able to work with this unpromising format to produce insightful and innovative thinking on contemporary issues of governance and political economy and the best products of the system were undoubtedly able and accomplished, pursuing interests in areas such as mathematics, natural sciences and hydraulics. Provincial and local officials perforce found themselves engaged in many of the practicalities of public administration such as flood management, but none of this aggregated up into a focused effort of scientific inquiry and the prevailing intellectual ethos was one of disdain for anything that smacked of practicality.

As Confucianism became more entrenched as the state ideology, so the intellectual came to be seen as someone whose role was to put his intellect to the service of the state and not to question the premises on which the state was based. This is not to say that Confucian scholars were incapable of independent thought or the ability to exercise a challenge function within the framework of Confucian doctrine, which was in fact subject to extensive and controversial re-examination at various points by scholars such as Zhu Xi and Wang Yangming. But the idea that the main task of the intellectual should be to provide a rationale for state behaviour rather than to pursue the truth wherever it might lead sank deep roots. Meanwhile, though there were many scholars motivated by a genuine love of knowledge, study of the Confucian classics came to be seen first and foremost as a route to obtaining civil service positions and the wealth and status that they conferred. This mindset was pilloried by the eighteenth-century author Wu Jingzi in his satirical novel *Rulin Waishi—The Scholars*. Wu, himself the scion of a formerly wealthy family fallen on hard times, depicted a system characterised by dogma, intellectual rigidity, pretentiousness and moral turpitude, with some aspirants to high office driven literally mad by the pressures of studying for the official examinations.

None of these factors are in themselves convincing explanations as to why China failed to capitalise on its early technological and scientific achievements and to develop what Joseph Needham described as the methodology of modern science: "the application of mathematical hypotheses to Nature, the full understanding and use of experimental method, the distinction between primary and secondary qualities, the geometrization of space, and the acceptance of a mechanical model of reality."[11] Western education systems, typically much more elitist than a Chinese system that was in principle and practice open to all comers, focused on a knowledge of Latin, Greek, theology and ancient history at the expense of science and mathematics well into the nineteenth century. And Western elites cultivated a disdain for commerce and practicality that was every bit as lofty as that of their Chinese counterparts. What possibly gave the West the edge that ultimately led to the Industrial Revolution was a combination of intellectual liberalisation in the form of the

Reformation and a system of property rights that, in contrast to China's centralised imperial system of pervasive state control, incentivised and rewarded innovation by individuals. An additional consideration was that Britain, the initiator of the Industrial Revolution, had benefitted from a windfall of capital in the form of bullion stolen from the Spanish empire that created an enabling financial environment for innovation.

Two factors undoubtedly did make a difference, as Mark Elvin points out in *The Retreat of the Elephants*, an ecological history of China. The first was the absence in China of the concept of a "fact," which Elvin defines as:

> a publicly recorded and accessible statement about an observable aspect of the world, set in the context of a systematic evaluation of the evidence that yields an approximate possibility of its being true and subject to a continuing public scrutiny and re-evaluation... It depended upon the publication of reports through books and journals and the exchange of ideas through learned societies, universities, museums and other such institutions.[12]

Though China had books and some state academic institutions, most of this complex was missing. Elvin observes that the other ingredient largely missing in China was the idea of a scientific programme, a plan of collective systematic work of the kind designed in the late 1660s by Claude Perrault for France's Academie Royale des Sciences. Individual Chinese scholars often made perceptive observations about the natural order but none of this was ever aggregated up into a systematic and commonly accepted body of thinking. In essence, the Chinese system was not, as was the case with the pre-Reformation Christian church, institutionally opposed to scientific innovation. But neither was it sufficiently pro-science to achieve a critical mass of innovation.

For all that China seemed to stall scientifically and technologically just as the West had begun to focus on experimentation and mathematisation to establish the basis of a genuinely scientific method, China remained a wealthy and exceptionally well-governed state up to the point when, starting in 1839, the West forced it to open its markets to the outside world. Matteo Ricci, though critical of many aspects of Chinese culture, was generally positive about a state that, in contrast to a fragmented Europe plagued by dynastic and religious conflict, seemed large, unified and well-ordered.[13] To the extent that Western thinkers knew anything at all about China, they tended to be impressed by a state whose governance appeared to be in the hands of an educated rationalist corps of professional administrators and by an economy that was inter alia able to supply a vibrant demand for Chinese artefacts that collectively became known as chinoiserie and for that most prized of commodities, tea. Indeed, for many Enlightenment thinkers, notably the Austrian philosopher and mathematician Gottfried Leibniz, the Chinese model was worthy of emulation. But the eighteenth century, normally seen as the apogee of Chinese power and prosperity, was in fact a period of significant economic and social stress that traditional pre-industrial era capacities struggled to address.

China has experienced two major periods of economic revolution in the past. Mark Elvin describes the first revolution in the following terms:

> The mediaeval economic revolution...is associated with a shift in the center of China's economic gravity from the Northeast to the East. It was distinguished by more productive farming, especially of rice, by better transport, especially on water, by extensive commercialisation, and by the widespread use of money and written contracts. The populations of its cities at times reached more than a million. It used woodblock printing, and hence enjoyed increased literacy. It pioneered the first elements of mass production...and mechanisation as in the water-powered spinning of hemp yarn.[14]

This first revolution ushered in a long period of economic prosperity with only limited environmental impact. The second significant economic revolution came in the form of foodstuffs introduced by the Portuguese from the New World, including maize, potatoes, cassava and groundnuts, which could be planted in what had hitherto been marginal upland areas. The introduction of these new crops led to a population explosion in the eighteenth century and to significant environmental degradation as forest cover was stripped from hillsides to permit cultivation, resulting in soil erosion and increased flooding. As one scholar has described it,

> The population of China roughly doubled during the eighteenth century, from around 150 million in 1700 to around 313 million in 1794. The precondition for this expansion was China's capacity to develop new ways—and new places—for people to make a living. These ways and places included New World crops such as maize and sweet potatoes which made the hills yield a living to immigrants... All over China people were moving upward as well as outward: forested hills became flourishing sweet potato and maize farms until their soil eroded and became barely cultivable.[15]

In the wealthy provinces of China's eastern seaboard, agriculture became intensive to the point where it required more or less round-the-clock activity to sustain diminishing outputs. Households not primarily engaged in agriculture were involved in specialised production of artefacts such as porcelain, cotton and silk, often operating on such narrow margins that the incapacitation of a single family member could result in destitution. In defiance of Confucian doctrine that emphasised the importance of settled populations, many men were forced to abandon their homes and take to the road as itinerant beggars or monks. The stresses and psychoses engendered by such pressures are vividly brought to life in Philip Kuhn's book *Soulstealers*, which analyses an outbreak of collective hysteria that elicited the attention of the emperor and led to a nationwide witch-hunt for individuals supposedly guilty of taking men's souls by clipping their

31

queues (Chinese men had for generations worn their hair long until the Manchu imposed their own style consisting of the front half of the skull shaven with the hair at the back plaited into a long queue).

Pre-industrial Qing dynasty China was caught in a Malthusian trap. Indeed, the Qianlong emperor (1711–99 CE) reached the same conclusion as Thomas Malthus about the nexus between population growth and the availability of arable land that was at the heart of the pre-industrial economy some years ahead of Malthus himself. The country was effectively running ever harder to remain in the same place with the additional complication that, in a polity that actively discouraged immigration for fear that diaspora populations could develop subversive habits, China was unable to take advantage of the "overspill capacity" afforded by the New World to ease its population pressure. When finally significant numbers of Chinese workers were able to move to the USA in the 1840s to take part in the California gold rush and then to build the Pacific railroad, this was followed by the 1882 China Exclusion Act prohibiting further Chinese immigration.

China's Malthusian dilemma was summed up in 1793 by a Chinese scholar-administrator when describing the impact of an influx of Chinese settlers into the remote and inhospitable province of Guizhou, where the amount of farmland had:

> only doubled or, at the most, increased three to five times, while the population has grown ten to twenty times. Thus farmland and houses are always in short supply, while there is always a surplus of households and population... Question: Do Heaven-and-earth have a way of dealing with this situation? Answer: Heaven-and-earth's way of making adjustments lies in flood, drought and plagues.[16]

Of these, there was never any shortage.

2

CHINA MEETS THE WEST

When China came into contact with a technologically more advanced culture in the form of the British Empire the consequences were, as they invariably are in such circumstances, profound. British commercial interest in China had been growing since the early days of the British East India Company. The Qing emperors however took a very restrictive view of international commerce and confined Western traders to a small enclave in the city of Guangzhou from where they could trade for prescribed periods with designated Chinese counterparts. British traders had to pay for their purchases of Chinese tea, porcelain and silks with silver bullion but increasingly sought to substitute this with payments in opium from the East India Company's opium monopoly in Bengal with the result that opium consumption and addiction became a significant social and public health problem during the late Qing period. British merchants wanted better terms; in 1793 the British crown despatched the Irish peer Lord Macartney to China to negotiate direct, permanent access to Chinese ports and the establishment of an embassy in Beijing.

Macartney's interview with the Qianlong emperor was an object lesson in how two cultures can fail totally to connect.

Macartney, an urbane and thoughtful man, had sought to impress his interlocutor with gifts that demonstrated Britain's technological superiority, including clocks, telescopes and modern firearms. The equally urbane though by then tired and elderly Qianlong emperor, steeped in a mindset that held all foreigners to be barbarians whose only possible status could be as vassals of the Middle Kingdom, was unimpressed and rejected all Britain's requests. As he put it in a missive to King George III, "Our Celestial Empire possesses all things in prolific abundance and lacks no product within its borders. There is therefore no need to import the manufactures of outside barbarians in exchange for our own produce."[1] The idea of a permanent embassy in Beijing was completely at variance with the preferred Chinese model of tributary missions despatched to China for limited periods with the formal aim of acknowledging China's suzerainty over them—though in practice such missions were seen by those taking part more as lucrative trading opportunities.

A counterfactual history of Sino–British relations would interpret the Macartney mission as a missed opportunity to avert what happened next, a forcible opening up of China by the Western powers beginning with the First and Second Opium Wars—respectively 1839–42 and 1856–60—that led to the undermining of China's traditional political and economic structures and engendered a national crisis of confidence. In reality, the two sides were too far apart in mutual understanding for this ever to have been a realistic outcome. As in so many previous cases, the disruptive impact of a meeting of two cultures, one materially and technologically more advanced than the other, was brutal in its intensity. Between the late 1840s and 1945 a total of forty-one foreign concessions were set up in Chinese cities, mostly in the coastal area but also as far inland as Yunnan and Sichuan. These concessions enjoyed immunity from Chinese law—extraterritoriality—and were administered and policed by the foreign powers to whom they had been forcibly ceded. China's share of global GDP declined by roughly half as cheap foreign manufactures replaced traditional handicrafts and expenditure on opium leached silver from China's coffers. But the damage inflicted on the Qing dynasty's authority and prestige both domestically and internationally, though impossible to quantify, was arguably far greater. In the West, China was pilloried as the sick man of Asia, a term that was—briefly—to resurface in the context of the 2020 COVID-19 pandemic. The cost to China of missing the Industrial Revolution was to be a lengthy period of turmoil and a search for a modern identity that is at the heart of modern China's policies and strategies. This period of Chinese history has since become known as the Century of National Humiliation—*bai nian guo chi*—and has become a key driver in the Chinese Communist Party's efforts to promote China's image as a proud, sovereign, technologically advanced civilisation.

For China's Confucian elite the disruptive impact of the West was hard to comprehend or make sense of. On the one hand, the Western "barbarians" clearly possessed technological capabilities such as steamships, modern artillery and firearms and manufacturing capabilities far in excess of anything China could match. At the same time, Westerners appeared in Chinese eyes to be uncouth, uneducated and lacking in the most basic concepts of ethics and morality. How was it possible that such people had succeeded in humiliating a millennial civilisation governed in accordance with the time-honoured moral precepts of Confucianism and based on ritual that reflected the laws of heaven? China was not the only civilisation to confront this puzzle. The thirteenth-century Islamic scholar Ibn Taymiyyah, the go-to source of religious authority for modern jihadist groups, faced the same challenge when trying to make sense of the Mongol invasions of Syria, a state supposedly ordered in accordance with the word of God. His conclusion, to which as a life-long critic of the then-prevailing theological orthodoxy he was already predisposed, was that the state had not been sufficiently Islamic and needed to become more devoutly observant. A similar conclusion was reached by India's Deobandists following the suppression of the Indian Mutiny.

Some Chinese thinkers reached a similar conclusion, namely that the answer for China was to double down on Chinese tradition. Many Confucian scholars expressed their preference by opting to withdraw from public life. Others, among them the Chinese statesman Zhang Zhidong, one of the most outstanding graduates in his generation of Confucian scholars, argued for a hybrid approach known as the Self-Strengthening Movement, the aim of which he summed up in the phrase "Chinese learning for substance, Western learning for utility"— "*zhongxue wei ti, xixue wei yong.*" Meanwhile a young cohort of iconoclastic Chinese intellectuals advocated a wholesale repudiation of a Confucian culture which they saw as a barrier to essential modernisation.

During the second half of the nineteenth century, tradition and modernism struggled to coexist. The Qing dynasty, itself an alien dynasty still living in fear of manifestations of loyalty to the preceding Ming dynasty, sought to continue business as usual while keeping foreign interests as much as possible at arm's length. But the last Qing emperors had to contend with a succession of internal rebellions the most significant of which was the Taiping, itself an intriguing example of how the old and the new came together. The founder of what became the Heavenly Kingdom of Great Peace, Hong Xiuquan, was a failed candidate for the Imperial examinations. Exhausted and suffering a psychotic episode as a result of his failure, Hong while on his way home came across a pamphlet published by Christian missionaries. Having read it, Hong came to the realisation that he was the younger brother of Jesus Christ and raised a rebellion that combined anti-Qing sentiment with a kind of messianic Christian utopianism. The Taiping rebellion ravaged the Yangzi valley region for fourteen years, resulting in somewhere between twenty and thirty million deaths and widespread population displacement.[2]

The extent of China's failure to come to terms with modernity was dramatically illustrated by a humiliating naval defeat at the hands of the erstwhile client state of Japan in 1895. Efforts by the young Guangxu emperor to introduce reforms on the back of this defeat fell victim to a conservative coup led by his mother the Empress Dowager Cixi. But the failure of the anti-foreigner Boxer rebellion, which led to reprisals that included the burning of the Summer Palace and resulted in further concessions to foreign interests, was the beginning of the end. By 1906 the Imperial examinations were abolished and Chinese students encouraged to go overseas to obtain a modern education. Many of these students made common cause with a growing number of revolutionary groups often formed by exiles, who were eventually united by Dr. Sun Yat-sen into the Tongmenghui. Other revolutionary elements included anti-Manchu criminal groups such as the Green Gang and Hongmen, extreme Japanese nationalist groups who had aspirations to take over Manchuria, and elements within the New Army, a modern military force formed in the wake of China's defeat at the hands of Japan. Following a succession of rebellions throughout China, the last of which, the Xinhai Revolution, is seen as marking the end of the imperial system of government, the last Qing emperor, the six-year-old Puyi, abdicated in February 1912 in favour of a supposedly republican government headed by military strongman Yuan Shikai. A millennial system of government that all things considered had served China well had come to an end. But China's struggle to find a modern identity had only just begun.

As is so often the case, the Xinhai Revolution failed to live up to expectations. After a brief period during which the Empire was restored, China succumbed to a period of warlordism and instability which lasted into the 1930s. Some warlords were relatively progressive, as was the case with Yan Xishan, who ran a modernising administration in the province of Shanxi. Another was Feng Yuxiang, known as the Christian General, based in what is now Hebei province. A convert to Methodism, Feng had some eccentric habits such as baptising his troops with a fire-hose, but in contrast to many other warlords he maintained effective public order and banned prostitution, gambling and the sale of opium in the region he controlled. The majority of warlords were brutal and reactionary, treating the populations under their control as cash cows, actively promoting the opium trade but otherwise showing no concern for economic or social development. The result of their rule was widespread destitution, violence and population displacement.

The period following the collapse of the Qing gave rise to a ferment of intellectual activity as China's intellectuals sought desperately to find answers to the country's problems. One of the earliest Western ideologies to reach China was Social Darwinism—based on a misreading of Darwin's theory of evolution as implying the survival of the fittest rather than, as Darwin in fact argued, the survival of the most adaptable—as expounded in Thomas Huxley's *Evolution and Ethics* and Herbert Spencer's *The Study of Sociology*. Yan Fu, a graduate of China's naval school system established under the Self-Strengthening Movement, who translated Huxley's book into Chinese with the title *On Evolution*—*tianyan lun*—observed that this Western knowledge represented China's last best chance to survive in a rapacious and competitive world. As he put it, "The west is truly wealthy and powerful, therefore in today's policies we can have no other teacher than the west."[3] Other ideas eagerly explored included classic Western liberalism and socialism of the British variety as expounded by Henry George, an advocate of state expropriation of surplus value. The common factor was that these theories were studied less because of an intrinsic interest in the subject matter than because they were seen as the key to enabling China to become strong and prosperous again. This instrumentality in the acquisition of Western learning was to remain a consistent feature of China's struggle for modernity. So too was a focus that was rooted in concepts of national and racial identity.

With the desire to acquire Western knowledge came a repudiation of China's classical intellectual traditions. Hu Shi, one of the founder members of the New Culture Movement, wrote a satirical essay entitled "Chabuduo Xiansheng" ("Mr. Near-enough") in which he pilloried a supposed Chinese cultural disdain for precision as a major barrier to the adoption of modern science and technology. The New Culture Movement promoted the use of vernacular literature in preference to a classical Chinese, a highly compressed literary language incomprehensible when spoken; an end to Confucian patriarchal culture and the promotion of female emancipation (Henrik Ibsen's *A Doll's House*, in which the heroine Nora walks away from an oppressive marriage, became an iconic text for China's modernisers); democratic and egalitarian values; a repudiation of Chinese exceptionalism; a reinterpretation of China's classical texts; and a focus on the future rather than the past. Mr. Science and Mr. Democracy—*sai xiansheng* and *de xiansheng*—were portrayed as the two answers to China's problems.

The perceived backwardness of traditional Chinese culture was perhaps most dramatically portrayed in the short stories of Zhou Shuren, better known by his pen-name Lu Xun. Zhou, who came from a scholar-gentry family in Shaoxing, a town justly famed for the quality of its rice wine, was one of many young Chinese who in the late nineteenth and early twentieth centuries went to study in Japan, a country that in contrast to China had successfully embraced modernity whilst maintaining its own distinctive identity. While in Japan he studied medicine but subsequently opted to become a writer on the grounds that this would enable him to exercise greater impact as an advocate of change. One of his best-known stories, "Kong Yiji," portrays a failed candidate for the traditional examinations system who is physically and mentally broken by years of profitless churning through the Confucian classics. A ragged, stick-thin figure mumbling to himself in snatches of classical Chinese incomprehensible to his fellow townsmen, Kong Yiji scrapes a living through begging and petty theft before dying an ignominious and unmourned death. Another story, "Medicine," tells of a parent who seeks to cure his son's tuberculosis by feeding him a bread roll soaked in the blood of an executed criminal as recommended in a traditional Chinese pharmacopoeia. In a final ironic twist, the criminal in question turns out to be a revolutionary involved in an abortive effort to overthrow the Qing dynasty.

The New Culture Movement helped to infuse a new generation of Chinese students with a sense of political awareness and engagement that came to a head in 1919 during the Versailles Treaty negotiations that followed the end of World War I. In 1917 China had entered World War I on the Allied side, sending 140,000 Chinese workers to France to provide logistic support for the British Army. At the Versailles Treaty negotiations that followed the Allied victory China had sought recompense for its contribution to the war effort with demands that included the abolition of privileges for foreign powers in China such as extraterritoriality and the return of former German concessions in Shandong province which had been taken over by Japan at the start of the war. These demands were ignored and the Allies awarded the German concessions to Japan. This sparked student protests in Beijing that quickly morphed into strikes by students, workers and patriotic merchants across China's major cities. Faced with the prospect of severe economic disruption, the Chinese government refused to sign the Treaty of Versailles. On the face of it, this was a Pyrrhic victory in that the Chinese government failed to achieve any of its objectives. But the May Fourth Movement, as the protests became known, marked a turning point in China's evolution, a moment in which China's modernising forces coalesced and were able to exercise real effect. It was also a moment that invited a fundamental rethink of Western ideas and values in the light of the carnage of the Western Front, which had taken its share of Chinese lives, and the hypocrisy and double standards manifested by Western nations following the conflict. In the words of Yan Fu, "three hundred years of evolutionary progress have come down to nothing but four words: selfishness, slaughter, shamelessness and corruption."[4]

The fact that much of the activism of the May Fourth Movement took place in the cities was indicative of the role that urbanisation was to play in energising China's search for modernity. One city in particular, Shanghai, stands out as the place in which modern ideas and modern technologies came together to play a catalytic role in modern China's evolution. One of the first "treaty ports," Shanghai quickly evolved into one of largest and most modern cities on the planet—it for example had air-conditioned office buildings before Chicago—and exemplified the best and worst aspects of modernity. The city was divided into three main areas: the International Settlement, an amalgamation of what had previously been the British and US concessions; the French Concession; and the Chinese Municipality. The former two were self-governing with their own laws, police and military forces and powers of taxation. Shanghai was Asia's most important shipping and financial centre, with major Western banks and trading houses occupying prime positions on the Bund, which was modelled on the Liverpool waterfront, then one of the busiest ports on the planet. In the words of the 1933 *Handbook for China*, "The smoke stacks of many factories form a business-like pattern against the blue background of the sky, just as they do in London, or New York... On the shores there are huge ship-building plants, warehouses, cotton mills, silk filatures, oil tanks, docks and a busy line of railway [sic]."[5] Many of these industrial facilities were foreign-owned but there were also successful Chinese entrepreneurs some of whom were able to compete successfully with Western-owned businesses for contracts in areas such as ship-building.

As in other major cities of the era, the opulent lifestyles of the elite, which earned Shanghai the title of "Paris of the East" depended on the labour of an impoverished proletariat that flocked to the city from all over China and lived and worked in generally appalling conditions. Westerners by and large enjoyed a privileged status—though that did not extend to the numerous White Russian refugees who fled to Shanghai after the October Revolution and who often worked in menial roles including prostitution. But Shanghai also gave rise to a substantial Chinese middle class who eagerly embraced modernity and whose lifestyles were portrayed by Chinese writers such as Mao Dun. In the first chapter of his best-known book *Ziye* (*Midnight*), Mao Dun describes such a family meeting their elderly parent off a boat from the countryside and whisking him in a luxury limousine through the thronged neon-lit streets of Shanghai, an assault on his senses so shocking that the elderly gentleman suffers a stroke. This passage, arguably one of the most vivid ever written in modern Chinese, exemplifies the chasm that then existed between China's modernising cities and a vast countryside where little had changed in centuries.

Shanghai was also a vital crucible for developing and disseminating ideas. China's first modern newspaper, the weekly

English-language *North China Herald* began publishing in 1850 with a daily edition, the *North China Daily News* following in 1864. *Shen Bao*, the first modern Chinese-language newspaper, in fact owned by a British entrepreneur, began publishing in 1872 (prior to that, the nearest thing China had to newspapers were illegal reprints of information contained in the *Capital Gazette*, a newsletter of official court actions and edicts intended to be read only by officials but often leaked to local printers by corrupt clerical officers). Major Chinese-language publishing enterprises included the Chung Hwa Book Company and the Commercial Press. A film industry which was to reach its heyday in the 1930s and '40s began in 1909. Meanwhile Shanghai was home to two of China's most prestigious universities, St Johns and Fudan, which trained generations of Chinese students in modern subjects. Shanghai's foreign settlements had since the late Qing served as a "safe space" in which reformers and revolutionaries could enjoy sanctuary from the reach of the Chinese state.

The idea that was ultimately to exercise the greatest traction over modern China took concrete form in Shanghai in 1921. The disenchantment of many Chinese intellectuals with Western liberal ideas following the Treaty of Versailles was matched by an interest in Marxism following the October Revolution in Tsarist Russia and the establishment of the Soviet Union. Initial interest in Marxism centred on Peking University where Professors Li Dazhao and Chen Duxiu established a Peking Socialist Youth Corps in 1920 with help from Grigori Voitinsky, a representative of the Comintern, an organisation set up by the new Soviet administration to foment the spread of communism internationally. Mao Zedong, who was to go on to head the Chinese Communist Party (CCP), was then working in the library of Peking University under Li Dazhao. The CCP's beginnings were modest. Its first ever congress consisted of thirteen delegates initially meeting in Shanghai's French Concession before decamping to a boat on South Lake in Zhejiang province to avoid arrest by the French authorities.

Comintern support for the newly-formed organisation was vital for the CCP's survival. But at that point Stalin, who had taken over the leadership of the Soviet Union, was more interested in the potential offered by veteran revolutionary Sun Yatsen's Guangzhou-based Guomindang (KMT) party. Though Guangzhou at that point exemplified many of the worst aspects of warlord rule, it was a major port with many international links and strong labour unions that amounted to an industrial proletariat, in Marxist orthodoxy the essential prerequisite for revolution. Another Comintern agent, Mikhail Markevich Gruzenberg alias Borodin, was dispatched to Guangzhou to liaise with Sun while Stalin decreed that the CCP should form a united front with the KMT. The KMT, though still espousing Sun Yat-sen's People's Three Principles—*sanmin zhuyi*—of nationalism, democracy and people's livelihood, was restructured on communist lines. The Comintern also helped establish the Whampoa Military Academy to train officers for what was to become the Northern Expedition of 1926–27, the aim of which was to overthrow the warlords and re-establish a unified Chinese government.

The CCP–KMT alliance proved to be of short duration. Sun Yat-sen's successor General Chiang Kai-shek, whose own ideology is perhaps best described as neo-Confucian, disliked and distrusted the communists and when his army reached Shanghai in 1927, turned on them, massacring over 5,000 CCP members. Attacks on the CCP were orchestrated in Beijing and Changsha by warlord allies of Chiang. From that point on the KMT— which became known as the Nationalists—and the CCP were effectively at war. The CCP was driven from the cities and came close to being destroyed when KMT forces, by then under

German military tutelage, drove them from their rural bases and forced them onto what subsequently became glorified as the Long March, a year-long trek from Jiangxi in south-eastern China to remote areas of Shaanxi in the north-west. A temporary truce between the two organisations following the outbreak of war with Japan in 1937 changed little, and following Japan's defeat a civil war led in 1949 to Chiang Kai-shek's withdrawal to Taiwan and the establishment of the People's Republic.

While the CCP was located in its base area in Yanan, in the loess hills of Shaanxi, it carefully cultivated an image of egalitarianism, simplicity of lifestyle, rectitude and commitment to serving the people that sought to draw a contrast with a KMT regime that had acquired a reputation for extreme venality and oppression. The CCP's reputation attracted many idealistic young Chinese adherents from Nationalist-controlled areas, and Edgar Snow's book *Red Star Over China*, based on a—carefully stage-managed—visit in 1936 to the Yanan base area, burnished the CCP's image internationally. Resistance against the Japanese has become an important part of the CCP's creation myth but in practice they allowed the KMT to do the bulk of the fighting and focused instead on rebuilding their ranks. In 1940 Zhou Enlai, reported in a secret missive to Stalin that as of August 1939 China had suffered one million military casualties of which just 31,000 were from the Communist Eighth Route Army and New Fourth Army.[6] Mao Zedong used this period of relative peace to reinforce his paramount role in the Party leadership and to build a uniquely Chinese form of communism at odds with Soviet orthodoxy. Mao was a uniquely complex character whose own theoretical understanding of Marxism was limited and who sought intellectual inspiration more in Chinese classical and mediaeval texts such as the *Romance of Three Kingdoms* (*sanguo yanyi*). While in Yanan Mao sought to impose his model of Marxism–Leninism and Mao Zedong Thought through a series of rectification campaigns which drew on the now familiar tech-niques of meticulous analysis of a subject's past, self-criticism and coercion to achieve thought-reform. Much worse was to follow.

The CCP inherited a country ravaged by war, the majority of its population living close to subsistence in the countryside. But China did still have some significant industrial capacity, particu-larly in its three north-eastern provinces. During the late Qing significant parts of this region, formerly the Manchu heartland, had been acquired as concessions by Tsarist Russia and had undergone a process of industrialisation and railway building. In 1931, following the Mukden incident, Imperial Japan had occu-pied the entire region, installing the last emperor of the Qing, Henry Puyi, as the ruler of what was termed Manchukuo. As in Korea and Taiwan, the Japanese proved to be highly efficient colonisers in that they quickly developed an extensive state-of-the-art industrial base and transport network run largely by the Japanese military. By the late 1930s Manchukuo was producing more steel than Japan. Post-liberation, the northeast became the heartland of China's heavy industry.

China was also able to benefit from significant Soviet assis-tance in the post-liberation era. In the words of a now-declassi-fied CIA report,

> Communist China achieved remarkable progress during 1950–57 in its programme of rapid industrialization and militarization, pri-marily because of the economic, military, technical, and the indus-trial support received from the USSR... Sino–Soviet relations have been greatly strengthened as a result of the willingness of the USSR to supply equipment and technical services valued at about $3.3 billion for the construction of major industrial enterprises in Communist China.[7]

China also received over $1 billion in loans and played host to some 10,000 Soviet experts. And the Soviet Union under-took to assist China with a project to build its own nuclear bomb, a commitment on which Nikita Khrushchev subsequently reneged. The love affair did not last. Relations began to fray following Khrushchev's secret 1956 denunciation of Stalin who, despite their differences, had served as Mao's role model, and were further strained by what Mao perceived as Soviet "capitulationism" towards the USA. In 1960, in response to growing Chinese antagonism, the Soviet Union withdrew all its advisors, leaving China with a large number of half-finished industrial projects to complete themselves. Although the Soviet Union did not ask China to do so, Mao Zedong decided to repay all outstanding debts within a compressed timescale under the slogan "not a penny less"—*lian yifen dou bushao*—at huge cost to the Chinese people, with agricultural produce originally destined for domestic consumption sold overseas to raise the necessary funds.[8] Meanwhile China was subject to a wide-ranging US technology embargo which severely impeded its efforts at modernisation.

But it turned out that nothing the USA could do to constrain China's development could compare with what the CCP under Mao Zedong was able to do to itself. Mao was obsessed above all else with class struggle. In the aftermath of liberation, he initiated mass campaigns in the countryside to punish and humiliate "landlords" and redistribute their land and possessions. These campaigns, which trampled over an age-old system of land rights based on complex contracts enforced by local courts, operated on a quota system which required CCP cadres to identify and eliminate at least one landlord per thousand population irrespective of an actual situation in which landlords were often either thin on the ground or non-existent. Throughout the nation, people were given class labels of "good," "middle" or "bad" depending on their perceived loyalty to the communist revolution; these categories would define individuals and determine their and their descendants' life chances for decades to come.[9]

The net effect of all this activity on both agricultural and industrial production was disastrous. And worse was to follow. Following the 1956 Hundred Flowers Campaign in which people were invited to express their views on the Party's performance and did so in coruscating terms, Mao launched an anti-Rightist Campaign which disproportionately targeted China's intellectual elite, including many patriotic Chinese intellectuals who had returned from overseas to make a contribution to the new China. Many were subject to ferocious criticism sessions, dismissed from their jobs, imprisoned and even killed. This was followed by an even greater self-inflicted catastrophe in the shape of the Great Leap Forward. As Frank Dikotter describes it in his book *Mao's Great Famine*,

> Between 1958 and 1962, China descended into hell. Mao Zedong, Chairman of the Chinese Communist Party, threw his country into a frenzy with the Great Leap Forward, an attempt to catch up with and overtake Britain in less than fifteen years. By unleashing China's greatest asset, a labour force that was counted in the hundreds of millions, Mao thought that he could catapult his country past his competitors. Instead of following the Soviet model of development which leant heavily towards industry alone, China would "walk on two legs": the peasant masses were mobilised to transform both agriculture and industry at the same time, converting a backward economy into a modern communist society of plenty for all.[10]

The concept underpinning the Great Leap Forward of catching up with and then surpassing the West—*ganchao*—has remained a key leitmotif of China's modernising aspirations. The result of this experiment was to send the Chinese economy into freefall and to bring about a famine in which Dikotter, extrapolating from a detailed examination of provincial archives, estimates as having caused the unnecessary deaths of forty-five million people either through starvation, malnutrition-related illness or murder. China's peasants were stripped of their property and possessions and herded into giant agricultural communes. Efforts to overtake the UK in steel production included the construction of small backyard smelters into which peasants had to put existing metal utensils in order to make steel of such poor quality as to be unusable. Faced with the imperative to maximise outputs, factory managers produced mountains of goods that were totally unserviceable at a huge cost in terms of misallocated resources.

After 1962 the madness came to a brief end as more gradualist policies were reintroduced and China's economy began to register annual growth of between 5 and 6%. But in 1966, in an effort to recover his diminished standing and restore his legacy, Mao launched the Great Proletarian Cultural Revolution, an effort to overthrow all that was left of the old China and to rebuild society from scratch. To implement his strategy Mao unleashed the anarchic potential of China's youth, urging them to "storm the citadel." Classes in schools and universities came to a halt as students attacked and humiliated their teachers and, in some cases, denounced their own parents for bourgeois practices such as possessing Western books, artwork and music. Mao's political opponents were denounced, imprisoned and killed. Hordes of Red Guards, clutching copies of Mao's little red book, swarmed across the country destroying much of China's cultural heritage. Intellectuals—the "stinking ninth" social category—were sent to work at menial tasks in rural communes to learn from the peasants and workers. One such intellectual was the astrophysicist and subsequent dissident Fang Lizhi who had previously suffered dismissal during earlier campaigns. When, as the initial chaos of the Cultural Revolution began to die down, Fang was able to resume work in 1972, his paper on the Big Bang Theory attracted much official opprobrium for challenging Marxist–Leninist orthodoxy of a steady-state, infinite cosmos.[11]

Educated youths—*zhiqing*—were also rusticated in large numbers, an experience graphically and humorously depicted in the film *Balzac and the Little Chinese Seamstress*. One such educated youth was Xi Jinping whose father Xi Zhongxun had been subjected to house arrest some years before the Cultural Revolution began, and who spent some years in the remote village of Liangjiahe in Shaanxi. Redness—ideological commitment—was to be prized over expertise. An indication of how far this anti-intellectual bias pertained is that Albert Einstein was the target of denunciation campaigns on the grounds that his Theory of Relativity challenged Marxist–Leninist orthodoxy that space and time were infinite. The only intellectuals to be spared Mao's wrath were those working on China's indigenous nuclear weapons project. When China finally came blinking into the daylight in late 1976, its people traumatised, its institutions trashed and public trust destroyed, it accounted for just over 1% of total global economic activity.

Yet the Mao years had not been an unmitigated disaster. Much progress had been made in developing China's human capital with literacy levels rising from just 20% in 1949 to nearly 70% in 1976 and life expectancy up from 30 to 66 years thanks to a nationwide system of basic healthcare. A national network of power grids had been built and industrial capital expanded. This left China well-placed to take advantage of the opportunities that were to come. And as anyone who has visited Mao's ancestral home at Shaoshan in Hunan province can attest, for many Chinese Mao remains an inspirational figure who despite his shortcomings did much to restore China's self-esteem and standing in the world.

3

CHINA GOES DIGITAL

Following the death of Mao Zedong in 1976 and the arrest shortly thereafter of his most fanatical followers, the so-called Gang of Four, veteran CCP leader Deng Xiaoping, denounced during the Cultural Revolution as the "number one capitalist roader," eventually emerged as China's de facto leader. In November 1978, at the Third Plenum of the Eleventh Party Congress, Deng announced the Four Modernisations, of agriculture, industry, national defence and science and technology—concepts that had first been articulated in the early 1960s after the Great Leap Forward. The process began with agriculture where the communes were broken up and land leased to farmers who signed production contracts with the state that permitted them to sell any produce surplus to quota on the free market. Individual initiative was encouraged and the Chinese people were supposedly told that "to get rich is glorious." Except they never were: what Deng Xiaoping actually said was that a section of the population should be allowed to become wealthy ahead of the rest—*rang yibufen ren xian fuqilai*.[1] Unbridled capitalism was never part of the plan.

At that point the state controlled all aspects of an individual's life. Existence revolved around the work unit—*danwei*—which effectively provided a cradle to grave system of welfare, albeit at the most basic level. The Four Modernisations aimed to change this expectation of the "iron rice bowl." Industrial modernisation began with the establishment of Special Economic Zones in which foreign entrepreneurs including from Hong Kong and the Chinese diaspora were encouraged to set up production lines to make goods for export, taking advantage of abundant cheap labour and tax holidays. Municipalities were empowered to set up township and village enterprises while the managers of state-owned enterprises were given greater latitude to run their operations with capital provided through a reformed banking system. Deng made clear that military modernisation, the necessity of which had been amply demonstrated by the People's Liberation Army's (PLA) poor performance during a 1979 incursion into Vietnam, would be contingent on progress in the other modernisations. The PLA were however given a consolation prize in the form of the right to earn revenue from arms sales and other forms of business such as the sale of military land for real estate development. Over the next decades many PLA commanders were to spend more time in the boardroom than on the battlefield.

Chinese science and technology were in a parlous state due to years of isolation from the global mainstream, the systematic disparagement of intellectuals under Mao and the collapse of the formal education system during the Cultural Revolution. A case in point was the semiconductor industry, which in the early 1960s had been more or less on a par with the USA thanks to the return to China of patriotic Chinese scientists who had studied in the United States.[2] The sector had however fallen far behind as these scientists were caught up in the vortex of political movements and forced to spend years performing menial tasks in remote rural areas. But China's universities and other key academic institutions such as the Chinese Academy of Science were quickly reconstituted, growing numbers of young Chinese despatched overseas to study in Western universities and links with Western academic institutions established. The mid-to-late 1980s in China were characterised by rapid liberalisation and openness to new ideas as the leadership sought answers to the challenges of modernisation from a wide and eclectic range of sources.

One of those sources was Alvin Toffler, an American futurologist whose two best-known books, *Future Shock* and *The Third Wave*, were remarkably prescient in predicting the transformational implications for human society of a then still-incipient information revolution: "linked to banks, stores, government offices, to neighbours' homes and to the workplace...computers are destined to reshape not only business, from production to retailing, but the very nature of work and, indeed, even the structure of the family."[3] Toffler's books were translated into Chinese and read by the leadership, including, reportedly, Deng Xiaoping himself. On a visit to Beijing Toffler was received by then-Premier Zhao Ziyang. At that point China not only had virtually no computers—even basic telephone lines were in short supply. But China's leadership was quick to spot the potential of Information and Communications Technologies (ICTs) for economic development. As early as 1983 Jiang Zemin, then Minister for Electronics Industry but later to become CCP Secretary-General and head of state observed that ICTs were "the strategic high ground in international competition...the discrepancy between China's level and the world's advanced level is so great that we must do our utmost to catch up."[4] China's leadership decided to prioritise the country's electronics industry, setting a growth target double that of the wider economy. China's Academy of Sciences invested in a start-up company that eventually became Lenovo, the world's largest manufacturer of personal computers. The China Academic Network was set up to link China's universities to each other and eventually to comparable institutions overseas. In 1994 the Chinese government took the first steps to connect China to the Internet and China's citizens began to go online two years later.

Meanwhile a series of events had shaken China's leadership, collectively posing what seemed like an existential threat to their hold on power. China's move towards a more market-driven economy during the 1980s had been accompanied by pressures for greater political liberalisation. An iconic video series, *River Elegy* (*He Shang*) crystallised the nature of the debate, drawing unfavourable comparisons between what it presented as the backwardness of China's closed, land-based, authoritarian culture with the outward-looking, maritime, liberal culture of the West. The Party leadership was split between conservatives and reformers but in 1987 CCP Secretary-General Hu Yaobang, who appeared not just to be a pragmatist but also a liberaliser, was forced from office. Hu's death in 1989 led to large numbers of students gathering in Tiananmen Square in the centre of Beijing demanding a series of reforms including greater government transparency and accountability, freedom of expression and an end to elite corruption.

As protests broke out around China involving not just students but also workers, Deng Xiaoping personally canvassed the commanders of China's military regions, claiming that failure to suppress the student movement would mean the end of the CCP. PLA troops entered Tiananmen Square on 4 June and fired on the protesters, leading to significant deaths and injuries, a sad irony for a Party which had co-opted the 1919 May Fourth student protests as part of its own creation myth. Five months later came the fall of the Berlin Wall, the reunification of Germany and the collapse of communism in Eastern Europe. In 1991 the Soviet Union finally collapsed under the weight of its own contraditions. The last of these events gave rise to major existential angst and much heart-searching within the CCP, whose leaders concluded that a major—though not the sole—cause of the Soviet collapse had been the inability of the Soviet economy to satisfy the material needs of its population. The CCP embarked on a desperate race to shore up its claim to legitimacy by delivering rapid improvements in the material circumstances of China's population. And what was referred to as the process of "informatisation" became an integral part of that race.

The term "informatisation," in Chinese "*xinxihua*"—信息化—is one of a number used in Chinese to equate to the English term "cyber," an exact translation of which does not exist. Chinese writers have coined the neologism "*saibo*"—赛博—when translating Western texts dealing with concepts such as cyber warfare but it is otherwise little used. The term "cyberspace" is commonly translated as "*wangluo kongjian*"—网络空间—meaning literally "network space," and "cyber security" as "*wangluo anquan*"—网络安全. When in 2014 President Xi Jinping talked of the need for China to transition from a large cyber power to a strong cyber power, he used the terms "*wangluo daguo*"—网络大国—and "*wangluo qiangguo*"—网络强国. The most usual translation of "Internet" is "*hulianwang*"—互联网—literally "mutual connection net." Almost all other neologisms coined to create a new cyber vocabulary have more or less exact equivalence with their English counterparts.

One of the things that makes China's digital ecosystem so distinctive is language. Though it is commonplace to talk about the Chinese language, there are in fact many dialects, often mutually unintelligible. Until Xi Jinping, who speaks standard Putonghua (literally: common speech), a form of the language based on the speech of an educated Beijing native, all China's leaders since Liberation have spoken with pronounced regional accents that even native Chinese speakers sometimes struggled to comprehend. What unites these different spoken forms is a common written language but one of such complexity that some of China's early reformers saw it as a major barrier to modernisation. Mao Zedong, who took great pride in his own distinctive "grass" style of calligraphy, told US journalist Edgar Snow that China might have to abandon the written language in favour of a romanised script as the price of pursuing modernisation[5]—though in the end he opted for a simplified form of the script long in use among the scholar class and which greatly facilitated the CCP's promotion of literacy. But even with simplified characters, learning written Chinese is a formidable undertaking requiring many hours of boring repetitive study. The largest Chinese dictionary, compiled during the reign of the Qing emperor Kangxi, contains some 70,000 characters, each made up of one of 214 radicals plus a more or less phonetic component. Of course many of the neologisms spawned by modernisation are not to be found in this dictionary, but such neologisms, many initially coined by Japanese scholars, are created by conferring new meanings on traditional characters either separately or in combination rather as Western scientists drew on Latin and Greek: thus for example the word for "electricity" is *dian*, literally "lightning," computer is *diannao*, literally "electric brain." Basic literacy in Chinese requires a knowledge of some 3,000 characters while someone with tertiary education would be expected to know around 10–12,000. A Chinese typewriter is in effect a small offset printing press that requires specialised training to operate. The idea of a portable Chinese typewriter was a contradiction in terms.

Computerisation has given the written Chinese language a whole new lease of life as technologies such as Optical Character Recognition have facilitated the computerisation of Chinese text. Early online inputting involved systems such as wubi that created characters in the same way they are written but virtually all inputting systems are now based on the standard form of romanisation, *Hanyu pinyin*. These offer the inputter a range of possible character options ranked in order of probability with predictive texting having developed to the point where the first option is almost always the right one. This compromise has proven remarkably effective though ironically it has led to a decline in people's ability to write characters, a phenomenon known as *tibi wangzi*—lifting the pen and forgetting the character—as the requisite "muscle memory" atrophies through growing disuse. Written Chinese is an efficient means of conveying information: generally speaking, an English translation of Chinese is normally a third longer than the original. So, far from being a barrier to the adoption of modern ICT, the Chinese language has, through a characteristic exercise in Chinese pragmatism, turned into a significant enabler.

In contrast to the United States which, after privatising ARPANET and unbundling its sclerotic telecommunications networks, had more or less left the development of the Internet to the private sector, China's approach to digitalisation from the outset took the form of a series of state-driven top-down initiatives integrated into the state planning system. The establishment of nationwide communications links and Internet connectivity necessarily involved collaboration with US corporations who had most of the technology China needed, and the US Chamber of Commerce in Beijing played an important catalytic role in forging these connections. Windows software, mostly pirated, became the "industry standard" for government offices and private users alike and as late as 2014 China faced the prospect of digital meltdown when Microsoft withdrew support for Windows XP, before concluding that they would have to make an exception for the Chinese market. Meanwhile US corporations such as Apple and Cisco, attracted like many others in the US manufacturing sector by low wages and production costs, transferred much of their basic manufacturing to China though in the main retaining their high-value design and software production capabilities within the USA. However, from 1996 China adopted an industrial strategy towards telecommunications networks whereby foreign corporations were excluded in order to foster the development of an indigenous sector. This was to prove critical not just to developing domestic networks but also to China's ability to project digital power overseas through national champions such as ZTE and Huawei.

As it became evident that the Chinese state was serious about promoting informatisation, growing numbers of young Chinese engineers and entrepreneurs, many of whom had been educated overseas and had acquired experience in Silicon Valley, returned to China and created their own ICT start-ups. Their focus was not on first-principles technical innovation but rather on the innovative application of the ideas they had learnt in Silicon Valley to create customer-facing online services that offered consumer convenience and were designed to take account of local conditions and cultural preferences. The Chinese government created an enabling environment for these companies through the Ministry of Science and Technology's Torch programme, which promoted the development of Science and Technology Industrial Parks offering tax breaks and other benefits to companies designated as hi-tech enterprises. Beyond that, companies were left largely to their own devices within a still weakly regulated environment and found themselves engaged in the most raw and elemental form of capitalist competition. The US-trained ICT entrepreneur Kai-fu Lee in his book *AI Superpowers* describes China's Internet ecosystem as:

> a coliseum where hundreds of copycat gladiators fought to the death... It was the domestic combatants who pushed each other to be faster, nimbler, leaner and meaner. They aggressively copied each other's product innovations, cut prices to the bone, launched smear

campaigns, forcibly deinstalled competing software and even reported rival OS to the police.[6]

Major US service providers such as eBay, who saw China as just another segment of a one-size-fits-all global market to be managed out of the USA, simply could not survive in such a distinctive and hyper-competitive environment and were eventually compelled to withdraw.

By the mid-2000s the broad outlines of a distinctive Chinese Internet ecosystem had begun to emerge. The Chinese Internet was at once similar to but also different from that of the West. Chinese websites tended to be much more crowded and "busier" than Western counterparts, operating on a "push" rather than a "pull" basis which offered a more passive browsing experience for users. Most users accessed the Internet for entertainment with online gaming becoming so popular that even the PLA had to make a virtue of necessity by allowing it within the military on the grounds that gaming assisted in the development of strategic thinking. Other uses included dating services, online shopping and, inevitably, pornography despite the fact that it is illegal in China. Initially most users accessed the Internet via Internet cafés—*wang ba*; personal computers and laptops were still beyond the reach of most consumers. But the arrival of smartphones in the mid-to-late 2000s saw a massive surge in mobile access. China's entrepreneurs developed a growing range of apps designed to reduce the frictions of life in urban China while manufacturing phones that were both cheap and offered functionality in some respects superior to that of Western competitors. The range of online services available to users became nothing short of staggering in its variety. Online food and beverage delivery services became so cheap and pervasive that ordering a single cup of coffee represented a rational consumer choice— though a terrible environmental one as China's already polluted rivers became choked with single-use plastic containers. Young single middle-class urban ladies reluctant to get married but under continuous pressure from their families to do so were able to relieve this pressure by going online to hire a "fiancé" who could accompany them on annual trips home during the Spring Festival. Video streaming meanwhile became both a form of entertainment for young single people and, for the more enterprising, or more willing to engage in risqué online behaviour, a means of earning what were often significant sums.

Since joining the World Trade Organisation in 2001 China's economy witnessed a dramatic period of double-digit growth based on rapid industrialisation focused on export markets. This growth was accompanied by large-scale urbanisation and the creation of a middle class numbering some 300 million. While remarkably successful in generating GDP growth, this process of rapid industrialisation had significant downsides in the form of widespread pollution, over-capacity, misallocation of resources, growing inequality and the emergence of an economy which Premier Wen Jiabao described in 2007 as "unstable, unbalanced, uncoordinated and unsustainable."[7] Promoting the development of e-commerce and the integration of the digital and real-world economies through the Internet Plus initiative became an important plank in the government's efforts to rebalance the economy away from an excessive reliance on exports and towards domestic consumption and to address the problems of under-development in western China and rural communities. China's Internet entrepreneurs responded with initiatives that included Singles Day—*guanggun jie*—on 11 November, a one-day orgy of online consumerism which in 2017 generated revenues totalling US$ 44.5 billion.

Online retail companies like Alibaba, untypical in that its founder Jack Ma was home-grown and had no background in IT, developed online payment systems that enabled China's consumers to leapfrog the use of credit cards and move to what is now close to being a cashless society—to the point where even beggars now display signs with QR codes enabling them to accept electronic donations. The messaging and social media company Tencent has, through its WeChat social media platform, which is similar in function to Twitter, evolved into an online one-stop shop—or as Kai-fu Lee has called it, a digital Swiss army knife— where users can communicate, shop, find entertainment, pay bills and taxes and obtain bank loans with minimal formalities. The wealth of data that a company like Tencent can glean about its users enables it to make far more confident judgements about suitability for loans than China's banks—which in any case have always regarded retail clients as an irritating distraction from the conduct of normal business amounting to little more than lending to state-owned enterprises (SOEs). China's online payment and banking systems are in effect posing a challenge to traditional retail banking but beyond that may, if they become more globally prevalent, ultimately have the effect of displacing the US dollar as the global reserve currency if the USA cannot come up with its own digital currency.

China's biggest Internet service providers became international household names under the acronym BAT, standing for Baidu, Alibaba and Tencent. The latter two companies listed in Hong Kong and New York respectively and are among the ten most highly valued corporations on the planet. But within China's hyper-competitive market they could not rest on their laurels. All three at various times faced significant difficulties affecting confidence in their brands—in the case of Alibaba the prevalence of counterfeit goods advertised on their sites; in the case of Tencent concerns about whether the Chinese government has visibility of social media posts; and in the case of Baidu, an unfortunate reputation for accepting payments for ranking search results and for delivering those that included unreliable advice about medical treatments. These latter led to cases of suicide by individuals who had invested their life savings in such treatments only to discover that they were the modern equivalent of snake-oil. China's private Internet companies, notwithstanding the massive contribution they made to China's economy, were periodically reminded that they existed at the pleasure of the Party-state and behaviour seen as contrary to the Party-state's interests and priorities would incur substantial penalties. A case in point is that of the multi-media platform Bytedance, which has since become internationally prominent through its US-based subsidiary TikTok. One of the company's most popular products was the Neihan Duanzi app which enabled users to circulate jokes (*duanzi*) and humorous video clips. In 2018 Neihan Duanzi was closed down by the State Administration of Radio and Television for hosting "vulgar and improper content," with the company's CEO delivering a grovelling public apology which just about rescued the rest of the business.[8] The closure of Neihan Duanzi was also a potent reminder of the CCP's determination to exercise control over the country's online discourse and to hold service providers accountable for the content on their services.

From the outset, the Chinese Party-state was attuned to the risks that came with the Internet in the form of information flows that challenged the Party's narrative or which might otherwise prove socially destabilising. As soon as the Internet was established China's Ministry of Public Security was given responsibility for policing it. In 1997 China's State Council promulgated the Computer Information Network and Internet Security, Protection and Management Regulations. Couched, as is true for all Chinese legislation, in vague, broad-brush terms that afford the authorities almost limitless latitude to decide what is or is not legal, these regulations banned:

> online incitement to resist or violate the Constitution, laws or administrative regulations; incitement to overthrow the government or the social system; incitement of division in the country or efforts

to obstruct national reunification; incitement of hatred or discrimination against national minorities; dissemination of falsehoods; distortions of the truth, rumours or messages that disrupt social order; promotion of feudal superstitions, sexually suggestive material, gambling, violence or murder; promotion of terrorism and incitement of other criminal activities, including insulting and slandering people; attacks on the reputation of state organisations; and any other activities that run counter to the Constitution, laws or administrative regulations[9]

—in effect a shopping list of all the things that keep the Party-state leadership awake at night.

In 1998 China inaugurated the Golden Shield Project with the aims of excluding undesirable foreign content whilst also monitoring domestically-generated content that might prove subversive. Controlling content from outside China was relatively straightforward as China had only six International Exchange Points (IXPs) and information flows could be controlled using a combination of standard firewalls and filters. Access to many Western services including Twitter, Facebook, Google and the websites of many Western news services was blocked and although China-based users are still able to access such services using Virtual Private Networks (VPNs), use of such systems has been progressively clamped down on. This aspect of the project, which has been referred to as the Great Firewall of China, affords the state visibility of those—relatively few—Chinese who seek to access banned material from overseas and, where necessary, the ability to intervene to prevent them. The Great Firewall has elicited criticism from foreign, in particular US, companies doing business in China on the grounds that it constitutes a restrictive practice that violates China's WTO obligations. Such companies can however use—expensive—Chinese VPNs to escape the Great Firewall, presumably on the basis that these can easily be monitored by the security authorities.

Managing domestic content generated by China's 800 million "netizens" looked to be much more of a challenge particularly in the case of early blogging services such as Weibo on which comments posted were universally accessible. In the early days of such services, China's netizens used micro-blogging to draw the attention of the Party-state to a host of official abuses and malfeasance involving corruption—by then pervasive—and incompetence and in so doing enjoyed a degree of tacit support from a central government that had always found it hard to obtain visibility of what was happening at a provincial and local level. Examples include exposing a notably corrupt CCP cadre, referred to as "Brother Watch," who was photographed wearing a succession of luxury watches each costing many times his official salary; officials in Wenzhou who sought to cover up a high-speed train crash by burying the wrecked carriages with dead passengers still on board; and officials in Tianjin who sought to minimise the impact of an explosion in a chemical storage facility situated illegally close to a residential area. On a more positive note China's central, provincial and local administrations made proactive use of social media to engage with populations to monitor and respond to popular concerns. For example, the Ministry of Public Security, responsible for policing, put out an app enabling netizens to communicate directly with their local police forces.

A more difficult area to manage was commentary on foreign policy. Since 1989 China has implemented a "patriotic education" programme focusing on China's humiliation at the hands of the West with the aim of promoting nationalism as a unifying force within Chinese society. The results have been evident online whenever China perceives itself to have been wronged or slighted, as happened in 2005 when a statement by UN Secretary-General Kofi Annan that Japan should be considered for a permanent seat on the UN Security Council elicited widespread outrage. The result was an outpouring of angry social media posts that quickly led to street protests and attacks on Japanese commercial premises. This was tolerated by the state up to the point when protesters turned their ire on the Chinese government for failing to deal more robustly with Tokyo, whereupon a clamp-down on anti-Japanese messaging was instituted. More recently the Chinese government has sought to leverage nationalist sentiment within China to generate social media posts attacking Hong Kong residents involved in protests against the introduction of an extradition bill that would permit Hong Kong residents to be extradited to China. Among those posting messages attacking the protesters are a cohort of young patriotic women known as the "Fan Girls"—*fanquan nu* (not to be confused with the "little pinks"—*xiao fenhong*—individual female teenage bloggers given to putting out overblown patriotic messaging on a range of issues). In this case individual protests have formed part of a much larger state-sponsored exercise involving the creation of bots generating pro-regime messages on Western social media platforms such as Twitter and Facebook.[10]

As time has gone by the Chinese Party-state has developed a more all-encompassing suite of capabilities to monitor and control online discourse and has also become progressively less tolerant of online dissent, with so-called "Big Vs," bloggers enjoying a large public following, being progressively closed down. Service providers have been made responsible for policing their own content and an insistence on real-name registration by users has limited the scope of netizens to post comments anonymously. It is estimated that the Ministry of Public Security has established a network of censors at provincial and municipal levels numbering two million, with the ability to draw on ever more sophisticated data-mining and other technical tools. In addition the Chinese state can rely on the efforts of the Fifty-Cent Party—*wumao dang*—so called because of apocryphal claims that they are paid fifty cents by the government for every post they produce to engage in online discussions and nudge them in directions more favourable to the official line; in fact it turns out that most of these posts are made by civil servants. Posts deemed to have contravened what are often opaque red lines can be taken down within minutes of being posted. Examples of memes and expressions deemed unacceptable are constantly changing. In 2014, during the Occupy Hong Kong movement, protesting the Chinese government's imposition of restrictions on the candidate-list for the role of Chief Executive, banned terms included "Hong Kong," "barricades," "Occupy Central" and "umbrella"—the latter, used by protesters to protect themselves against police pepper spray, having become the informal symbol of the protest movement. Following the Sunnylands summit between presidents Obama and Xi Jinping in 2013, one Chinese netizen incurred the ire of the censors by comparing Xi, who, juxtaposed with the tall, lithe figure of Obama looked rather portly, to Winnie the Pooh. This meme was to resurface in 2018 when Xi Jinping announced the end of term-limits on the position of President of the People's Republic, leading to a rash of pictures of Winnie the Pooh clutching a jar of honey with an accompanying text that read "Find something you love and stick with it"—*zhaodao yiyang ni suo zhongai de shiwu, ranhou yong bu fangshou.*[11]

These examples illustrate the inventiveness of China's netizens in finding ways of getting around an ever more restrictive censorship regime. The relative phonemic impoverishment of the Chinese language creates the possibility of using multiple homonyms and puns while the richness of China's classical literature offers scope for oblique allusions that an educated audience can be expected to pick up on. The result is a cat-and-mouse game between netizens and censors that has given rise to a counterculture of dissidence with its own lexicon. Emblematic of this counterculture is the "grass-mud horse," depicted graphically as a beast resembling an alpaca. The words *cao ni ma* (草泥马) can also be written as 肏你妈 (the same phonemes but with different tones), meaning "fuck your mother." Another widespread term in this lexicon of cyber dissidence is "river crab"—*hexie* (河蟹)—which, if written using the alternative characters 和谐 refers to the activities of the censors in seeking to "harmonise" public discourse. A more recent example that has more international connotations is the "rice rabbit," the Chinese characters for which sound like "Me Too." The fact that China's netizens refuse to be cowed by a pervasive system of online surveillance does not however change the reality of what the US academic Rebecca MacKinnon has referred to as "networked authoritarianism."[12] This approach accepts that in the digital age people will have access to more information and more means of self-expression than would be true in a traditional authoritarian society. Rather than fight this, the authorities seek to channel it by allowing a degree of online discourse that creates an impression of freedom and agency whilst ensuring that behaviour causing concern can rapidly be identified and closed down. At the same time the authorities can seed the public discourse in ways favourable to their objectives. For now at least the Chinese Party-state has achieved information dominance over its population and that situation seems unlikely to change for the foreseeable future.

4

CHINA'S LEADERSHIP

VERSION 3.0

Xi Jinping's assumption of office as CCP Secretary-General and head of state in 2013 marked a major inflection point in China's economic and political evolution. Xi himself is a particularly interesting figure. His father, Xi Zhongxun, was one of the founders of the People's Republic and was an economic pragmatist who, under Deng Xiaoping, pioneered the concept of Special Economic Zones. Xi Zhongxun had been subjected to house arrest by Mao Zedong before the Cultural Revolution—a development that may well have saved him from the harsher fates meted out to some of his fellow CCP leaders. Xi junior was rusticated to the remote Shaanxi village of Liangjiahe, an experience that appeared not to have shaken his belief in the CCP. When the Cultural Revolution ended, Xi was able to study at Tsinghua University following which his father arranged for him to serve as secretary to Geng Biao, a former comrade-in-arms during the civil war and by then vice-premier for foreign affairs and military industry and secretary-general of the CCP Central Military Commission. The three years Xi spent with

Geng amounted to a major formative experience, teaching him much about strategic thinking and the skills and disciplines needed to advance through the Party ranks as well as giving him a grounding in military affairs.[1] Following this apprenticeship Xi served in the provincial administrations of Hebei, Fujian and Jiangsu before being catapulted into the position of Shanghai party secretary following the previous incumbent's arrest on charges of corruption. Shortly thereafter he was appointed to the CCP's Standing Committee, serving as Hu Jintao's vice-president and deputy-chairman of the Central Military Commission.

Whereas Hu Jintao was a technocrat, an engineer by training who had worked his way up through service in the CCP Youth League, Xi Jinping was what is termed in China a "princeling"—*wangzi*. The princelings had been a reality since the founding of the People's Republic as China's new communist leadership sought to instil in their offspring a sense of belief in the Party's right to rule whilst ensuring that they enjoyed a privileged upbringing. The princeling identity was reinforced and to a degree formalised in 1989 when, following the suppression of the Democracy Movement, the Party's founding fathers agreed that the government should select one child from each of their families and move them up through the political system on the grounds that, in the words of General Wang Zhen, "Nobody is more reliable than our own children. We need our own children to protect the red China that we have established."[2] The original group of princelings consisted of the sons and daughters of the so-called "eight immortals," senior CCP leaders who had joined the Party before Liberation: Deng Xiaoping, Chen Yun, Li Xiannian, Peng Zhen, Yang Shangkun, Bo Yibo, Wang Zhen and Song Renqiong. It was subsequently expanded to encompass the offspring of all senior leaders at a national and regional level, in the process becoming a powerful and hugely wealthy political faction convinced of their entitlement to rule and to derive material benefits from their privileged status. Xi's membership of this group may account for his self-confident manner that is in marked contrast to that of his predecessor, who maintained an aura of impenetrability as a defence and survival mechanism.

Xi's appointment came at a complex and convoluted period in China's domestic politics. Though he had presided over a period of unprecedented economic growth and prosperity, Hu Jintao's tenure was coming to be seen within leadership circles as characterised by political and ideological drift. Powerful economic vested interests stood in the way of the further economic reform seen as necessary to address growing inequalities and to prevent China becoming stuck in a middle-income trap—a situation in which a country that has attained a certain income level due to its particular advantages then becomes stuck at that level. China's military and security agencies had come close to being uncontrollable and unaccountable fiefdoms, and corruption had reached levels that risked eroding the CCP's claims to legitimacy. Adherence to Marxism–Leninism amounted to little more than lip service with many of China's new middle-class professionals seeing membership of the CCP as just another line on their CV.

In the run-up to Xi's nomination, veteran leaders including former premier Li Peng and former CCP Secretary-General Jiang Zemin were manoeuvring to ensure that whoever was appointed would safeguard their and their families' interests. Meanwhile in the western megalopolis of Chongqing, the modernising anglophone Party Secretary and Politburo member Bo Xilai, seen by many in the West as the very model of a modern Chinese politician, was engaged in what amounted to a US presidential-style electoral campaign entirely at odds with Chinese political norms of behaviour which demand prospective leaders to be self-effacing. Bo's efforts to secure the Party leadership imploded spectacularly after his security chief Wang Lijun sought asylum in the US consulate in Chengdu, claiming inter alia that Bo and his wife Gu Kailai had been involved in the murder of British businessman Neil Heywood. This episode, which offered a rare insight into the back-workings of Chinese leadership politics, resulted in Bo being dismissed from his posts and, in 2013, sentenced to life imprisonment for corruption while his wife received a suspended death sentence. The febrile nature of leadership politics at that juncture can be judged by the prevalence of rumours of prospective military coups and by speculation about the significance of a two-week period during which Xi Jinping disappeared from public view. This disappearance has never been publicly explained though one plausible account suggests that Xi used this period to lobby his fellow princelings to support his agenda of cracking down on elite corruption and bringing the PLA to heel.[3]

From the outset Xi adopted a very different leadership style from his predecessors, marking a significant shift away from the collective leadership model imposed by Deng Xiaoping to insure against a return to Maoist excess and towards a much more high-profile personalised style. The Chinese term that best describes Xi is *dafang*, meaning someone with a poised, easy and unaffected manner, qualities that make for natural leadership. But it quickly became apparent that with the poise came an unshakeable focus and determination, accompanied by a deep-rooted belief in the validity and superiority of Marxist–Leninist ideology. As he put it in a 2013 speech in which he set out his stall to the Politburo, "we must concentrate our efforts on... building a socialism that is superior to capitalism and laying the foundation for a future in which we will win the initiative and occupy the dominant position."[4] One of Xi's first leadership actions was to implement a campaign against corruption that, in contrast to earlier such campaigns, has lasted for years and has to date netted close to two million "tigers"—high officials—and "flies"—lesser figures.

Corruption has always been a feature of Chinese political culture. As economic development got under way in the 1980s, it became pervasive, with CCP cadres, who were required to work long hours to achieve demanding targets in return for low remuneration, feeling justified in seeking a share of the profits from a private sector which their efforts had enabled. Indeed, during the 1990s and early 2000s any CCP cadre who sought to live up to the Party's austere ideals by refusing to engage in such practices would have found himself—in China's male-dominated political culture, it would almost invariably have been "him"—in an impossible position, forfeiting the cooperation of the population necessary to achieve his targets and hence risking demotion.[5] Levels of corruption gave rise to the phenomenon of the "naked official"—*luoti ganbu*—meaning one whose family were all resident outside of China and who would himself join them once he had embezzled enough. The risk of imprisonment or even execution was seen as an acceptable price to pay for securing the family's future. All members of the Party nomenklatura had substantial funds and property holdings overseas and their offspring would normally secure foreign residence through either study or business investments.

Xi was well aware that every hand was dipped in the blood of corruption and was able to use this knowledge to bring to heel critics and opponents. These included Zhou Yongkang, former Secretary of the CCP Political and Legal Committee with oversight of the police, procuratorate and intelligence and security services (Zhou did not help his case by using his powers covertly to monitor the personal communications of senior CCP leaders); and Generals Xu Caihou and Guo Boxiong, both members of the CCP Central Military Commission who had presided over a culture of corruption in which all senior PLA appointments had been purchased, at the most senior level for sums as high as US$ 3 million. The campaign against corruption had a significant international element, Operation Fox Hunt, which resulted in several hundred officials who had absconded overseas with embezzled state funds being brought back to China to face punishment. Operation Fox Hunt was the subject of a film of that name while the campaign against corruption was the subject of a well-made TV drama series entitled *In the Name of the People*— *renmin de mingyi*.

In one of his first speeches after assuming office Xi set out his vision for the "great rejuvenation of the Chinese race" (*minzu*) which he also referred to as the China Dream. In his work report to the 19th Party Congress five years later, he set out three goals: that China should become a moderately prosperous society— *xiaokang shehui*, a Confucian concept—by 2020; to have "basically realised socialist modernisation" by 2035; and to have become a leading global power by 2049, the centenary of the founding of the People's Republic. Xi's conviction that only the CCP could achieve these goals fed into a relentless focus on the promotion of ideology; a shift away from the civilianisation of government that had taken place under Deng Xiaoping towards greater Party involvement in day-to-day administration; and a progressive crackdown on non-governmental and civil society organisations seen as challenging or competing with the CCP's hold on power. Central Party Document Number Nine, formally entitled "Briefing on the Current Situation in the Ideological Realm," circulated in 2013 and leaked by journalist Gao Yu, who was subsequently imprisoned, listed seven taboo issues—*qige bujiang*: Western constitutional democracy—including the separation of powers, a multi-party system, general elections, an independent judiciary and a "nationalised" army; universal values; civil society; economic neo-liberalism; press freedom; historical nihilism, which meant dwelling on the CCP's mistakes; and questioning reform and opening-up and socialism with Chinese characteristics.[6] What was to become "Xi Jinping Thought on Socialism with Chinese Characteristics for the New Era"—otherwise referred to as "Xi Jinping Thought" and set out in two dense volumes entitled *The Governance of China*—was adopted into the CCP's Constitution after the 2017 19th Party Congress at which Xi Jinping proclaimed that "north, south, east, west and centre... the Party controls everything." Party members were required to engage in extensive study of "Xi Jinping Thought" including by downloading an app with the title "Study a Strong Nation"—in Chinese *xuexi qiangguo*, where the word-play involving Xi's surname is anything but accidental—on which they were required to answer online quizzes on the material they had read with a system of rewards and penalties depending on their scores.

Xi's efforts to impose greater ideological conformity can be seen as the culmination of an internal intellectual debate that had been ongoing since Deng Xiaoping's reform and opening-up had begun. Rather as had happened in the late nineteenth and early twentieth centuries, during the 1990s, a period of relative intellectual liberalisation, China's intellectuals had explored ideologies ranging from liberalism and social democracy through to authoritarianism and neo-Maoism, the latter almost as serious a challenge to the Party's authority as liberalism. The current of thinking that proved most influential within the Party leadership was a form of neo-authoritarianism promoted by scholars such as Hu Angang, Wang Shaogang and Jiang Shigong. Mostly Western-trained and drawing on a wide variety of Western sources, they were opposed to the proposition that there could be only one—Western—path to development. They saw a strong centralised state as the only way to mitigate growing inequalities and they rejected Western notions of electoral democracy, civil society and the neutrality of law as being at odds with achieving that outcome. They were strongly influenced by the ideas of the Weimar intellectual and Nazi collaborator Carl Schmitt on issues of state sovereignty and the law and the impossibility of achieving a modus vivendi with political opponents. The key elements of their thinking boiled down to asserting the superiority of political sovereignty over the rule of law, arguing for a repoliticisation of the state, a rejection of universalism and an assertion of Chinese exceptionalism.[7]

Another important intellectual influence was Wang Huning, a Shanghai-based academic who from 1995 worked in the CCP Central Party Research Office before entering the CCP Secretariat in 2007. In 2012 he was elected to the CCP Central Committee and in 2017 was made a member of the Politburo Standing Committee, the first person with a research and policy background to make it to the apogee of Chinese political life. In the course of this trajectory Wang acted as the architect of the contributions to Marxist–Leninist theory that all Chinese leaders are expected to produce, in the case of Jiang Zemin, the "Three Represents," in that of Hu Jintao the "Harmonious Society" and "Scientific Outlook on Development" and in the case of Xi Jinping, the "China Dream." Wang, who has published prolifically on a range of issues including national sovereignty, governance, ecology and corruption, has always rejected the neo-authoritarian label but his writings on governance closely track those of the neo-authoritarians in areas such as the need to take account of political, cultural and social conditions and on the importance of stability and a strong centralised leadership. Wang is not opposed to democratisation but argues that this should be the product of intra-Party debate rather than being externally imposed.[8] Wang's best-known work, *America Against Itself* (*Meiguo fandui Meiguo*), which compares the US ideal with the contemporary reality, identifies excessive individualism as a major vulnerability and something China should at all costs avoid.

One of Wang's initiatives appears to have been selectively to co-opt aspects of traditional Chinese thought with the aim of demonstrating that the CCP represented a legitimate continuation of China's millenarian traditions. The focus has been on Confucian concepts of hierarchy, the subordination of the individual to the interests of the collective and an emphasis on the traditional Confucian values of benevolence, righteousness, honesty, integrity and social harmony, the latter with reference to the concept of the "Great Unity," the Confucian ideal state in which all mankind lives in peace and in harmony with nature. In the words of an article in a 2017 edition of the *Liberation Army Daily*, "today communist ideology and the common ideology of socialism with Chinese characteristics exemplify the search for values imparted and inherited by the Chinese people over the ages: the process of Sinification of Marxism involves fusion with the essence of China's traditional culture and alignment with China's concrete realities."[9]

One of Xi's earliest organisational initiatives was to use the mechanism of the Leading Small Group (LSG) to take a hands-on approach to government. The Leading Small Group is a long-established device used by both the Party and the State Council, China's highest non-Party body, to exercise a policy guidance, coordinating and monitoring role across China's sprawling and highly stove-piped bureaucracy and is designed to cut through bureaucratic barriers and bypass vested interests.[10] When Xi assumed office there were already some fifty LSGs in existence, headed by a range of senior Party and state figures. Xi has added substantially to that number, of which he himself chairs eight. The LSGs, which seldom publicise their composition or agendas, are served by a secretariat the head of which derives significant authority from proximity to the leadership. Of the LSGs chaired by Xi, the most consequential are probably the LSG for Comprehensive Deepening of Reform, which meets monthly and covers a wide agenda, the National Security Council—which, contrary to the expectations of many foreign observers, has not evolved into something resembling its US counterpart, being primarily concerned with domestic security issues—and the LSG on Cyber Security and Informatisation.

The creation of a new LSG on Cyber Security and Informatisation chaired by Xi was a clear recognition of the centrality of cyber capabilities in delivering his ambitious policy agenda but also a recognition of how far China still lagged behind the USA. As in the West, China's institutional response to the evolution of the Internet was initially piecemeal and fragmented. Key players in managing the process included the Ministry of Industry and Information Technology (MIIT), which dealt with technical and regulatory issues relating to postal and electronic communications, the production of electronic and information goods and software and the promotion of China's knowledge economy; the Ministry of Public Security (MPS), which was responsible for policing the Internet; the CCP Propaganda Department; and to a lesser extent the Ministry of Foreign Affairs, which has the formal lead on international negotiations relating to international cyber security and cyber governance. The net result was that, as Xi Jinping observed in a 2014 speech inaugurating the new LSG, China had become a big cyber power but now needed to transition to becoming a strong cyber power. This would require greater central direction and coordination. In 2014 the Cyber Administration of China (CAC) was set up with a remit to develop and implement policy in relation to China's Internet. The CAC provided the secretariat for the LSG on Cyber Security and Informatisation and it was this proximity to Xi Jinping that provided it with real authority. The LSG also benefitted from inputs from an Advisory Committee for State Informatisation comprising sixty-six of China's top scientists and engineers in the field of ICT, many of them Academicians.

The CAC's first head was Lu Wei, a larger-than-life figure with a talent for self-promotion whose background was as a journalist for the state news agency Xinhua and later as a senior official in the CCP Propaganda Department. In the latter capacity Lu had shown an early realisation that unlike traditional media the Internet, as a substrate that enabled information to be communicated directly and instantaneously in a variety of formats, needed to be managed differently. Up to that point China, while advocating internationally for a concept of cyber sovereignty whereby states should have the right to control content passing through their national networks, had been somewhat defensive about its censorship of the Internet. Lu Wei by contrast was unabashed and forward-leaning in seeking to justify China's approach. Speaking at the World Economic Forum's 2014 Summer Davos meeting in Tianjin, Lu drew an analogy between the Internet and a traffic system: "If it has no brakes, it doesn't matter how fast a car is travelling. Once it gets on the highway you can imagine what the end will be. And so, no matter how advanced, all cars must have brakes."[11]

Lu sought to promote China's vision through the World Internet Conference (WIC), the first iteration of which was held in November 2014 in Wuzhen, a traditional Zhejiang canal town that had been turned into a major—and somewhat Disneyfied—tourist destination. Hopes that this would become an event attracting the presence of world leaders went unrequited. Most Western states either stayed away or were represented by relatively junior in-country diplomats. CEOs of US and other Western technology companies were also largely absent. Panel discussions were highly scripted, leaving no room for open debate. An attempt to get delegates to sign up to China's policy of Internet sovereignty by slipping copies of a draft document under the bedroom doors of delegates at 11.00 pm on the final evening of the conference met with concerted pushback and had to be shelved. The 2015 Conference was attended by Xi Jinping, whose keynote address laid emphasis on cyber sovereignty, the importance of maintaining order in cyberspace and a governance system based on a multilateral approach. This latter concept carries particular significance since it seeks to privilege the role of national governments in global cyber governance in contrast to the existing multi-stakeholder approach which simply treats governments as one of many players. The World Internet Conference, though still failing to attract top-level Western participation, has settled into an exercise that focuses more on representation by developing countries and enables China's sprawling cyber community to communicate with itself. Meanwhile its originator Lu Wei was in 2016 arrested on charges of corruption and replaced by Xu Lin, a low-key self-effacing official in the Shanghai administration, in every respect Lu Wei's polar opposite. The CAC was initially guilty of overreach by trespassing on what the Ministry of Public Security regarded as its responsibility for policing online conduct and content, an initiative that met with predictable pushback. Since then it has cemented its role as the oversight organisation for Chinese Internet policy and its status has been elevated to that of a Commission—*weiyuanhui*.

In 2014 Xi had observed that there could be no national security without cyber security. In this regard China had a long way to go.[12] One consequence of a relentless focus on content security was a corresponding lack of focus on network security, with the result that China's domestic Internet was extremely vulnerable to malign actors, both domestic and international. According to the International Telecommunications Union's 2018 Cyber Security Index China ranked 27th in the world in terms of overall cyber capability, behind countries such as Turkey, Denmark, Germany, Egypt, Croatia, Italy and Russia—an unenviable situation for an aspirant cyber superpower.[13] Cyber criminality, in the form of online fraud, data theft, blackmail and libel became an issue of growing concern to China's expanding middle class and risked calling into question the feasibility of integrating

China's online and real-world economies envisaged in Premier Li Keqiang's Internet Plus strategy. Meanwhile the revelations of rogue NSA contractor Edward Snowden about the extent of the USA's global reach—notwithstanding the fact that many of Snowden's claims were inaccurate—raised concerns about issues such as the cyber security of critical infrastructure that had never previously been among leadership preoccupations. China's weak cyber security made it a favoured springboard for international cyber criminals seeking to conceal the origins of their attacks; China's Computer Network Emergency Response Team (CNCERT) has reported that foreign-based advanced persistent threat attacks directly threatening national security were becoming normal.

From 2014 onwards the Chinese government launched a blitz of organisational reforms and legislation to address this issue. At the public level an annual Awareness Week for National Cyber Security was introduced offering guidance to China's netizens on how to behave and stay safe online. A Cybersecurity Association of China was established in 2016 to align government, industry and academia around a common set of security objectives, and China's National Information Security Standardisation Technical Committee has introduced over 300 security standards covering critical infrastructure protection and product review. Key pieces of legislation addressing cyber security include the 2014 National Security Law that inter alia mandated national security reviews for all foreign investments that "impinge or might impinge on national security," and for foreign investments involving key material or technologies including information technology products and services; a Counter-terrorism Law that required all telecommunications and Internet service providers to supply encryption information to Chinese law enforcement agents; and a Cybersecurity Law that emphasised the importance of maintaining cyber sovereignty, set out broad prohibitions on various forms of online activity and required service providers to ensure real-name registration for services and to block and report illegal activity. It also effectively required all data relating to Chinese citizens to be stored within China unless permission was given for it to be exported.

Aspects of these laws attracted criticism from China's foreign business community and from civil rights organisations as potentially discriminatory and infringing on Intellectual Property (IP) rights of foreign companies. Such legislation was however in many ways analogous to that of Western countries and collectively represented a long overdue effort to impose order on China's "wild East" cyber environment characterised by pervasive online fraud including sales of counterfeit goods and disregard for privacy. The same is true for efforts to impose better protection for IP and consumer data. What China is currently engaged in represents a coherent and in many ways creative approach to Internet regulation that takes careful account of Western initiatives such as the European Union's General Data Protection Regulation. China's Cybersecurity Law does in fact list the protection of individual data privacy as an objective and this has been fleshed out in the 2018 Personal Information Security Specifications. There is however an important carve-out enabling the state to access data "affecting national security, the national economy and the people's livelihood."[14] The broad outlines of Chinese cyber regulation are now clear. They involve wide discretion in interpretation and enforcement that is characteristic of all Chinese law; a premium placed on social stability and the security and interests of the state; and enhanced scrutiny for foreign entities operating in China. This regulation is an important component of Xi Jinping's aspiration, set out in the "Four Comprehensives," which constitute part of his contribution to Marxist–Leninist theory, to perfect the use of rule by law to govern China—not of course to be confused with rule of law, which as Central Party Document Number Nine makes clear is something he is not prepared to countenance.

Expertise in cyber security is at a premium throughout the world and China is no exception. Relatively few Chinese universities offer courses in cyber security and such courses as exist are to be found within computer science departments, with the attendant risk that they focus on the purely technical aspects of cyber security at the expense of the institutional and human factors. China's private cyber security sector is still embryonic. The two industry leaders are ChinaSoft and China Cybersecurity, subsidiaries of state-owned enterprises, and there are some 400 fully private companies, in no way comparable in size or capabilities to US private sector counterparts such as Symantec, Mandiant or Crowdstrike. Almost all of them rely on software from foreign vendors. In the USA and other Western countries incentives exist for "white-hat" hackers to report previous unidentified cyber vulnerabilities. But in China such behaviour is actively discouraged as it is perceived as jeopardising the reputation and profitability of the company concerned.

Reliance on foreign cyber products has become a key preoccupation of the Chinese leadership. Despite efforts to promote digital indigenous innovation China remains dependent on some key foreign inputs from what have been termed in the Chinese media the "Eight Guardian Warriors"—*ba da jingang*—namely Cisco, IBM, Google, Qualcomm, Intel, Apple, Oracle and Microsoft. As late as 2014 Chinese government departments and the Chinese military were so dependent on Windows XP software that when Microsoft announced its intention to close down support for the product, the resultant outcry obliged them to make an exception for China. Microsoft subsequently announced that XP users would get a free upgrade to Windows 10. In security terms the situation was made worse by the fact that much of the Windows software used was pirated so did not even benefit from regular security upgrades. Efforts by the Chinese government and the Chinese military to replace Windows with indigenous operating systems that do not rely on US-origin open-source software such as UNIX have to date proven unsuccessful. The same is true of efforts to replace Google's Android system for mobile phones. In 2016 Xi Jinping observed that "The situation that our country is under others' control in core technologies of key fields has not changed fundamentally."[15] In pursuit of its objective of having networks that are "secure and controllable"—*anquan kekong*, China has launched a Made in China 2025 strategy with the objective of ensuring that by 2025 at least 70% of manufactures in ten key sectors, including communications technologies, will be indigenously manufactured. How realistic this is remains to be seen, though it is clear that the Chinese state is throwing huge resources at the problem and seeking to incentivise China's private sector. China's greatest deficits in information technology are in the realms of software and the manufacture of high-performance microprocessors, and for all the talk of technical decoupling it seems unlikely that China will be able to eliminate dependence on foreign technologies entirely. The degree to which it can reduce such dependence is likely to vary significantly.

Initiatives such as Made in China 2025 and regulations that appear to discriminate against foreign companies have inevitably raised questions about whether China really does want to remain globally connected or whether in fact its priority is to insulate itself from potentially harmful influences by practising a kind of digital autochthony. It is unlikely that Chinese leaders and thinkers would ever view the issue in such starkly binary terms, preferring instead to think in terms of a continuum that requires constant policy adjustments in the light of specific circumstances. China knows it cannot close itself off from the world since its economy has become so dependent on global engagement. At the same time the Chinese Party-state needs to insulate itself against threats emanating both from its own population and from threats posed by "hostile foreign forces" seeking to implement policies of "peaceful evolution"—undermining and eventually overthrowing the CCP. The response has been to promote the development of what has been termed by some Western scholars a techno-security state using technology not merely to monitor but rather to shape opinions and behaviours in ways favourable to the interests of the Party-state. This hugely ambitious project merits separate and detailed analysis.

5

CHINA, THE TECHNO-SECURITY STATE

The Chinese state is hardly unique in being preoccupied with security. The provision of security goods is arguably the most fundamental responsibility for any state and failure to provide them calls into question the state's raison d'être. In China's case security concerns have historically taken the form either of foreign invasion across land borders or domestic insurrection. China's history is replete with examples of both phenomena. In the pre-modern era the main external threat to China came in the form of invasions by nomadic and semi-nomadic "barbarian" Turkic or Tungusic tribes, with such invasions often taking place during periods of climate-induced economic stress such as the seventeenth century mini-Ice Age that coincided with the Manchu invasion.[1] Dealing with these risks required a proactive diplomatic and border-management approach that included dynastic alliances—a common theme in Chinese poetry is the hardship and homesickness suffered by Chinese princesses married to foreign khans; the development of economic relations that involved trading manufactured goods and agrarian produce for the cavalry mounts that China could not produce in adequate numbers; and a constant state of military readiness involving large standing armies and the development of infrastructure that included what eventually became the Great Wall of China. The utility of the latter was less about keeping barbarian hordes out of China—it seldom achieved that objective—than providing a logistics and communications network which enabled troops to be rapidly deployed across often difficult mountainous terrain to wherever they were most urgently needed.

An equally serious threat to security, and one much harder to control, came from indigenous insurrections, which often took the form of movements rooted in folk religion such as the Yellow Turbans who came close to overthrowing the Eastern Han; the fourteenth century Red Turban rebellion that led to the overthrow of the Mongol Yuan dynasty and whose leader Zhu Yuanzhang became the first Ming emperor with the regnal name Hong Wu; and the late eighteenth century White Lotus rebellion which, though defeated, significantly undermined the stability of the Qing dynasty. One of China's best-known novels *Shuihu Zhuan*, first translated into English by the US sinologist Pearl Buck as *Water Margin*, is situated in such an (imaginary) period of dynastic breakdown and makes reference in its early chapters to the Yellow Turbans. The novel charts the exploits of a group of outlaws and martial arts practitioners who have been driven to a life in the criminal underworld—*jianghu*, literally rivers and lakes—by corrupt and oppressive officials at a time of dynastic weakness. The central question the book addresses is what individuals are to do at a time when the established laws and norms of society no longer apply.

The challenges to regime security posed by such movements over the course of two millennia have left their imprint on China's political DNA and explain the CCP's neuralgia about religion and "feudal superstition." This neuralgia explains their response to Falungong, a quasi-religious movement based loosely on Buddhist metaphysics combined with traditional qigong meditation and breathing techniques. Falungong emerged in the early 1990s, a time when many Chinese were seeking to fill a post-Tiananmen spiritual void through religion, and initially enjoyed support from a CCP which had itself promoted qigong, stripped of its traditional religious connotations, as a healthy form of exercise. But as the movement grew to 70 million members, close to the size of the CCP, the Chinese authorities took fright and tried to close it down. In April 1999 the CCP leadership compound at Zhongnanhai was surrounded by some 10,000 Falungong adherents sitting cross-legged on the ground in a silent protest against a growing climate of repression. The ability to organise such a protest without detection was due to the use of new communications technologies such as mobile phones and online bulletin boards, the precursors to social media—and the fact that significant numbers of the intelligence services, police and military proved to be Falungong adherents. This incident led to a full-blown crackdown, with Falungong declared a "heretical sect"—*xie jiao*—and its adherents rounded up and put in labour camps amid widespread claims of ill treatment.[2] The movement, whose leader lives in the USA and which produces a globally distributed newspaper, *Epoch Times*, has remained a thorn in the CCP's side and is a priority target for China's intelligence services. Indeed, efforts to track and suppress Falungong supporters outside China may have been the driver for China's intelligence services to begin what has now become a pervasive campaign of global cyber espionage covering a much wider range of targets.

The Chinese Communist Party sees itself as a vanguard elite possessed of superior knowledge but facing the challenge of converting to its cause a host of social and interest groups inherently opposed to it. The CCP was not given power by the Chinese people through the ballot box but rather took it at gunpoint, albeit with some level of concurrence from a population exhausted by conflict and disillusioned with the Nationalist government. The issue of legitimacy is one with which the CCP has always struggled both domestically and internationally and this has shaped its approach to how security is maintained. In essence the people—or to use Mao's preferred term, the masses—cannot be trusted and have to be subjected to constant and pervasive oversight and control. In the pre-information era such control was maintained largely through a system in which all aspects of an individual's existence were regulated by the state. The state determined where people could live and work, whether and to whom they could get married, and what quality of food and clothing they could access. The rural population were effectively held prisoner in the countryside. Urban dwellers, who mostly lived in housing assigned by their work unit, were given residence permits—*hukou*—tying them to a particular city. Residential districts had neighbourhood watch committees whose members policed all comings and goings, noting and reporting anomalous activity. Each individual had their own file—*dang'an*—at the local police station containing details of every aspect of his or her life and behaviour. An example of how effective this could be is demonstrated in the film *Beijing Bicycle*. In the film, the free-spirited heroine is impregnated by an older married man and the two of them effect an illegal abortion in the man's home. The abortion is successful but is quickly followed by a visit from the police. It turns out that the foetus has been discovered in a nearby rubbish bin wrapped in pages from the newspaper *Guangming Daily*, a relatively highbrow publication aimed at the intellectual elite. And the police know beyond any possible doubt that in this particular neighbourhood the man is the only person who reads this newspaper.

As economic reform and large-scale urbanisation took hold, these measures of control were no longer fit for purpose and required updating to cope with very different circumstances.

Those in the West who criticise China's perceived lack of freedoms often fail to appreciate how much things have changed since the Mao era. Middle-class urban dwellers, of whom there are an estimated 300 million, now have the freedom to live where they like, choose what career path they will follow, move around China at will and travel overseas. From being an all-encompassing presence, the state now plays no more part in people's day-to-day existence than is true for most Western liberal democracies—if anything, rather less. In return all they have to do is not challenge the CCP's right to rule. The CCP seeks legitimation by virtue of its ability to meet the needs of its citizenry and to offer them the prospect of a better life; and by promoting nationalism to the point where the CCP arguably no longer sees itself as part of a global movement in the way that, on paper at least, the Soviet Union did. For all the focus in Western media of the foreign policy and defence aspects of Xi Jinping's work report to the 19th Party Congress, the reality is that the bulk of his report addressed domestic issues focusing on quality of life.

But while life is incomparably better for most Chinese, the Chinese economic miracle has produced losers as well as winners. These comprise everything from peasants displaced from their land by corrupt officials with little or no compensation; urban migrants unable to obtain residence documents enabling them to access housing and public services, sometimes publicly disparaged by officials as "low-end people"—*diduan renkou*; and urban middle-class "Nimbies" objecting to polluting factories being built near their homes. Urban China has even witnessed the emergence of a nihilistic counter-culture—*sang wenhua*—whose adherents, referring to themselves with ironic self-deprecation as *diaosi*—literally pubic hairs—reject aspirational middle-class values. Popular protests are commonplace. The CCP obsessively monitors these, though figures for the number of such protests have not been published since 2005;[3] a key performance measure for Party officials is the ability to resolve such protests quickly and with minimal publicity. This normally involves buying off the protesters with promises that go unfulfilled, then arresting the perceived ring-leaders on vague charges of disturbing public order or subverting the authority of the state.

As indicated in the preceding chapter, a key element of social control consists of pervasive monitoring of online communications, with the CCP relatively confident that it enjoys sufficient technology dominance to identify and quickly snuff out anything that might potentially represent an anti-Party movement. With this greater control of public discourse has come a greater emphasis on control of traditional mass media and the arts. During the 1990s China witnessed a surge of investigative reporting that revealed multiple examples of official corruption and malfeasance. This kind of reporting has been progressively stifled. *Nanfang Zhoumo* (*Southern Weekly*), a newspaper owned by the Guangdong Communist Party but which had made its mark reporting issues such as the sub-standard building practices behind the collapse of school buildings in the 2008 Sichuan earthquake and poor working conditions in factories operated by the Taiwanese electronics manufacturer Foxconn, no longer engages in such controversial reporting. The monthly journal for intellectuals *Yanhuang Chunqiu* (*China Through the Ages*), run by liberals and reformers who were also members of the CCP nomenklatura and which contained articles challenging Party orthodoxy, decided to close down in 2018. Meanwhile, as Xi Jinping made clear during a widely publicised 2016 visit to *People's Daily* and the state news agency Xinhua, the only acceptable role for the state media is to "love the Party, protect the Party, and closely align themselves with the Party leadership in thought, word and action"[4] and project positive energy—*zheng nengliang*. Journalists working for state media are now required to have their political credentials examined as a condition of continued employment.

Mirroring Stalin's observation that writers were "the engineers of the human soul,"[5] Mao Zedong in 1942 convened the Yanan Forum on Art and Literature in which the key messages were that art and literature should serve the Party and that writers and artists should seek inspiration from the lives of the rural masses and, by ridding themselves of bourgeois thinking through a process of struggle, undergo a spiritual transformation. The net result of this was a slew of unreadable novels with titles such as *Yanyang Tian* (*Days of Radiance*) and *Ou Yanghai zhi Ge* (*The Song of Ou Yanghai*) portraying the triumph of communism, and paintings and films that were unabashedly propagandistic and of questionable artistic merit. This trend reached its nadir during the Cultural Revolution when Mao Zedong's wife Jiang Qing, in a former life a not very successful Shanghai film actress with the stage name Lan Ping, launched her eight model operas—*yangban xi*—which for a time became the only entertainment available.

As the post-Mao modernisation process took hold China's writers and artists began to find their voice, but relations with the Party were always uneasy and censorship still widespread. The 1990s films of the talented "Fifth Generation" cineaste Zhang Yimou, including *Red Sorghum*, *Raise High the Red Lantern*, *Ju Dou* and *The Story of Qiu Ju*, won international plaudits but could not be shown in China as they were perceived to dwell excessively on the darker aspects of Chinese society. (Zhang has since been rehabilitated and was responsible for orchestrating the opening and closing ceremonies for the 2008 Beijing Olympics.) Yan Lianke, a writer whose works include *Dream of Ding Village*, depicting the lives of rural AIDS sufferers, and *Serve the People*, a satire on Communist Party morality featuring graphic sexual content and scenes of iconoclasm, has seen his works intermittently banned. On television, reality shows, soap operas and comedies reflecting everyday contemporary life have increasingly given way to series set during the anti-Japanese and civil wars that glorify the role of the CCP and vilify their opponents. In 2014 Xi Jinping resurrected the spectre of the Yanan Forum in a speech in which he urged China's artists and writers to produce works that were both artistically outstanding and also promoted core socialist values. Meanwhile China sought to tame Hollywood through a combination of investment and rationing the number of foreign films shown in China to the point where no Hollywood producer is now prepared to make films that will offend the CCP's sensibilities. The CCP has also shown skill and creativity in using social media and online gaming to promote patriotism among China's youth using cultural icons to whom young people can relate.[6]

An important element in conditioning the outlook of the masses is promoting a sense of paranoia about the threats to China's unity and stability supposedly posed by "hostile foreign forces," a term that features regularly in leadership speeches and articles in state-run media. At bottom the CCP is a Leninist organisation, born in an atmosphere of clandestinity and conspiracy and requiring the existence of a hostile "other" to justify its existence. Since 2014 China has instituted a "National Security Week" during which its citizens are urged to be on the lookout for foreign intelligence agents and to protect China's secrets. This is accompanied by films and graphic stories showing naïve young Chinese girls seduced by their wicked Western boyfriends into divulging classified information—which in China can mean virtually any information—only to be brought to book by the stern guardians of the law. This process extends even to primary school children, as evidenced by a photograph displayed on Chinese social media showing young children from a Xi'an primary school dressed in 1930s uniforms, standing in front of the Xian Incident memorial holding a banner that proclaimed them to be "young intelligence workers enjoying happy summer holidays while engaged in patriotic educational activities."

For the CCP the ultimate prize has always been the ability to condition public behaviour towards "correct" thought and actions in ways that naturally and effortlessly reinforce the Party's hold on power. This was neither a new concept nor one unique to China. Many societies sought to achieve similar outcomes through a combination of theology and realpolitik, as evidenced by the European concept of the Divine Right of Kings. In a Confucianist society, the fact that the emperor was on the throne was seen as evidence that he enjoyed the Mandate of Heaven. Any effort to oppose his rule or to behave in ways at variance with imperial orthodoxy ran counter to the Mandate of Heaven and was by definition morally reprehensible. The way to deal with unorthodox behaviour was to pre-empt it through a combination of rigorous social controls and education.

Following the collapse of the imperial system, China's modernisers perceived a need to reshape the psychology of the Chinese population in order to promote more public-spirited and less selfish behaviour, with Nationalist leader Chiang Kai-shek calling for the psychological reconstruction—*xinli jianshe*—of the Chinese people. The modernisers believed they had found an answer in the concept of "mental hygiene," which had come into vogue in US psychiatric circles during the 1920s and '30s. This concept held that the human psyche was infinitely malleable and that what determined human behaviour more than anything else was environmental conditioning. To this was added the concept of eugenics that had arisen out of the Social Darwinist idea of the survival of the fittest. Combined, these techniques could ensure a population that would consist of healthy, well-adjusted and socially compliant adults.

Such thinking resonated strongly with young Chinese scholars studying in US universities during the Nationalist era not least because the connotations of racial fitness that were a core part of Social Darwinism enjoyed widespread appeal. As with other branches of Western learning, their interest in psychiatry was resolutely instrumental: how could this knowledge contribute to China's modernisation by enhancing the mental resilience of its population and getting them to behave in ways that would facilitate the creation of a modern society? Within Nationalist China the concept of mental hygiene—*xinli weisheng*—became immediately politicised. Anyone failing to conform to the ideals of the Nationalist Party, which by then had adopted many of the trappings of National Socialism, should be regarded as suffering from a form of mental illness. Such "mental illness" was however not specific to a particular individual but rather something potentially injurious to the state and hence requiring state intervention.[7]

For the original proponents of mental hygiene, communism was seen as one of the forms of deviant behaviour that required pre-emptive intervention to eradicate. In an ironic twist, under the CCP, it was rejection of communism that came to be seen as a mental disorder. From the moment it seized power the CCP instituted programmes of thought reform that sought to create a compliant population using the by now familiar techniques of self-criticism and what came to be called brain-washing—*xinao*. This process involved a forensic examination of all aspects of an individual's past life with the aim of highlighting "incorrect" behaviour and compelling him to produce self-criticisms on a repeated basis leading to a repudiation of all former behaviours and thinking and an embrace of the "correct" world view. How effective this approach is in effecting fundamental change is open to doubt. In all likelihood the impact may be similar to hypnosis, which can work with subjects who are inherently suggestible but not on those who are more strong-minded. What it may however do quite effectively is break the spirit of those subjected to such pressurised tactics, leading them to adopt the line of least resistance. Such techniques have been in the main reserved for Party members and recalcitrant intellectuals during periods such as Mao's 1950s rectification campaign. For the great mass of society, the constant and unchallenged assertions produced by the CCP's Propaganda Department and reinforced through mechanisms such as the Patriotic Education Campaign, which highlights the humiliations suffered by China at the hands of the West and the indispensable role of the CCP in rectifying this, suffice—as long as the CCP delivers on its key commitments.

The CCP is now in the process of knitting together a suite of administrative and technological capabilities designed to address the challenges of maintaining social order in a modern consumer-driven society through what amounts to the creation of a techno-security state. In addition to its efforts to control the public narrative Beijing seeks to use technology to control public space to ensure compliance with its norms and values, with the risk that this will increasingly spill over into control of private space. Control of physical space is achieved in urban areas through a grid management system that was piloted in 2004 and rolled out across the country in 2015. The grid management system has echoes of the *baojia* system introduced by the Song dynasty administrative reformer Wang Anshi. Based on networks of ten households, *baojia*'s primary purpose was to provide militia services but the groups of ten households were also held collectively responsible for ensuring the good behaviour of their members. The grid management system involves the subdivision of the smallest administrative unit, the county (*xian*), into smaller zones, with one individual appointed to each zone to provide regular reporting on issues such as population size, housing, amenities and social organisations within the zone.

The grid management system is complemented by the Skynet project,[8] launched in 2005, which has involved the creation of a nationwide network of high definition video cameras providing round-the-clock coverage of major urban districts, streets, schools and business centres and coverage of secondary sites such as minor streets. These cameras are linked to vehicle registration and facial recognition software, the latter a technology in which China has become a world leader. Skynet is linked to the Safe Cities initiative, designed to provide warning of natural disasters and to enhance urban management and public security. A further embellishment has been the Sharp Eyes Project—*xueliang gongcheng*—inaugurated in 2015, which aims to extend surveillance coverage to rural areas which are more lightly policed than the cities but also to enhance security at the interface between urban and rural areas. The aim of Sharp Eyes is to establish 100% video coverage of key public areas and important facilities by 2020 to create a full cross-network of surveillance data. In the Shandong city of Linyi, where the project was first trialled, a programme was launched under the strapline "all households are monitors"—*huhu dou shi jiankong yuan*—whereby the cable TV boxes in households were all given access to security video feeds enabling citizens to report crimes simply by pressing a button. A significant innovation of the Sharp Eyes programme is in linking video cameras covering the entrances to private dwellings and other locations such as hotels and shops to the Skynet network.[9] China's urban residents are becoming used to receiving texts notifying them of infractions such as jaywalking or illegal parking for which they have been fined. In Shenzhen and Fujian jaywalkers, in addition to being fined, are publicly shamed by having their photographs displayed on large LED screens. Most appear ready to accept a trade-off between a reduction in personal privacy and a safer and better-run urban environment but tend to draw the line at such surveillance being extended to genuinely private places such as homes.

The far western province of Xinjiang has become a test-bed for this complex of surveillance and monitoring capabilities. Xinjiang, meaning "new frontier," has never been fully integrated with the rest of China, sometimes coming under Chinese administrative control but at other times enjoying autonomy and in the 1930s and 1940s even a brief period of independence before becoming subsumed in the People's Republic as an autonomous region. Until well into the 1990s Xinjiang's population was predominantly Uighur and Kazakh, though a significant number of Han Chinese had settled there in the 1950s and '60s, comprising what was termed the *bingtuan*—brigades—essentially communities of armed settlers serving as a colonial militia force.[10] Starting in the 1990s a state-induced wave of Han immigration into Xinjiang has reduced the Uighur to a minority. Xinjiang was always a sensitive region by virtue of its long border with the Soviet Union and because it was the location for China's nuclear weapons programme. Xinjiang is also fundamental to China's efforts to develop its Belt and Road Initiative (BRI), a significant component of which involves connecting China more directly with markets in Central Asia, the Persian/Arabian Gulf and Europe through road and rail links.

During the Mao era the traditionally Muslim Uighur population was unable to practise its religion but following reform and opening-up mosques were reopened, religious education introduced into Xinjiang schools, Uighur language news media and books published and connections with the wider Islamic world re-established with Uighurs and other minority Islamic groups such as the Hui being permitted to perform the Haj. While most Uighurs practised a quietist form of Sunni Islam, some were attracted to the more extreme teachings of Saudi Wahhabism and graduated from there to adherence to the jihadist doctrines espoused by al Qaeda leader Osama bin Laden. By the time of the 9/11 bombings the East Turkestan Islamic Movement (ETIM), comprising several thousand Uighur jihadists, was one of many Afghanistan-based transnational jihadist groups that had sworn *baya'at*—fealty—to bin Laden, subsequently migrating to the Federally Administered Tribal Areas of Pakistan and from there to Syria where they comprise part of the al Qaeda umbrella group Jabhat Fatah al Sham. ETIM aspires to create an Islamic state in Xinjiang and since the 1990s its sympathisers have undertaken a series of unsophisticated but nonetheless deadly terrorist attacks both within Xinjiang and elsewhere in China. China was quick to align itself with US president George W. Bush's Global War on Terror, seeing this as providing international validation for an approach that addressed burgeoning Uighur separatist tendencies by equating them with terrorism.

In 2017 China moved to a new level of social control in Xinjiang. Drawing on techniques previously used to control Tibet, another autonomous region susceptible to separatist tendencies, dense networks of surveillance cameras combined with facial recognition technology were set up in all towns and cities—in reality every city in Xinjiang consists of two cities, one Uighur and one Han Chinese, separated by a large square and a statue of Mao Zedong. Police posts and checkpoints were established at intervals of one or two hundred metres and physical checks of Uighur residents were supplemented by technical means including the mandatory uploading of mobile phone apps enabling individual movements and social media behaviours to be monitored at all times and the widespread collection of biometric data including DNA. Surveillance cameras were installed in private houses and Uighur families found themselves required to accommodate Han Chinese "guests." Over and above high levels of physical security the Chinese state has set out to sinicise the Uighur population by outlawing many of the external manifestations of Islamic observance such as beards for men and veils for women, the public use of Arabic script to write the Uighur language and the use of the Uighur language in education. The process has since spread to China's Hui community, consisting of Muslims who have long since assimilated most aspects of Chinese culture, and to all other religions including Christianity and Judaism, with the small historic Jewish community in Kaifeng experiencing a crackdown on religious practice.

In 2018 reports began to emerge of large numbers of Uighurs being placed in custom-built detention centres where they were pressured to renounce Islamic behaviour and adopt Chinese lifestyles including the consumption of pork and alcohol.[11] After initially denying the existence of such facilities, estimated to hold between 1 and 1.5 million people, the Chinese state then acknowledged that they did exist but that their purpose was educative; the aim was to eliminate the risk that Xinjiang's Uighur population would succumb to Islamist extremist propaganda and to provide them with vocational training and tuition in the Chinese language so that they could enjoy a good economic future. In essence this approach amounted to treating Islamic behaviour as a mental aberration that could be cured with the right conditioning. It also represented a repudiation of a long-standing Chinese policy dating back to Liberation whereby China was conceived of as a multi-ethnic state with fifty-six officially recognised ethnic minorities in favour of the imposition of a single—Han—culture. China's initially defensive response quickly turned into a defiant assertion that this programme constituted a major contribution to global counter-radicalisation. This programme of forced cultural assimilation attracted no significant official response from the Islamic world, with only Malaysia's prime minister Dr. Mahathir Mohamed being honest enough to admit that China's global economic heft made such behaviour difficult to challenge.

The response in Western liberal democracies has been more forceful, with the US Senate passing a Uighur Human Rights Policy Act calling for sanctions against Chinese officials and a prohibition on the export of US goods and services to Chinese state agents operating in Xinjiang. More consequentially, in October 2019 the US Department of Commerce added eight

Chinese technology companies to its Entities List, meaning they were no longer able to purchase components from US companies without US government approval. The companies included Hikvision, the world's largest producer of video surveillance technology, SenseTime Group and Megvii Technology, both specialising in facial recognition software, and iFlytek, which specialises in speech recognition technology. The fact that these companies remain heavily reliant on Western components testifies both to China's continuing vulnerability and to the complicity of a number of Western companies in enabling the development of China's techno-security state.[12]

But while China has remained publicly unapologetic about its Xinjiang policy, it has had to take into account both internal reservations about the policy manifested through the leaking to international media of large quantities of classified Party documents setting out in detail what the policy consists of and how it should be implemented, and non-government responses in the Islamic world. An example of the latter can be found in Malaysia, a country that has always had an uneasy relationship with China due to long-standing political and cultural tensions between the country's Malay Muslim majority and its substantial Chinese minority population. In response to reports that the Chinese state was planning to rewrite religious works including the Quran to reflect socialist values, the head of the Malaysian Consultative Council of Islamic Organisation wrote:

> The rewriting of the Quran will be seen as a war against Islam and Muslims around the world will definitely stand up to rebuke this policy. We remind China not to cross the red line. The already massive repression of Uighur Muslims has been heavily criticised by the international community and the Muslims will not tolerate such abusive policy to alter the most sacred text of Islam.[13]

In late 2019 a senior Chinese official announced that all those who had undergone the original vocational training had "graduated" and found work. In reality what seems to have happened is that many Uighur detainees have been released on condition that they sign contracts to work in factories close to their original detention centres.[14] Meanwhile Xinjiang has experienced a significant outflow of Han Chinese who find the security environment onerous and oppressive, thereby threatening to reverse the demographic engineering process that since the 1990s has led to the Uighur becoming a minority within their own region.[15]

The two last pieces in this jigsaw of social control are the Smart Cities initiative and the Social Credit scheme. China has enthusiastically adopted the Smart Cities programme, accounting for 500 projects out of a global total of 1,000. This initiative is based on collaboration between municipal administrations and private sector companies and focuses on the delivery of different capabilities depending on perceived municipal priorities. One example is Hangzhou's City Brain project undertaken by Alibaba, which provides AI-enabled analysis of road conditions, enabling officials to optimise traffic flows by altering traffic light sequences and permit swifter passage for ambulances and other emergency service vehicles. Others include Shanghai's Citizen Cloud project, a cloud-based platform accessible via a mobile app which enables citizens to access a range of government services, and Guangzhou's regional health information platform, which makes patient records easily available to healthcare professionals and which is supplemented by a hospital app enabling patients to make appointments and access other healthcare services from a digital one-stop shop. The benefits of such technologies are self-evident. But the Smart Cities initiative also constitutes the interface at which technologies designed to optimise efficient urban living can also be optimised for social control.

Much has been written in the Western media about China's Social Credit system, which is normally described as "Orwellian." Many Western media reports talk of a nationwide system in which both the financial and personal behaviour of individual citizens, including online behaviour, are aggregated into a single score. Those with high scores receive rewards such as easy access to loans while those with low scores are penalised in various ways including not being able to buy tickets for high-speed rail journeys or send their children to better schools. China's own propagandists have characterised the system as one that will "allow the trustworthy to roam everywhere under heaven while making it hard for the discredited to take a single step."[16] This may well be the ultimate objective though the reality is more complex and messier.

The idea of social credit was first introduced in a State Council document published in 2014. Its primary aim was to deal with the pressing problems of a low trust society characterised by high levels of corruption, fraud and counterfeiting (there is virtually nothing in modern China that has not been counterfeited, including infant milk formula and eggs). A particular problem was the inability of courts to enforce legal judgments against businesses and individuals, who often evaded enforcement by simply moving to another province. The primary focus of the document was on improving the trustworthiness of government bodies and the commercial sector with the focus very much on financial and regulatory behaviours. Regulatory agencies were each required to draw up two lists, black and red. The former comprised businesses and individuals which had violated existing laws and regulations while the latter comprised entities and individuals with a good record of legal and regulatory compliance. A system of MOUs enables all regulatory agencies to have visibility of each other's lists and to impose additional penalties on those who have violated a particular law or regulation.

Various experimental regimes have been launched around the country in conjunction with private sector companies, such as the Alibaba spin-off Ant Financial's Sesame Credit, which offers rewards for those with good credit scores—in essence a combination of Experian plus a loyalty card reward scheme. But in 2017 the central government decided that none of these schemes would be rolled out at a national level and the focus is now on encouraging local governments to develop their own systems without prescriptive guidance on what these should contain or what if any systems of penalties and rewards should be applied. Some cities have rolled out schemes that award each citizen a single score based on their compliance or otherwise with existing laws. In other cases, such as those of Fuzhou and Nanjing, social credit metrics are being merged with existing systems for providing social services but without social credit scores being allocated.

The original intention set out in the 2014 State Council document was to have a national social credit system in place by 2020 but it seems improbable that the existing patchwork of local schemes can be aggregated up to a comprehensive national scheme within the stipulated time-scale, nor is that necessarily the intention. As the China research group Trivium has put it:

> China's central government doesn't see its own role in the SCS as an assigner of scores, but rather as a record keeper, whose job is to consolidate government files into a central database of social credit records, and then through that database, provide state agencies, city governments, banks, industry associations, and the general public with data on individuals and companies so they can make their own evaluations. The master database of social credit records has already been built: it's called the National Credit Information Sharing Platform (NCISP) and a significant amount of the data it contains is open for public sharing.[17]

Meanwhile the National Development Reform Commission, which has overall responsibility for implementing the social credit system, has encouraged private sector tech companies to develop social credit apps, an example of which is the Debt Default Checker—*laolai chaxun*—developed by the Xiamen

Tuoke Internet Technology Company—which enables companies and individuals to ascertain who is on the central government's Defaulter Blacklist.

China's techno-security state is becoming and in many respects is already a reality and raises uncomfortable questions about the relative strengths of authoritarian states vis-à-vis liberal democracies. On the face of it the CCP is well on the way to consolidating its control over its population to a degree that precludes any kind of effective internal challenge to its authority. And the CCP's ambitions to eliminate threats to its hold on power do not stop at China's geographical borders. As Samantha Hoffman has observed, the CCP's concern for its political and ideological security is not something that is bounded by geography.[18] China has shown an increasing propensity to take action overseas to address perceived threats to its security. And it has taken a leaf out of the USA's book by seeking to apply its laws extraterritorially to foreign private sector companies that do business in or with China. This was the case with foreign airlines who were told that failure to categorise Hong Kong, Macao and Taiwan as part of China in all their publications irrespective of whether they were available in China would adversely affect their social credit scores. The extent and implications of this expansion overseas is only now starting to become apparent as the Chinese Party-state seeks to defend its values and narrative using the threat of denial of access to Chinese markets as its primary lever. It is also seeking to normalise the Chinese approach internationally including by making its surveillance systems available to other states and by such means as seeking a redefinition of human rights at the United Nations by prioritising the right to economic development.

As Leon Trotsky is supposed to have observed, while an autocrat is in power his demise seems inconceivable; once he has been deposed it seems inevitable. It has been suggested that the natural span for a one-party state is seventy years[19] based on examples that include the Soviet Union and Mexico's Partido Revolucionario Institucional (PRI). There was some evidence of concern within the Chinese Communist Party as this potentially fateful deadline approached—and then passed without serious incident. If anything, objective evidence points to growing levels of popular satisfaction within China about their government's performance. In the words of a detailed survey conducted over many years by the Harvard Kennedy School's Ash Center:

> Even in 2003, the central government received a strong level of satisfaction, with 86.1% expressing approval and 8.9% disapproving. This high level of satisfaction increased even further by 2016, but such increases were minimal because public satisfaction was already high to begin with. By contrast, in 2003, township-level governments had quite negative satisfaction rates, with 44% expressing approval and 52% disapproving. However, by 2016, these numbers had flipped, with 70% approving and only 26% disapproving. These increases in satisfaction are not just limited to overall assessments of government performance. When asked about the specific conduct and attributes of local government officials, increasing numbers of Chinese citizens view them as kind, knowledgeable and effective.[20]

This is hardly evidence of a population feeling ground down and oppressed and suggests that what matters most to Chinese citizens is competence and delivery—areas in which the performance of Western liberal democracies is coming under question. For now at least it seems that the convenience and security offered by the various components of the techno-security state outweigh concerns about any restrictions on personal freedom they may impose. How long that will last is another question.

6

CHINA, THE INTELLIGENCE STATE

State-on-state espionage has a murky status in international law. International humanitarian law, otherwise known as the Law of Armed Conflict (LOAC) does afford espionage a legitimate role in armed conflict on the basis of a clear distinction between war and peace—which is becoming progressively less meaningful in an era of "grey zone" warfare. Espionage in peacetime is more contentious. Since it necessarily involves interference in the affairs of another sovereign state it could be seen as an internationally wrongful act as specified in the United Nations Charter. And to the extent that such espionage interferes with or impacts on the rights of individuals, for example by eavesdropping on their communications, it could be seen as a violation of human rights law. But there is nothing in international law that explicitly prohibits state-on-state espionage, and international law, like English common law, is broadly permissive, meaning that anything not expressly prohibited is allowed. More to the point, international law is still in large measure a reflection of state practice, and most states either practise espionage or reserve the right to do so in pursuit of national security and national advantage.

China is no exception to this rule. Espionage has been a recognised facet of Chinese statecraft since at least the Spring and Autumn period (777–476 BCE) as evidenced by its codification in Sunzi's *Bingfa*, normally translated as *The Art of War*, and in subsequent works of strategy such as *The Thirty-Six Stratagems—sanshiliu ji*. Modern China's approach to espionage has been shaped by the early experiences of the Chinese Communist Party (CCP), which came into existence in a period of widespread hostility to communism, leading inevitably to a culture of intrigue, clandestinity and paranoia intrinsic to a Leninist organisation. During the 1930s and '40s the CCP fought a savage no-holds-barred intelligence war with Chiang Kai-shek's Nationalist forces, with the CCP's intelligence apparatus under the control of Zhou Enlai (who went on to become prime minister under Mao Zedong).[1] From 1949 onwards China had to contend with a climate of global hostility exacerbated by Mao's efforts to promote an international communist revolution focused initially on the states of Southeast Asia. Meanwhile the threat from Chiang Kai-shek's Taiwan-based Nationalist forces, still committed to retaking the Chinese mainland, presented a major security challenge which involved extensive use of espionage by both parties.

Intelligence agencies engage in covert collection using a variety of means including human intelligence—HUMINT—and signals intelligence—SIGINT. They also to varying degrees engage in covert action, which can entail efforts to shape the behaviours and policies of other states. These efforts can include anything from colluding with opposition groups to overthrow a government through to bribing politicians and journalists to promote particular policies or discredit others. During the 1950s China's efforts to foment revolution were however driven less by the intelligence agencies than by a range of CCP entities that included the United Front Work Department, the Overseas

Chinese Affairs Office and the CCP Central Liaison Department, all of which covertly promoted links with entities such as the Indonesian Communist Party (PKI), which launched an unsuccessful coup against President Sukarno in 1965, and the Communist Party of Malaya, which launched an insurgency against the British colonial administration during the 1950s.

During this period China's main intelligence service, previously known as the Social Affairs Department and subsequently the Investigation Department of the CCP (ID/CCP), was primarily taken up with addressing domestic threats to the CCP. Foreign intelligence successes were few and far between and were mostly run by the Ministry of Public Security (MPS), which was responsible for counter-intelligence and counter-espionage. Known cases focused against the West included Larry Wu-Tai Chin, a young interpreter who was infiltrated into US government service in China before the establishment of the People's Republic. Chin joined the CIA-controlled Foreign Broadcast Information Service, from where he provided his MPS case officers with high-grade intelligence on Sino–US relations and other topics until his retirement in 1981. Chin was subsequently betrayed by a defecting Chinese intelligence officer in 1985 but committed suicide before he could be tried.[2] Another well-known case is that of the French diplomat Bernard Boursicot, recruited in Beijing through his relationship with transgender Chinese opera star Shi Beipu, a story that was turned into the modern opera *M. Butterfly*. At the outbreak of the Cultural Revolution the ID/CCP became an instrument for persecuting Mao's domestic opponents under its then head Kang Sheng, who in the 1940s had presided over a purge of intelligence personnel deemed—largely incorrectly—to have collaborated with either the KMT or Japan.[3] During the ensuing chaos the ID/CCP was taken over by the military and its operations ground to a virtual halt.

Once the Cultural Revolution had ended and Deng Xiaoping's reform and opening-up had got under way, China's intelligence agencies were given both a makeover and a new mission. In 1983 a new civilian intelligence agency, the Ministry of State Security (MSS), was formed, combining the intelligence collection and analysis departments of the ID/CCP with the counter-intelligence and counter-espionage divisions of the Ministry of Public Security (MPS), which became primarily a police and public order agency. The remit of the MSS was "to ensure the security of the state through effective measures against enemy agents, spies and counter-revolutionary activities designed to sabotage or overthrow China's socialist system."[4] The MSS was both an internal security service and a foreign intelligence service. In exercising the latter role it found itself in direct competition with the Second Department of the PLA General Staff (2/PLA), which was engaged in open-source intelligence collection via a global network of defence attachés, some of whom maintained limited intelligence liaison relationships with their host governments, and in covert collection operations using non-official cover officers (NOCs) operating under a range of business and academic identities.

An important mission for China's intelligence services was to collect scientific and technical intelligence to enable China's modernisation programme, a requirement that was formalised in 1986 through Plan 863. This plan, initially proposed to Deng Xiaoping by China's nuclear scientists, was designed to reduce Chinese dependence on Western technologies in areas deemed to be strategic, including bio-technology, space, information technology, lasers, energy, automation and new materials.[5] Much of what Plan 863 aspired to achieve came through legitimate forms of activity, including culling information from open-source publications, the establishment of joint ventures with Western companies and the outright purchase of certain technologies. But espionage also played a significant role. Numerous actors such as businessmen, academics and students were pressed into service to collect whatever information they came across in the course of visits to Western countries or engagement with scientists from those countries. The initial focus was on the USA, and China was able to exploit the ease of access afforded by an open society to engage in low-level incremental collection activities described by a former FBI counter-intelligence official as a "thousand grains of sand approach."[6] By no means all the covert collection activities were undertaken or directed by China's intelligence services, which initially focused their attention on advanced military technologies, an area in which China lagged significantly behind the West.

One advantage the Chinese intelligence services were able to exploit was a Chinese diaspora community that was disproportionately represented in classified US defence programmes. Such individuals, many of whom still had family in China, were susceptible to appeals to assist China with its own development—and could often be made to feel guilty about enjoying comfortable lives in the West while their compatriots—*tongbao*—had suffered poverty and deprivation. This covert collection effort proved remarkably successful, enabling China to acquire technologies for nuclear warhead miniaturisation, quiet submarine propulsion, and the B1 and B2 strategic bombers. The fact that it was done incrementally over a long period—the collection effort against the W88 miniaturised nuclear warhead took twenty years to complete—made it difficult for the US authorities to justify the resources needed to investigate or prosecute. The result, as illustrated in David Wise's book *Tiger Trap*, based on the study of court records and interviews with former FBI counter-intelligence officials, was a handful of prosecutions resulting in almost no major convictions. Even Katherine Leung, known by the FBI codename Parlour Maid, who was prosecuted as an

MSS double agent (she had succeeded in seducing her FBI case officers and effectively ended up running them), received only a judicial slap on the wrist.

The advent of modern ICT proved to be a game-changer for China's intelligence services, turning what had previously been a cautious and risk-averse community—the Boursicot case had required prime ministerial approval—into one that engaged in pervasive collection activities with few if any political constraints. To begin with, the principal entity engaged in this digital collection effort was China's signals intelligence—SIGINT—agency, the Third Department of the PLA General Staff (3/PLA). Until the 1980s 3/PLA had limited reach beyond China's immediate periphery, and in an age where SIGINT collection was to some extent a function of physical proximity to information flows, China's isolation put it at a disadvantage. This began to change in the 1970s when as part of the US–China rapprochement initiated by President Richard Nixon, 3/PLA operated two US-built SIGINT stations at Qitai and Korla in Xinjiang to collect telemetry on Soviet missile tests and space launches and to monitor anti-ballistic missile and nuclear warhead tests. By the 1990s 3/PLA had established a chain of listening stations along the coast of Myanmar, including Great Coco Island in the Andaman Sea, and had acquired two former Soviet listening posts in Cuba, at Bejucal and Santiago de Cuba, targeting US communications. In addition, 3/PLA began to conduct SIGINT collection operations out of Chinese embassies whilst also conducting a growing range of tactical naval collection operations.[7]

By the early 2000s it became evident that China's intelligence agencies were engaged in a pervasive global campaign of cyber espionage. It is likely that this campaign began with efforts by the MSS to target foreign-based Falungong supporters and other dissident groups such as Free Tibet, the latter through an operation that became known in the West as Ghost Net. But as it became evident that there existed vast treasure troves of data on computer systems that were either poorly defended or not defended at all, this campaign extended to foreign governments, NGOs focusing on human rights and private sector corporations. The first such operation to be made public was known by the codename Titan Rain, targeting the unclassified networks of numerous US agencies including the Department of Defense, FBI and the Sandia National Laboratories responsible for the US nuclear weapons programme.

The fact that the information collected was unclassified did not diminish its value. In the pre-information era intelligence agencies focused exclusively on the collection of classified information not in the public domain. But in the information age a combination of bulk collection plus artificial intelligence programmes using machine learning enables patterns to be identified and conclusions drawn that would not be apparent from reading single classified documents or debriefing individual human sources. Governments are hence having—slowly and belatedly—to rethink concepts of secrecy and security and how to apply protections to data that would not previously have merited such consideration.

The primary focus of China's cyber espionage campaign was on the collection of foreign Intellectual Property (IP) in pursuit of the country's modernisation objectives. As with earlier Chinese collection activities, it was not only the intelligence agencies who were involved: much of the collection effort, described by those on the receiving end as "noisy and repetitive," was undertaken by freelance groups of hackers operating with broad concurrence from the Chinese state and, when required, in conjunction with the intelligence agencies—which themselves often moonlighted for state-owned enterprises (SOEs) and other private sector entities. In contrast to Russia, whose hackers were at pains to avoid detection, Chinese attackers made little effort to cover their tracks. The data they sought matched more or less exactly the science and technology priorities set out in successive Chinese Five-Year Plans and their activities were closely aligned with the rhythms of the Chinese working day. What set China's cyber warriors apart was their persistence and the ingenuity with which they used social engineering to identify ways into their targets, starting at the outer ring and working their way inwards. They were also skilled at attacking the networks of ancillary bodies such as contractors and legal firms associated with particular contracts whose networks contained much valuable data but whose levels of security awareness were lower than those of their principals.

Many Western commercial companies were unaware that they were under attack or did know but affected not to care. Those that did know often chose not to make an issue of the fact for fear of jeopardising their commercial prospects in China, or harboured a misplaced conviction that China could copy but not innovate, so Western companies would always be able to maintain their edge. An example of the consequences of such an approach is provided by Nortel, in 2000 the world's largest and most advanced telecommunications company and one of the brightest jewels in Canada's economic crown. By 2009 Nortel had filed for bankruptcy as the result of a sustained campaign of Chinese cyber theft enabling Chinese telecommunications companies such as Huawei, aided by generous state subsidies, to reverse-engineer Nortel products and sell them at prices with which Nortel itself could not compete.[8] Warnings by Nortel's chief security officer Brian Shields about the threat from Chinese cyber espionage were dismissed by senior management as the jeremiads of "someone who always cried wolf."[9] Even warnings from Canada's security and intelligence agency CSIS were disregarded. And although the Canadian government were painfully aware of what had been done, they too remained silent out of a combination of embarrassment at the ease with which such a prominent national asset had been taken apart and a reluctance to put at risk their wider relationship with China. Companies that did speak out or instigated lawsuits against Chinese companies for IP theft, as was the case with Cisco and Motorola, often found themselves subject to retaliatory Chinese state actions in the form of anti-trust or anti-money laundering investigations, leading them to withdraw their suits.

Such behaviour is hardly unique: all major economies owe some of their initial success to industrial espionage. In the early eighteenth century a young Englishman, John Lombe, commercialised the emerging technologies of Britain's Industrial Revolution by smuggling back from Piedmont the techniques for spinning strong yarn from silkworm threads (a technology the Byzantine empire had centuries earlier stolen from China). Lombe acquired this knowledge by the not very sophisticated but nonetheless effective means of creeping into Piedmontese sericulture factories at dead of night and making drawings of the spinning machines by candlelight. He took this stolen IP back to Britain and with his brother built the world's first modern factory in Derbyshire using water-powered looms.[10] The young American republic similarly owed much of its early commercial success to stolen British manufacturing techniques. More recently Japan and South Korea have both faced significant allegations of industrial espionage during their rise to economic prominence. It is hardly surprising that China should have opted to follow suit. But as with so much else about China the difference lies in the exceptional scale and impact of their activities, and in the fact that in the cyber domain espionage may also be a prelude to sabotage, creating an additional layer of risk for companies and other entities whose networks have been penetrated.

By the early 2010s the level and intensity of Chinese cyberattacks against US corporations was on the way to becoming a

major irritant in Sino–US relations. The US government however had limited scope to retaliate directly against China due
both to the reluctance of many victims of cyber espionage to
acknowledge such attacks and the fact that there was an asym-
metry of vulnerability between the two countries. Put simply,
there was much China wished to steal from the USA but a lot
less that the USA wanted to steal from China. US espionage
activities against China, which certainly included a significant
cyber component, as evidenced by the revelations of rogue NSA
contractor Edward Snowden, were focused on the collection of
what might be termed traditional national security targets such
as government strategic intentions and military capabilities. A
further problem for the USA arose from the inherent difficulties
of attributing a cyberattack to a beyond-reasonable-doubt standard
in a domain that offers so many opportunities to disguise the
origin of a particular attack by routing it through multiple inter-
mediate points. It would in principle have been possible for the
USA to cut China off from the Internet and Chinese leaders
certainly feared this possibility but such an act would have
seemed a disproportionate response potentially tantamount to a
declaration of war.

Instead, the US government sought to dissuade China from
engaging in state-sponsored industrial cyber espionage by drawing a distinction between espionage conducted for legitimate
purposes of national security and espionage undertaken for economic purposes, something that was not legitimate (by law, US
intelligence agencies were prevented from collecting this kind of
intelligence for the benefit of US corporations; their activities in
this arena consisted of pursuing what might be termed a "level
playing-field" agenda, collecting intelligence with the aim of
ensuring that US corporations were not disadvantaged by rivals
employing underhand means such as bribery to secure contracts).
China however rejected this distinction, pointing out that eco-

nomic development was vital to China's national security. Failure to escape the middle-income trap or to further improve living standards could translate into levels of social disruption that could prove fatal for the CCP's continued hold on power. And in off-the-record exchanges Chinese officials observed that industrial cyber espionage represented condign retribution for China's century of humiliation at the hands of the West and for the West's withholding of technology from China after Liberation under the COCOM arrangements that remained in force until 1994. In 2014 the USA lost patience and publicly indicted five officers of the Shanghai-based 3/PLA Unit 61398 for cyberattacks directed against the USA's nuclear, metallurgy and solar energy sectors. The indictment included satellite imagery showing the location of Unit 61398 and photographs and detailed biographical details of the five officers concerned. This was followed by US threats to apply financial and other sanctions against Chinese companies judged to have benefitted from stolen US IP, action which if taken to extremes would have had a devastating effect on the Chinese economy. In 2015 presidents Barack Obama and Xi Jinping jointly pledged that neither country would engage in cyber espionage against commercial targets.

For a while this agreement appeared to be delivering the intended result. The level of visible cyberattacks against the USA and its Five-Eyes intelligence partners the UK, Australia, Canada and New Zealand diminished by as much as 90%—though this was accompanied by a corresponding rise in the level of attacks directed against targets in Europe, Japan and other advanced economies that did not have the same level of attribution capabilities the USA had so dramatically demonstrated. The reduction in cyberattacks coincided with a major military reorganisation designed by Xi Jinping—who in addition to his many other roles was Chairman of the CCP Central Military Commission—to promote professionalisation within a PLA the senior leadership of which had become mired in corruption to the point where virtually all of China's generals had purchased their appointments. As part of this reorganisation, 3/PLA had been integrated into a new Strategic Support Force with a remit that encompassed offensive and defensive information operations, electronic and space warfare. 3/PLA were instructed to cease moonlighting for the private sector and to focus their energies on developing military cyber capabilities.

It was not long before the MSS took advantage of the resultant gap in the market. During the early years of Xi Jinping's tenure the MSS had been under a cloud. Three vice-ministers had either been dismissed or arrested: one for allowing the MSS's resources to be used to covertly monitor leadership communications including those of Xi Jinping himself at the direction of the disgraced head of the CCP Political and Legal Commission Zhou Yongkang; another whose private secretary was found to be a long-time CIA agent; and a third for corruption.[11] The MSS sought to make up lost ground by launching a series of operations targeting not individual private sector companies but rather managed service providers, entities that provided cloud-based computing and data storage services for multiple private sector companies. The technologies they targeted were dual-use, i.e. with potential military applications, hence arguably not in breach of the letter of the agreement reached with the USA. An example of this phenomenon is the hacking group identified by the US cyber security company FireEye as APT 41 (APT standing for Advance Persistent Threat). APT 41 appears to combine promiscuous targeting of strategic intelligence that includes the technology priorities set out in Made in China 2025—China's strategic plan to increase levels of indigenous manufacture in key technologies—political intelligence and intelligence on developments such as mergers and acquisitions in strategic industries with criminal exploits undertaken for personal gain.[12]

The emergence of the MSS as the lead agency focusing on industrial espionage also resulted in an increase in traditional HUMINT techniques. Speaking to the Washington-based think-tank CSIS in August 2020, US Assistant Attorney-General for National Security John Demers highlighted the extent of what he referred to as the "man on the inside" cases in which individuals within US companies had been suborned into stealing the intellectual property of the corporations for which they worked. He also highlighted the use by China of the Thousand Talents programme to illicitly procure IP. The overt aim of the Thousand Talents programme is to attract leading-edge scientists and others with specialised knowledge to work in or with China and there is nothing illegal about this. But in a growing number of cases academics and scientists have been inducted into the programme while remaining in the USA and failing to tell their employers or the federal government of their involvement. Demers also attributed the US decision to close China's consulate in Houston to the important coordinating role it had played in the collection and return to China of stolen IP.[13]

It is hard to determine how effective a contribution to China's economic and technical progress such espionage has made. In some cases, the nexus is readily apparent, an example being China's rapid development of a nationwide high-speed rail network based on stolen Japanese technology—though even here a failure to fully understand some aspects of the technology that had been "acquired" resulted in 2014 in a major rail crash with multiple deaths and injuries. In other areas success has proven more elusive, as evidenced by China's persistent failure to develop indigenous aero engines for passenger aircraft despite a massive campaign of espionage undertaken under the direction of the Jiangsu State Security Bureau (SSB)[14] involving large-scale cyber espionage undertaken by non-state hacker groups combined with the recruitment of human sources inside target companies. The kinds of technology least amenable to such an approach tend to be those where results are the product of many years of incremental learning and what in German is termed *fingerspitzgefuehl*—the kind of intuitive knowledge that only comes with prolonged experience and for the acquisition of which there are no short-cuts. Moreover, industrial cyber espionage eventually produces diminishing returns and, in order to give rise to continued economic growth, needs to give way to innovative research. This is undoubtedly starting to happen in China as companies that initially relied on IP theft and imitation have now become genuine innovators in their fields with a consequently greater interest in seeing better IP protection within China. This is an issue the government has begun to address with some innovative legislation and a system of courts that have real teeth and in which foreign plaintiffs have begun to fare disproportionately well. But overcoming China's addiction to IP theft is likely to prove hard. Continuing high levels of Chinese espionage appear to be driven by a number of factors. These include the imperative of meeting demanding targets in relation to Made in China 2025, and the simple fact that Chinese industrial cyber espionage has developed into a self-sustaining ecosystem comprising many interest groups whose power and prosperity are bound up with such activity.

Chinese espionage has not just focused on acquiring technology. It also plays a growing role in enabling China to exercise global effect both by acquiring intelligence on foreign governments and shaping a global environment favourable to China's interests. In addition to substantial quantities of intelligence derived from cyber operations, China's intelligence agencies have been equally energetic in recruiting human sources. In an ever more technologically enabled world, intelligence from human sources—HUMINT—still has an important role to play. Many cyber exploits are enabled by human sources on the inside, a case in point being the Stuxnet attack on the SCADA systems controlling Iran's illegal centrifuge enrichment programme into which malware was allegedly introduced by an engineer whose role was to update the system. And although cyber intrusions can provide access to large volumes of valuable data, human sources still have a vital role to play in explaining how the policy-makers of other states see the world and why they take the decisions they do. Until relatively recently China's intelligence agencies were reticent about recruiting non-Chinese sources—and they retain a strong preference for relying on ethnic Chinese due to cultural affinities and the ability to exercise greater control through leverage over family members in China. However, it is now clear that they have the confidence to recruit foreign sources and in the case of the USA and other Western European countries have shown ingenuity in using social media as a targeting tool.

A case in point is that of Kevin Mallory, sentenced in May 2019 to twenty years' imprisonment for spying for China. Mallory, a Chinese linguist who had worked as a CIA case officer, was unemployed and heavily in debt when, in 2017, he was contacted on the professional networking site LinkedIn by a Chinese national purporting to be a representative of a Shanghai-based think-tank looking for an expert on foreign policy. Mallory's LinkedIn profile did not explicitly identify him as a former CIA officer but this would have been apparent to anyone familiar with the terms used by CIA officers when preparing post-retirement CVs. Invited to China to attend an expenses-paid meeting, Mallory was recruited, tasked, paid and supplied with covert communications.[15] Another former CIA officer, a Defense Department employee, and a former US State Department employee have all either been indicted or sentenced for spying on behalf of China in 2019. The latter, Candace Claiborne, a low-level administrative officer, was paid tens of thousands of dollars by the MSS for what can only have been low-grade operational intelligence. Four years earlier China's intelligence agencies had scored a major coup by hacking into the database of the US Office of Personnel Management (OPM), which held the personnel records of 21.5 million US federal government employees including sensitive information about their financial, marital and other personal problems. Because the US intelligence community had refused to store the personnel data of its employees on a database known to be poorly defended, any CIA officers using State Department or similar US government covers could be readily identified by virtue of their absence from the OPM database. Meanwhile the CIA's own China operations suffered a major setback when, between 2010 and 2012, some twenty of their Chinese agents were either killed or imprisoned due to a previously undetected vulnerability in the covert messaging systems with which they had been equipped.[16] Recruiting and running agents in a closed high-surveillance society such as China is self-evidently a much harder proposition than in an open society such as the USA, and replacing these assets will not have been easy if indeed it proved possible at all.

China's intelligence community has also been able to take advantage of China's more general global expansion, particularly in the field of telecommunications, to enhance its global collection effort. China's telecommunications national champions Huawei and ZTE have provided modern telecommunications networks throughout the developing world, potentially giving them access to large volumes of data. And China is currently providing various forms of AI-enabled surveillance technology to sixty-three countries according to a September 2019 report by the Carnegie Endowment for International Peace—though the report notes that almost as many countries had received similar technology from the USA and other Western states.[17] In 2012 a new headquarters complex for the African Union, built by the

China State Construction Engineering Corporation, was inaugurated in the Ethiopian capital Addis Ababa. Five years later it transpired that confidential African Union data had been transferred from the new complex every night between the hours of midnight and 2.00 am to servers located in Shanghai. China's government predictably denied any involvement.[18] Meanwhile China's intelligence agencies have become more brazen in efforts to silence critics and dissidents living overseas through intimidation and even kidnapping, as in the case of the Hong Kong-based bookseller Gui Minhai who was rendered to China from Thailand in 2015.

China's intelligence agencies have now developed a global reach that exceeds their wildest ambitions in terms of their ability to collect volumes of intelligence. What is less clear is the impact this collection effort has had on top-level Chinese policy-making. There is little public detail available about China's intelligence apparatus or the ways in which intelligence is used to inform policy. In 2016 China published an intelligence law that achieved the remarkable feat of not identifying by name any of China's intelligence agencies nor giving any indication of their size, composition, budgets or remits—beyond a very general statement that they operate within China's laws. No reference was made to the role of intelligence in policy-making nor to the existence of any central intelligence assessment mechanism performing the roles undertaken in the USA by the National Intelligence Council, the UK's Joint Intelligence Committee or the Australian Office of National Intelligence in pulling together intelligence from all available sources and producing agreed national assessments. Similarly China appears to lack any established crisis management mechanism for quickly bringing the top leadership together to address international crises, with the result that in previous such situations, such as the 2001 collision between a US reconnaissance aircraft and a Chinese fighter jet, the US government was unable to make high-level contact with Chinese counterparts for some days.

The Hong Kong protests that erupted in June 2019 in response to a proposed extradition bill that would enable Hong Kong residents to be extradited to mainland China suggest that these mechanisms either do not exist or are dysfunctional. China's leadership was visibly blindsided by events in Hong Kong and it became clear that they had been listening only to voices telling them what they wished to hear—a problem not unique to China—rather than reading hard-headed intelligence assessments of the realities, if indeed such assessments were produced. All intelligence agencies struggle with the challenge of telling truth to power but the problem is especially acute within authoritarian regimes. As the former chairman of the Soviet KGB Vladimir Kryuchkov observed, the value of the KGB's intelligence sources was often vitiated by the need to analyse their product through a filter of ideological preconception.[19] Ultimately the greatest value an intelligence agency can provide is to reduce uncertainty for policy-makers and provide them with a sense-making narrative that can help them put in context and assess the significance of particular events. It is unclear to what extent China's intelligence agencies are able to perform that role, given that China's leaders possess a clearly defined worldview based on certain beliefs that are unchallengeable.

Chinese espionage, particularly the cyber variety, has achieved a scale and intensity never before experienced. It has become a major destabilising factor in relations with the USA and has had a damaging effect on international trust. Foreign companies operating in China now take it as a given that their data will be stolen and their Chinese employees compelled to report on their employers. Few foreign businessmen or other professionals on short-term visits to China will now risk bringing with them any electronic media that might afford access to their corporate databases. The threat from China is not merely to the intellectual property that represents the economic future of these states but, in extreme scenarios, their very ability to function as societies. China has for some time been reconnoitring the USA's power grids and other facets of US critical infrastructure apparently with a view to sabotaging these systems in times of crisis.[20] Nor is the threat merely one of espionage or sabotage. China needs to be understood as an intelligence state where, in contrast to liberal democracies, covert techniques are woven into the fabric of the state, as was the case with the Venetian Republic in the sixteenth and seventeenth centuries.[21] This reality is reflected in an Intelligence Law that requires citizens and organisations to provide the Chinese intelligence agencies with assistance. It has far-reaching implications for how China is seeking to shape the world in pursuit of its national interests.

7

A WORLD ORDER WITH
CHINESE CHARACTERISTICS

For most of its history China had nothing that could be termed
a foreign policy, only a border management and security policy.
That is not to say that the China of antiquity was entirely cut off
from external contact with the wider world, though in the pre-
modern era China's geography, with deserts and mountain ranges
to the west and the Pacific Ocean to the east, undoubtedly had
an isolating effect. The Han dynasty and the Roman Empire
were known to each other and several times exchanged envoys.
The US sinologist Homer Dubs claimed that descendants of a
Roman legion captured by the Parthians at the battle of Carrhae
made their way east and established a city in China,[1] a claim that
was not taken seriously initially but for which some evidence has
now been unearthed. Most contact however took place indirectly
through Parthian and Kushan intermediaries who controlled the
Eurasian trading route that became known as the Silk Road.
During the Tang dynasty, perhaps the most cosmopolitan in
China's history, the then-capital Chang'an, now Xian, played
host to a wide range of foreign merchants while many of the girls

employed in the Tang capital's bars and brothels were red-haired, green-eyed Central Asians; the barbarian whirling girls—*hu xuan nu*—that were the subject of an anonymous snatch of doggerel from that era.[2] During a period of religious fervour that characterised the early part of the Tang dynasty, India was looked up to as the source of the Buddhist sutras, the efforts to acquire which gave rise to one of China's best-known works of late mediaeval literature, *Xi You Ji*—*The Journey to the West*. For a brief period during the Mongol Yuan dynasty China was, albeit involuntarily, part of a Eurasian empire that encompassed Russia and extended into Eastern Europe.

China's approach to statecraft was rooted in the Confucian concept of hierarchy. During the Spring and Autumn and Warring States periods that followed the collapse of the Zhou dynasty, successor states were engaged in a constant struggle for hegemony and empire. The Westphalian concept of equality between sovereign states never took hold. China's concept of statecraft instead equated sovereignty with supremacy, based on the Confucian concept of *tian xia*—all under heaven—in which the ideal was global rule by an enlightened leader who was a moral exemplar and who hence enjoyed the mandate of heaven. In practice, Chinese statecraft conceived of the world in concentric circles. China and sinicised states such as Vietnam constituted the inner ring of civilised human beings; the outer ring consisted of barbarian tribes whose unwillingness to adopt Chinese mores rendered them sub-human in Chinese eyes. It was conceptually impossible for China to treat barbarians as equals. When the Turkic Xiongnu nomads sought such an arrangement with the Han their overtures were rejected out of hand.[3]

China's relations with other states were conducted through what is known in the West as the tribute system, though as the US sinologist Mark Mancall has pointed out there exists no such term in Chinese.[4] The tribute system was a convenient fiction, rather like the Holy Roman Empire in its latter phase, which provided a conceptual framework within which diplomacy could be conducted. States would send annual tribute missions to China where, in return for pledges of allegiance, they would be granted lucrative trading privileges. So lucrative were these arrangements that merchants from surrounding states would often travel with diplomatic credentials that their Chinese hosts knew to be bogus but which it suited both parties to accept as genuine even though the costs to China, in terms of hosting and entertaining their visitors, was disproportionately high.[5] And while treating with other states on a basis of equality was theoretically unacceptable, China could be pragmatic when the occasion demanded. Faced with a Russian state rapidly expanding into regions of Siberia which China saw as falling within its ambit, the Qing dynasty concluded China's first ever bilateral diplomatic agreement, the 1687 Treaty of Nerchinsk, which delineated the border between China and Russia and permitted a permanent Russian diplomatic presence in Beijing.

Until the arrival of the Western powers in the mid-nineteenth century China's main external security threat came from nomadic and semi-nomadic tribes located to the north and west. Policy was focused on keeping them at arm's length through a combination of dynastic marriages and economic incentives. After the brief burst of extroversion evidenced through the fifteenth century naval expeditions of Zheng He, the Chinese state became progressively more inward looking. Jesuit priests such as Matteo Ricci achieved some traction through their superior mathematical and technical skills but China's rulers were studiedly incurious about the countries from whence these priests and scholars originated. Similarly, in the eighteenth century the European vogue for chinoiserie made a significant contribution to the Chinese economy but China's rulers manifested no interest in learning about the states whose demand gave rise to this lucrative trade.

During the latter part of the nineteenth century China's reaction to the Western powers was also to try as far as possible to keep them at arm's length but the impact of their collective presence in China demanded a more pragmatic and flexible response. This involved sending missions overseas to learn from the West, which extended to eminent figures such as the modernising—and in China still controversial—statesman Li Hongzhang, who travelled extensively and, while in London, struck up a friendship with the inventor and entrepreneur Sir Hiram Maxim.[6] It also involved learning the art of statecraft as practised in the West; China proved a quick study, as evidenced by its foray into gunboat diplomacy in the 1870s when it despatched a warship to the Mexican port of Veracruz in response to reports of abuses of immigrant Chinese workers. And while China was at a disadvantage with respect to the more technologically advanced countries of the West, the Chinese state still managed to register some important diplomatic advances. From the 1920s onwards many foreign concessions were recovered, starting with Shandong, a former German concession transferred under the Versailles Treaty to Japan, a development that had triggered the May Fourth Movement. Under Chiang Kai-shek's Nationalist administration China also registered an important cultural victory when it persuaded Hollywood to abandon its stereotyped and demeaning representation of Chinese people, then invariably played by white actors, as the price of access to the Chinese market.

By 1945 China had largely put what the CCP came to term the Century of National Humiliation behind it. The foreign concessions were gone, though the colonies of Hong Kong and Macao remained, and China enjoyed a place at the world's top table by virtue of its position as a permanent member of the newly-formed United Nations Security Council. The nation was severely impoverished as a consequence of the Sino–Japanese war and some of its north-eastern territories were under Soviet occupation, but it is possible to imagine a very different future that China might have enjoyed had it been able gradually to consolidate its position as a status quo power in a period of relative peace and security. In the event a four-year civil war put paid to any such prospect and the regime that took power in Beijing in 1949 had no interest in pursuing a gradualist agenda either at home or abroad. In this context it was unsurprising that the creation of the People's Republic in 1949 should have given rise to a more assertive foreign policy. Under Mao Zedong China quickly emerged as a major disruptive force bent on taking on the forces of US imperialism through direct military engagement in the Korean peninsula and through the promotion of communist subversion throughout Southeast Asia and Indo-China. Mao's Three Worlds theory was a significant impetus for what was to become the Non-Aligned Movement. But this initial burst of revolutionary zeal proved short-lived. Relations with the Soviet Union, which had never been straightforward, declined rapidly following Khrushchev's 1956 denunciation of Stalin and Mao's disgust at a new Soviet policy of peaceful coexistence with the West. China's weak economy meant that it had little to offer the rest of the world, and as the country became embroiled in the politics of class struggle China became largely friendless. When Richard Nixon visited China in 1972 with the aim of forming a strategic relationship to contain Soviet military expansionism, he found a country that was isolated, angry and resentful.

As Deng Xiaoping's economic reforms took hold, China effectively opted not to have a foreign policy beyond doing the essential minimum to ensure a climate of peace and stability in which to pursue modernisation. China was content to be a free-rider on US-supplied security goods in the Asia-Pacific region and was at pains to behave as a status quo power. Sanctioned by the international community following the 1989 suppression of the

Democracy Movement, China followed Deng Xiaoping's dictum of keeping a low international profile, a strategy that became known as "hide and bide."[7] In 2001 China's already fast-developing economy became turbo-charged following its entry into the World Trade Organisation (WTO) on developing country terms, a development that would prove to have momentous implications both for the global financial system and the global balance of power. This translated into a much greater overseas presence as China sought to secure sources of raw materials, develop new markets for its products and seek investment opportunities. With growing economic power came increasing political influence and self-confidence. By the time Hu Jintao became CCP Secretary-General in 2003 China's emergence as a major power had begun to raise questions about what sort of power it would be.

In the late 1990s China had promoted a new security concept which held that Cold War concepts of competing and antagonistic blocks were outdated and that the way for states to enhance their security was through diplomatic and economic engagement.[8] Implicit, though not yet explicit, in this concept was China's concern about a continuing network of US alliance relations with states around China's periphery seen as part of a containment strategy. The new security concept evolved into the concept of China's peaceful rise—subsequently renamed China's peaceful development. This concept sought to persuade the world that China would be sufficiently self-aware to avoid what Graham Allison was later to refer to as the Thucydides Trap, namely the risk that growing tensions between a rising and an incumbent power could lead to war. China embarked on a good neighbours policy, settling long-standing territorial and border disputes with all its neighbours except India, developing economic relations with states in the Asia-Pacific region, and taking up membership of regional institutions that included the Association of Southeast Asian Nations (ASEAN), the Asia-Pacific Economic

Cooperation Forum (APEC) and the Shanghai Cooperation Organisation (SCO), which encompassed Russia and Central Asian states of the former Soviet Union. It also played a positive role in efforts to prevent North Korea from acquiring nuclear weapons through its participation in the Six-Party Talks.

2008 however proved to be a major turning point. China's hosting of the Olympic Games that year was seen as a coming-out party, an opportunity to showcase a new, modern forward-looking country. But international protests about repression in Tibet accompanied the Olympic torch as it made its way around the world and amid a welter of negative publicity it seemed to the Chinese leadership that the West was determined to rain on China's parade. That same year witnessed the global financial crisis, which hit China particularly hard, destroying the economic raison d'être of entire Chinese cities, plunging tens of millions of Chinese workers into unemployment and necessitating the establishment of a US$ 700 billion fund to mitigate the most immediate effects of the crisis. For China's leaders the financial crisis was a moment of epiphany, calling into question the validity of the Washington Consensus doctrine of liberal economics and the fitness for purpose of the post-World War II global governance institutions.

Yet though Beijing's instinct was to blame the USA for the crisis, in reality China shared much of the responsibility. As the UK-based economist Diana Choyleva has observed, the global financial crisis was the product of a "clash between two very different economic systems within a global trade and financial system largely set up to serve open markets."[9] China's approach to world trade was based on pegging its currency to the US dollar while refusing to allow the free movement of capital, opening its markets only selectively, controlling the cost of borrowing and energy and privileging the state sector. For the decade prior to the crisis, the economic relationship between the USA and

China appeared to be delivering significant benefits to both. China registered double-digit economic growth while US and other Western consumers were able to borrow cheap money generated by China's savings glut to purchase Chinese-made consumer goods. So benign did the arrangement appear that it led Mervyn King, former governor of the Bank of England, to refer to the period 1998 to 2008 as the NICE decade, as in "non-inflationary, constantly expansionary"[10]—though rather than extolling this arrangement, King was seeking to emphasise that it was unsustainable. Eventually Western consumers reached the peak of sustainable borrowing and at that point the financial system imploded at least in part due to China's unwillingness to play by the rules.

Meanwhile the USA had become increasingly concerned by a Chinese military expansion catalysed by the 1990 First Gulf War which had showcased hitherto unseen US military technologies such as precision-guided conventionally armed missiles and sophisticated electronic warfare capabilities. The realisation of how backward the PLA had become sparked a Chinese version of the US Revolution in Military Affairs. This, over the next two decades, saw the PLA evolve from a low-tech, mass-mobilisation land-based force with minimal capacity to project force beyond China's borders to a modern all-arms force based around a blue-water navy, a range of short and intermediate-range missiles, a modern air force and an ambitious programme of digitalisation. Concern about the implications of a programme whose purpose appeared to be to constrain the USA's ability to operate militarily in the Western Pacific led to President Barack Obama declaring a pivot into Asia, in part a recognition that the Bush administration's focus on counter-terrorism campaigns in the Middle East and Afghanistan had distracted the USA and led it to underestimate the strategic impact of China's growing power. Militarily, the pivot into Asia was of little consequence, involving no significant redeployments of personnel or capabilities. It did however involve a significant recommitment to the USA's regional alliance relationships, a development which China, ringed about with US military bases and lacking any real allies of its own, interpreted as evidence of a continued US commitment to a containment strategy. The USA reinforced that perception by maintaining a sedulous disinterest in China's proposal for a new kind of great power relations.

A further concern to China's leadership was the spate of "colour revolutions" that began in 2003 with Georgia's so-called Rose Revolution, all involving manifestations of popular discontent with governments perceived as autocratic and uncaring about citizens' welfare. During Iran's 2009 Green Revolution, the fact that the US State Department asked US social media companies to suspend routine maintenance to enable protesters to continue using their messaging systems simply reinforced what was already an article of faith among China's leaders, namely that these revolutions were being instigated and fomented by the US government—and that China might well be next on the US hit-list. A related concern was the West's apparent commitment to so-called neo-interventionism, based on the UN doctrine of the Responsibility to Protect, which held that in circumstances where a government was unable to assure the safety of its own population, other states should intervene to do so. This doctrine, promoted by UN Secretary-General Kofi Annan in 2005, ran contrary to China's long-held advocacy of a strict interpretation of Westphalian national sovereignty which precluded any interference by one state in the internal affairs of another no matter what the context. The 2003 US invasion of Iraq, the 2011 Franco–British intervention in Libya that led to the overthrown of Muamar Qadhafi and the US limited—and ultimately ineffectual—intervention in Syria following an uprising against the regime of Bashar al Assad the same year, all suggested to China's leaders that the aggressive instincts of the USA and its Western allies remained undiminished and might well be directed against them.

While Chinese thinking about the international situation was driven by perceptions of external threat and the machinations of "hostile foreign forces," it also had a significant positive side. Since the mid-1990s Chinese official pronouncements on foreign policy had spoken of China being in a period of strategic opportunity.[11] This saw the world as being in a period of relative peace and stability, affording China the circumstances to pursue its economic development objectives. As China's economy grew and the country's global power increased, there arose a conviction based on the Marxist concept of historical determinism that the USA and the West more generally was in irrevocable decline and that China's moment had come. This began to translate into a more extrovert, assertive and even aggressive foreign policy.

This change first became evident in the South China Sea where China had always had competing claims with other ASEAN states to islands and reefs. During the period of the good neighbours policy China had sought to address this issue by encouraging other claimant states to engage in joint exploitation of oil and mineral resources. But in 2009 China reasserted claims to the seas within the so-called nine-dash line, originally a claim made by the Nationalist government in 1947[12] and which encompassed virtually the whole of the South China Sea, including areas claimed by other states as part of their exclusive economic zones based on the UN Law of the Sea Convention (UNLOSC). China also embarked on a major programme of building on what would otherwise have been uninhabitable reefs, with many of these facilities becoming militarised despite a commitment by President Xi Jinping to Barack Obama not to do so. A 2016 judgment by the Permanent Court of Arbitration in a case brought by the Philippines government ruled that the nine-dash line had no validity, a judgment that Beijing, which had refused to take part in the proceedings, flatly rejected. China used naval paramilitary forces—coastguard and fisheries protection vessels—to enforce its claims, preventing other states from fishing or conducting oil exploration in areas it claimed within the nine-dash line. It also sought to discourage "freedom of navigation" naval patrols by the USA and its allies on the basis of innocent passage, the right of warships to transit territorial waters without having to seek prior permission of the state controlling those waters—an interpretation which China is not alone in questioning.

From a strategic perspective China's desire to control the South China Sea is entirely understandable. In addition to the existence of significant oil and mineral reserves on the sea-bed, 80% of China's energy imports and nearly 40% of its foreign trade pass through the South China Sea. And the South China Sea, together with the East China Sea over which China has declared an Air Defence Identification Zone, is bounded to the east by the so-called first island chain, which stretches from Japan through Taiwan and the Philippines to Borneo and Vietnam, all actual or potential US allies. China is hence vulnerable to a naval blockade that would have a devastating effect on its economy and on its ability to deploy its newly-developed blue-water naval forces, which could find themselves bottled up in their bases in time of conflict. In the longer term, China has aspirations to control not just the waters up to the first island chain but also to the second, which stretches from Japan through the Marianas, the Caroline Islands and Guam where the USA has substantial military bases. In effect China's long-term aim is to drive the USA out of the Western Pacific.

The appointment of Xi Jinping as CCP Secretary-General in 2012 effectively marked the end of the Deng era of "hide and bide," though this was never made explicit. In a speech in

November that year at the National Museum of China Xi spoke of the China Dream—*zhongguo meng*—which he described as the great rejuvenation of the Chinese race. This was a vision for a prosperous China with a developed-world economy, at ease with itself and with the world more generally. Xi proposed two centennial goals: to turn China into a moderately prosperous society—*xiaokang shehui*—a term borrowed from Confucianism and not further defined, by 2021; and to build a strong and prosperous economy by 2049. At around the same time, Xi advanced the concept of a community of common destiny for mankind—*renlei mingyun gongtongti*—which was subsequently translated (less accurately) as a community of common future for mankind. He also advanced what became known as the Belt and Road Initiative (BRI), a major global programme of infrastructure development designed to link China more directly with global markets. The community of common destiny concept was so vague and ill-defined that it largely passed Western policy-makers by, while the BRI initially seemed like a solution in search of a problem. It has however since become apparent that these two concepts together represent a deliberate strategy to reshape the global order in ways favouring Chinese interests, potentially resulting in a world subject to Chinese hegemony.

Since Xi Jinping took office China's state-controlled media has published countless articles and opinion pieces arguing that the post-World War II global governance arrangements are no longer fit for purpose and in need of revision. Developed by the USA and its allies at a time when many of the world's states were still colonial possessions, these arrangements are seen by Chinese commentators as privileging Western values and political systems while failing to accommodate alternative systems. China's narrative portrays it as a system based on zero-sum thinking and great-power politics in which a small number of states take decisions affecting the whole world. This leads to a world that suffers from a democratic deficit, a governance deficit, a development trap, a growing gap between rich and poor and multiple security challenges from issues such as terrorism and climate change. The community of common destiny for mankind purports to offer an alternative model that is inclusive, tolerant of political and cultural diversity and abjures hegemonism, colonialism, interference in the internal affairs of other states, the imposition on others of specific political and ideological systems and the establishment of spheres of influence. It rejects Western international relations theories supposedly based on great power contestation and alliance relations and the propositions that globalisation and modernisation must equate with Westernisation. It offers the Chinese model of development and "Chinese wisdom" as something for other states to consider emulating while emphasising that each state should develop in accordance with its own culture and "national conditions."[13]

A key element of the community of common destiny concept is the self-image of China as a morally superior power concerned about the well-being of all mankind in contrast to a USA that is depicted as motivated by narrow and selfish concerns and whose politics are dominated by special-interest groups. This approach draws on traditional Chinese concepts of governance that date back to the pre-Christian era, in particular the concept of *tian xia*—all under heaven. As mentioned in earlier chapters, this concept, which first appears in the *Shang Shu*, an ancient compilation of the sayings of the mythical emperors Yao and Shun and the rulers of the Shang and Zhou dynasties, was developed by Confucius and later Confucian philosophers such as Mencius (Mengzi) into the political ideal of a state in which peoples coexist harmoniously under an enlightened ruler upon whom had been conferred the Mandate of Heaven (*tian ming*)—as supposedly happened during the Western Zhou dynasty (1046–771 BCE).[14] It is also bound up with a self-image of China as a peaceful non-expansionist power, a self-image more than some-what at odds with the reality of China's recorded history.

Although China decries the Western alliance system, the community of common destiny has been described by State Counsellor Yang Jiechi as a "non-aligned alliance" in which participating states are expected to "stand on the side of China or at least to be neutral."[15] And while China publicly argues for a world in which all states are equal regardless of size, in 2011 Yang let slip the reality of China's inherently hierarchical attitude to international relations at a meeting with ASEAN states in which, exasperated by ASEAN pushback over China's South China Sea policy, he observed that "some states are small and others are big and that is just a fact."[16] Intriguingly Jiang Shigong, one of the neo-statist intellectuals who has been a vocal advocate of Xi Jinping's policies, published an essay on the intellectual website Ai Sixiang in April 2019 in which he examined the role of empires in global governance. Jiang presents the concept of empire as a rational evolution from lesser structures of governance and seems to be suggesting that a global empire with Chinese characteristics would benefit humanity. There is no indication that this essay represents official Chinese thinking—but given the author's standing with China's leadership it offers food for thought.

The community of common destiny is acknowledged to be a work in progress and numerous institutes have been set up in Chinese universities and think-tanks to put flesh on the bones of the concept. It is however possible to extrapolate from work already published and statements made by senior Chinese policy-makers broadly what the practical implications of the community of common destiny for mankind might actually mean for mankind. In essence it would be a world under a loose Chinese hegemony. It would be a world in which the legitimacy of the CCP was accepted; a world in which China's interests and priorities would be internalised by other states and not contested on pain of sanction; and it would be a world in which the interests of great powers, i.e. China, would take precedence over customary international law. Chinese thinkers have closely examined the UK and US hegemonic models and have rejected both as being impractical and unsustainable. In particular China wishes to avoid replicating a US model that involves a global network of some 800 military bases to sustain the role of global policeman. Whatever else China may aspire to be, it is quite clear that it does not want to replace the USA in that role. At the same time, whilst criticising US hegemony, China is far from sanguine about the prospect of the USA withdrawing too precipitately from its global policing role, fearing the prospect of what US academic Joseph Nye has referred to as the Kindleberger Trap, an effective absence of hegemonic power that risks creating global instability.[17]

The BRI is seen by Chinese thinkers as the primary mechanism for bringing about the community of common destiny. The thinking goes that as economic links grow closer states will appreciate the benefits of developing closer political and security links with China. With closer engagement will come a greater identity of interests and values. There are many facets to the BRI and many rationales for the project. It is partly about efforts by a state that has always had limited trust in markets to secure supplies of raw materials and markets for its manufactured products. It is about exporting some of the considerable excess industrial capacity that China has built up during its dash for growth—and the pollution that has accompanied that, as evidenced by plans to build coal-fired power plants around the world whilst promoting the use of clean energy at home. It is an exercise in soft power and signalling. It is a concept that China has sought, so far unsuccessfully, to have recognised by the United Nations as a contribution to international peace and security. At bottom it appears to be an attempt to shape a sinocentric world economic order with China at the centre of a global web of economic relationships in which high value activities are concentrated at the centre with the periphery contributing either raw materials with little in the way of added value, or acting as markets for Chinese goods and services.

Initially the BRI was somewhat ill-defined and confusing and suffered a lot from the opportunism of Chinese entrepreneurs jumping on the bandwagon by claiming that projects with no state backing were part of the BRI. Some of the initial projects were badly conceived and generated much adverse publicity, a case in point being the construction of a port in Hambantota in Sri Lanka. This construction left the Sri Lankan government facing unsustainable levels of debt which led to the port being leased to China for ninety-nine years, giving rise to international accusations that the aim of BRI was to acquire strategic assets through the creation of "debt traps." When in the summer of 2018 Beijing held a BRI review conference it was clear that Chinese officials were unable to give Xi Jinping a reliable indication of the number and value of BRI projects in existence. In his speech to the review conference, Xi characterised the first five years of BRI as in effect a ground-clearing exercise during which many important lessons had been learnt. The BRI has now been added to the national and Party constitutions, leaving no doubt as to the centrality of the project. As of April 2019, when the second BRI forum was held, it was announced that China had signed 170 agreements with 125 countries with a total value of US$ 90 billion. Plans for total expenditure are as high as $8 trillion.

A key challenge for BRI is security. Much BRI infrastructure is being or will have to be built in regions that are endemically unstable. This starts with China's own western regions, in particular Xinjiang, which goes some way towards explaining why Beijing has pursued the security policies it has. Further to the west, Pakistan plays a significant role through the development of the China–Pakistan Economic Corridor (CPEC) leading to the Chinese-built port of Gwadar. The corridor passes through Baluchistan, home to a violent separatist movement responsible for the deaths of a number of Chinese diplomats and contractors. As part of the conditions for CPEC, Pakistan, a country with chronic financial problems, has had to raise at its own expense an additional division of security forces to protect CPEC infrastructure. Meanwhile the ambition and expense of BRI projects had threatened to overwhelm the capacities of the Pakistani state. Pakistan is also in a more or less permanent state of stand-off with India, a strategic rival of China which has been at pains to avoid engaging with BRI.

There are in reality several different BRIs: a land transport component including Eurasian rail links and projects such as Malaysia's East Coast railway; a maritime component that includes port development and the leasing to China of existing ports such as Piraeus; a financial component including disbursements from China's Asian Infrastructure Investment Bank (AIIB); and a digital component. This latter is particularly important in terms of spreading Chinese influence through the provision of telecommunications services including the building of core backbone telecommunications networks by China's ICT national champions Huawei and ZTE. In 2019 Huawei alone was involved in some eighty telecommunications projects around the planet including laying undersea fibre-optic cables. In cases where China has built core backbone ICT networks these come with all the monitoring and surveillance capabilities available to the Chinese state and to that extent can be seen as a vector for exporting Chinese values or at least generating concurrence for such values. More broadly, China's efforts to wire the world are reminiscent of what the UK achieved in the nineteenth and early twentieth centuries when, through Cable and Wireless, it established a global telegraphic network that conferred significant commercial, strategic and security benefits—including the ability to eavesdrop on the telegraphic communications of major powers.

Discourse Power and China's "Glass Heart"

A key component of China's foreign policy strategy is the development of China's discourse power—*huayuquan*. At present the Chinese Party-state perceives that global discourse is dominated by Western media organisations and Western concepts such as universal values that are anathema to the CCP. China therefore needs to become proactive in making its own message globally predominant using the same propaganda techniques that have been and remain central to its exercise of domestic political and social control. The aim of what Xi Jinping has termed "telling China's story well"[18] is to pre-empt threats to the Party-state's hold on power by suppressing critical commentary and challenges to the CCP's ideology while seeking to shape the international discourse on issues of governance and values in ways favourable to China. It also aims to nurture an already entrenched nationalist sentiment in China's population and to demonstrate that only the Party-state can promote the Chinese people's interests and defend their dignity. This involves the mobilisation of comprehensive national power, with the effort spearheaded by two Party organisations: the Central Propaganda Department, whose role is self-explanatory; and the United Front Work Department (UFWD), described by Mao Zedong as one of the CCP's three "magic weapons"—the others being Party-building and the PLA.[19] The role of the UFWD is to engage with influential non-Party elites and opinion formers both in and outside China and encourage them to lend support to the CCP.

For many years the influence of the CCP Propaganda Department outside China was nugatory. Few foreigners were interested in reading turgid, jargon-laden and poorly translated outputs of China's state-controlled media. And all too often aspects of Chinese culture with genuine soft power attraction, such as the early films of the cineaste Zhang Yimou, were effectively disowned by the Party for sending the "wrong" messages. But as Nikita Khrushchev once observed, quantity has a quality of its own. In recent years China has engaged in a broad-spectrum effort to put out China's message at an estimated cost of US$ 10 billion a year. This includes a new London-based international news channel, China Global Television Network, employing experienced Western journalists at salaries far above what they could earn elsewhere; marketing Chinese news broadcasts and Chinese TV programmes throughout Africa and Latin America at prices that undercut competitors such as BBC and Al Jazeera; paying prestigious Western media outlets such as the *Washington Post* and the *Telegraph* to carry supplements such as *China Daily*—a credible candidate for most boring newspaper on the planet; purchasing media outlets such as the Hong Kong-based *South China Morning Post*; and hiring at inflated salaries lobbyists and members of national elites to advocate for China in their own countries—a process known as elite capture. It is impossible to estimate the impact of this sustained onslaught but its cumulative impact over time cannot lightly be disregarded.

The primary focus of the UFWD is on Chinese diaspora communities, particularly in countries where these diasporas are well-represented in the political, cultural and commercial life of their host countries. No matter what their actual nationality, in the Chinese Party-state's eyes all ethnic Chinese are "sons and daughters of the Yellow Emperor" and their primary loyalty should be to China. In countries such as Australia, New Zealand and Canada the UFWD has orchestrated the payment of political donations, including to one Australian senator forced to resign as a consequence; promoted the candidature of Chinese parliamentarians, including in the case of New Zealand an individual who had previously worked in a university that trained linguists for China's signals intelligence agency; and sought to leverage the Chinese Students and Scholars Associations established in Western universities to provide recreational and community services for Chinese students to control the behaviours of Chinese students and ensure that they don't go native while overseas and to exercise pressure on the universities to pursue pro-Chinese policies such as not allowing speakers deemed anti-Chinese on campuses. Concern about the impact of these policies has led Australia, a country caught between its economic reliance on China and its reliance for security on the USA, to introduce legislation requiring the registration of foreign political agents and a ban on foreign political donations as well as a revision of its national security laws.

The cumulative effect of these policies has arguably been diplomatically counter-productive at least in the short term. But it reflects the fact that foreign policy is increasingly being driven by Party organisations whose agenda is primarily domestic and whose understanding of the world outside China is non-existent. A feature of this new assertive policy involves a forceful diplomatic response to any slight against China, either real or imagined. This ultra-sensitive approach, which some of China's netizens have called a "glass heart"—*bolixin*—has seen Chinese ambassadors around the world reacting aggressively to minor incidents such as when Chinese tourists are perceived to have been badly treated, and, latterly, engaging in slanging matches with foreign governments on social media platforms such as Twitter. More significantly, foreign corporations perceived to have infringed China's interests as in the case of foreign airlines listing Taiwan and Hong Kong as separate territories in their literature, have been informed that failure to take corrective action would impact adversely on their social credit scores inside

China. An even more egregious example of China's "glass heart" was the massive outpouring of patriotic sentiment in China which looked set to jeopardise the NBA's continued access to the lucrative China market in response to a single social media post by the general manager of the Houston Rockets which read "Fight for freedom, stand with Hong Kong."[20] Such responses are a reflection of the importance the CCP places on demonstrating to its own population that the CCP—and only the CCP—can stand up for China and project a strong image of the country. In the NBA case the international reaction and the resultant harm to China's image was so widespread that Xi Jinping intervened to dial down the tension. But while carefully nurtured, nationalist sentiment within China regarding such events is real enough and rooted in China's historical experience. It is also rooted in the CCP's abiding sense of insecurity, and is unlikely to give way to a more nuanced approach to diplomacy in the foreseeable future.

8

PROJECTING DIGITAL POWER

For the Chinese Party-state, cyberspace presents a unique opportunity to expand its global influence precisely because what is
still a relatively new domain has little in the way of internationally agreed rules of the road. In terms of practicalities cyberspace
remains very much a US construct, its evolution driven by major
US tech giants such as Microsoft, Google and Facebook whose
policies and practices in this domain are often more consequential than those of the US, or for that matter any other, government. In the late twentieth century roughly two-thirds of
Internet users were located in the USA and almost all global
Internet traffic was routed through US-based servers. The protocols used to route Internet traffic (TCP/IP) and ensure its
security (SSL) were developed by US engineers and scientists, as
was the Domain Name System (DNS), the Internet's global
address book. The institution responsible for administering the
DNS and assigning top-level domain names such as .us or .cn,
the Internet Corporation for Assigned Names and Numbers
(ICANN), set up in California in 1998 as a non-profit public
benefit corporation, was between 2006 and 2016 under the
supervision of the US Department of Commerce.

Internet governance was initially characterised by a high degree of informality. On the technical side, it consists of engineers and scientists meeting to decide on technical standards and protocols in organisations such as the Internet Engineering Task Force (IETF), membership of which is in principle open to anyone with the requisite technical knowledge but which in practice is dominated by US and other Western engineers. On the public policy side, it includes entities like the Internet Governance Forum, set up by the UN in 2006 to address issues of public policy in the digital domain. These and other entities such as civil liberties and human rights groups make up the multi-stake-holder governance model, a community comprising state and non-state actors dealing with different facets of a governance system likened by one German academic to the rainforest, a complex interdependent ecosystem.[1] No single entity was or realistically could be in charge of such complexity but the US first-mover advantage in practice gave it a preponderant role in shaping global Internet standards and practices.

This US-centric approach however proved hard to sustain as Internet use expanded and numerous states and entities such as the European Union began to demand a more collective and more formalised international approach to Internet governance. At the 2003 United Nations-sponsored World Summit on the Information Society (WSIS) China, together with the majority of developing countries, called for an international Internet treaty and the establishment of an intergovernmental Internet organisation to enable governments to exercise a leading role in the management of Internet resources. China and the group of developing countries known collectively as the G77 also argued for an approach to Internet governance covering all public policy issues, including e-commerce, cybercrime and content control, in contrast to a US approach that sought to confine discussion of governance to purely technical issues. In addition, China called for the International Telecommunication Union (ITU), the UN agency responsible for assigning and managing the radio spectrum, assigning satellite orbits and overseeing other technical aspects of pre-Internet telecommunications, to be given a leading role in Internet governance.[2] Following the 2003 WSIS meeting, various initiatives to promote global Internet governance ensued but none did anything to harmonise an increasingly polarised debate between on the one hand China, Russia and the G77 arguing for a government-led approach and on the other the USA and its allies—referred to as the like-minded—who advocated for the perpetuation of the decentralised status quo governance model. A particular concern for China and Russia was the fear that the USA might use its de facto control over the DNS to cut these countries off from the global Internet.

Battle was joined in 2012 at the ITU's World Conference on International Telecommunications (WCIT), the ostensible purpose of which was to review the ITU's International Telecommunications Regulations. These regulations had been promulgated in 1988, an era in which circuit-switched—i.e. point-to-point—communications had been provided almost exclusively by state telecommunications agencies and were no longer relevant to an information age dominated by packet-switched technologies—in which individual communications were broken into packets transmitted by whatever routes were most readily available to be re-joined only at their final destination—delivered by private sector corporations. At WCIT Russia and China again sought a leading governance role for the ITU and for an approach that gave a pre-eminent role to governments while the USA and its allies argued that the openness and inclusiveness of the multi-stakeholder model offered the best prospect of governing a rapidly evolving Internet environment. The result was a deadlock that remains unresolved. In 2016 the USA did make a concession by relinquishing its oversight of ICANN and transferring this to the private sector, but this did not satisfy China and Russia's demand for a more centralised government-led model.

Global Cyber Security

From the moment the Internet became a global reality, states began to express concern about its wider security implications. It was Russia which first raised the red flag in the form of a 1998 letter from Foreign Minister Igor Ivanov to the UN Secretary-General in which he warned of the dangers posed by "information weapons" and the risk of information warfare between states, the impact of which he equated with that of weapons of mass destruction.[3] This reflected Soviet-era thinking about information warfare and the criticality of securing a state's "information space" to prevent national morale being undermined by exposure to information that challenged the dominant state narrative. Information and culture were key fronts during the Cold War and the discrediting of the Soviet narrative through broadcasts by entities such as Radio Free Europe and the circulation of samizdat publications undoubtedly played a significant if unquantifiable role in the collapse of communism in Eastern Europe.

This approach resonated with a Chinese Communist Party that saw the collapse of the Soviet Union as an unmitigated disaster from which vital lessons had to be learnt if the CCP was not to go the same way. China's policies of reform and opening-up had increased the CCP's vulnerability to "peaceful evolution," the process whereby Western values and ideals subtly undermined the CCP's ideology leading to its eventual rejection, and the Internet was a major vector for Western ideas to permeate Chinese society. This perceived threat forms the basis of the 2013 PLA-produced film *Silent Contest—jiaoliang wusheng—* which portrays China as being in a life-and-death struggle with an unremittingly hostile West. As discussed in earlier chapters the Chinese Party-state was able to use technology to contain this threat domestically but to be fully successful the threat also needed to be contained at an international level. This would involve international diplomacy designed to shape a more favourable environment and where initially at least China could leave Russia to do the heavy lifting. It would also involve something that Russia, which had proven unable to commercialise its considerable cyber capabilities, could not do, namely use the growing power of its ICT champions to create facts on the ground.

After a period of inconclusive debate an international forum for discussing cyber security was established. The ponderously named United Nations Group of Governmental Experts in the Field of Information and Communications in the Context of International Security—mercifully shortened to UN/GGE—was set up in 2004 under the UN's First Committee, which deals with disarmament and threats to international peace. Within the UN/GGE Russia, China and ideologically aligned states such as Cuba argued for a focus on information weapons and the development of international principles to enhance global information and telecommunications. Russia proposed an international treaty to deal with such issues while China argued that the free flow of information should be subject to the "premises that national sovereignty and security must be safeguarded and that historical, cultural and political differences must be respected."[4] China also argued that each country had the right to manage its own cyberspace in accordance with domestic legislation, a proposition referred to as cyber sovereignty, the basic characteristics of which were described by vice-foreign minister Li Baoding in the following terms:

> The sovereignty principle in cyberspace includes at least the following factors: states own jurisdiction over the ICT infrastructure and activities within their territories; national governments are entitled to make public policies for the Internet based on their national con-

ditions; no country shall use the Internet to interfere in other countries' internal affairs or undermine other countries' interests.[5]

After a series of inconclusive meetings, the UN/GGE that
was convened from 2012–13 made something of a breakthrough
with a consensus that existing international law applied in
cyberspace as did state sovereignty—essentially offering something for everyone. This breakthrough was at least in part the
result of a change of approach by the USA in the face of the
revelations of rogue NSA contractor Edward Snowden about the
extent of NSA reach in the cyber domain through programmes
developed in response to a transnational jihadist terrorist threat
that had itself proven adept at using modern ICTs. The consensus reached in 2013 proved temporary, in that China in particular argued that international law should not include the Law of
Armed Conflict (LOAC) since to do so would be tantamount to
legalising cyber warfare. Following the failure of the 2016–17
UN/GGE to deliver a consensus report due to disagreements
about the right of states to respond within the cyber domain to
internationally wrongful acts, the UN/GGE process morphed
into a two-pronged exercise: a new UN/GGE on Advancing
Responsible State Behaviour in Cyberspace in the Context of
International Security consisting, as have previous UN/GGEs,
of representatives of some twenty-five states, and an Open-
ended Working Group (OEWG), membership of which is open
to all states. Meanwhile China and Russia have continued to
promote within the UN General Assembly a code of conduct
carefully drafted to appear innocuous and uncontentious but in
fact containing provisions that would enable states to override
international law in areas such as free expression and human
rights whilst also seeking to outlaw the production by other
states of content seen as prejudicial to national security, the
latter anathema to the USA in the context of the First
Amendment, which guarantees freedom of speech.

China's ambivalence about the applicability of the Law of Armed Conflict in cyberspace is thought by Western diplomats and intelligence personnel to reflect the degree to which it sees the cyber domain as giving it an asymmetric advantage. The USA as a highly network-dependent society is uniquely vulnerable to cyber disruption. And, as indicated in a previous chapter, the extent to which it holds valuable data on inherently insecure networks offers extensive possibilities for industrial cyber espionage. It follows that China has no interest in agreeing to any rules of the road that might either constrain its cyber activities against the USA or create conditions that might legitimise a US response, whether in-domain or cross-domain, to such activity. That said, China's military has expressed interest in exploring measures to ensure a degree of stability in the military use of cyberspace and has for some time been engaged in Track Two para-diplomatic activities to that end.

Re-making the Internet with Chinese Characteristics

As part of its efforts to exercise greater control over global cyber governance and security China began to "swarm" the international agenda, taking pains to be represented at all major international gatherings dealing with these issues. But a step-change came in September 2019 at a meeting of the International Telecommunication Union (ITU) in Geneva when a group of engineers from the Chinese ICT national champion Huawei gave a presentation on a New Internet Protocol—New IP. In essence this was a proposal to re-engineer the Internet using a top-down government-led model to be designed and built by China. The argumentation behind this proposal was that the Internet as currently configured had reached the limits of its possibilities and was unstable, insufficient for future needs and replete with security, reliability and configuration problems. The Huawei engineers claimed that the new system was already being built across multiple countries, though no details were provided. The new concept was due to be presented at a major ITU conference scheduled to take place in India in November 2020 with a view to obtaining formal ITU approval for the concept so that it could be officially standardised. This decision would be in the hands of governments with others in the multi-stakeholder community having no direct voice in the deliberations.[6]

The Chinese proposal elicited strong reactions from Western governments who feared that Chinese values and controls would be baked into the new system, with government Internet service providers able to determine at a granular level both who could have Internet access and what information they would be accessing. In the event that the proposal succeeded, China would be able to minimise the costs it incurs in blocking information from the global Internet since other states could be relied upon to do much of this work for it. It would also be able substantially to expand its global digital footprint by sharing its new system with other authoritarian states equally keen to exercise greater control over digital networks. The fact that Huawei had a lead role in developing and promoting New IP was particularly significant in view of the questions that have been raised about the nature of the company's relationship with the Chinese state, an issue that has come to the fore in relation to Huawei's aspirations to be a global leader in the provision of 5G telecommunications services.

Huawei: China's ICT National Champion

Until relatively recently few people outside of China had heard of Huawei. To the extent that they had, this was mostly in relation to Huawei's marketing of mobile phones with some attractive user features such as a high-definition camera. But in the space of thirty years Huawei has transitioned from being a small start-up focused on providing telecommunications services to rural China to become a global telecommunications giant with a large campus in Shenzhen incorporating a bizarrely eclectic mix of architectural styles, 180,000 employees, revenues in excess of US$ 100 billion and a presence in 170 countries. Together with ZTE, a smaller company that is state-owned and privately operated rather than fully private as Huawei purports to be, it has since 1996 had the status of "national champion" for the ICT sector and has a key role to play in China's strategy for becoming a major technology power. In particular Huawei has fallen under the international spotlight by virtue of its efforts to become a world leader in fifth-generation mobile telecommunications (5G), a gateway technology designed to provide levels of hyper-connectivity that will significantly increase the scope of the Internet of Things—in which millions of devices embedded in vehicles and domestic appliances are connected to the Internet—and will enable more effective development of an industrial Internet made up of autonomous manufacturing and other processes by providing high-speed low-latency connectivity. 5G will also play a significant role in the development of Artificial Intelligence (AI) by generating vast streams of data which are the "feedstock" of machine-learning. Domination of the global 5G market has become a key battleground in a wider geo-political contest between the USA and China and given Huawei's salience, it is important to achieve an understanding of exactly what this company is and what relationship it has to the Chinese state.

Huawei was founded in 1987 by Ren Zhengfei, a former engineer in the People's Liberation Army. Ren was one of a large number of military personnel demobilised in the 1980s without much in the way of state support and his response, to use the term then prevalent in China, was to "jump into the sea"—*xia hai*—by entering China's embryonic private sector. His first business venture having failed, he then reportedly started Huawei with an initial capitalisation of US$ 5,000 provided by five "friends of friends," selling telephone switches imported from Hong Kong. Huawei's initial focus was on supplying the much-neglected rural sector, after which it moved into the urban sector where it distinguished itself from other players by providing customer support for its products. Ren's first big break came with the sale of telephone switches to the PLA. By 1994 he was sufficiently established to receive a visit to one of his newly-built offices by then-president Jiang Zemin, during which he sold Jiang the proposition that the Chinese state should exercise control over its domestic telecommunications sector by excluding foreign competition, a policy formally implemented in 1996. This policy had to be relaxed once China had entered the WTO in 2001 and foreign companies have, slowly, been permitted to access the China market but only through joint ventures with Chinese partners; in practice China's telecommunications are still dominated by three companies, all Chinese.

Relatively early on in its evolution Huawei took a decision to move into international markets, opening offices in Texas and California in 2001 and 2002 respectively and in Sweden in 2003. The decision to go international was very deliberate and involved seeking advice from Western companies including McKinsey and IBM. An early coup for Huawei was a deal struck with the UK telecoms provider British Telecom (BT) in 2005 to provide equipment for a £10 billion upgrade of its core mobile network. Since then Huawei has become deeply embedded in the provision of 3 and 4G mobile telecommunications within the UK, other EU states and twelve US states, mostly rural and thinly-populated. The company has established a well-deserved reputation for the cheapness and reliability of its equipment and for a strong culture of customer service. But concerns about its links to the Chinese state have begun to impact on its commercial prospects in the developed world. In 2010 the UK government had become sufficiently concerned about the potential national security implications of reliance on Huawei equipment to establish a Cyber Security Evaluation Centre staffed in part by experts from the UK signals intelligence agency GCHQ to evaluate all Huawei components and software going into the UK's mobile networks. The Centre has to date found no evidence of any malign exploits—nor probably did it ever expect to—but has identified "significant technical issues in Huawei's engineering processes" which means it can "only provide limited assurance that all risks to UK national security from Huawei's involvement in the UK's critical networks can be sufficiently mitigated long-term."[7]

Huawei's own creation myth is of a proudly private company whose workforce are the sole shareholders, built by relentless hard work and sacrifice, which involved embracing the Chinese technology sector's much vaunted 9–9–6 culture of twelve-hour working days six days a week plus unpaid overtime. Ren Zhengfei instilled at Huawei a culture of military discipline and ferocious competition both within the company and externally—what has been termed the "wolf culture" (*lang wenhua*)—a mindset of achieving results at any cost inculcated in new employees through a military-style introductory boot-camp. Commentators familiar with Huawei's corporate culture describe a company that is quintessentially Chinese, characterised by a lack of transparency and trust, with key decisions being taken by a small group of senior managers. Foreign employees of Huawei have often complained of being excluded from decision-making processes and given a version of events totally different from that shared between Chinese managers. Even Chinese employees entering Huawei mid-career have claimed that they are treated as outsiders.[8] This closed, secretive and exclusionary culture is in marked contrast to that of China's other national champion ZTE, whose growth has been in part the product of acquisitions of foreign corporations and which has worked hard to promote an inclusive and diverse culture which Huawei actively eschews.

Huawei's lack of transparency has become an increasing problem as the company has become ever more globally prominent and has given weight to an alternative account of its origins and its relationship with the Chinese state. This version, current within US and other Western intelligence circles, holds that Huawei is in effect the creature of the Chinese intelligence services and that its remarkable growth owes much to significant state subsidies including from the PLA and other elements of the Chinese intelligence community.[9] In words attributed to US Deputy National Security Adviser Matt Pottinger, "The advantage Huawei has had is one of massive state subsidies to the tune of tens upon tens of billions of dollars that have allowed them to undersell the competition, kneecap the market and drive market competitors out of business."[10] Allegations of mutual collaboration include the sharing of stolen foreign intellectual property and a readiness by Huawei to provide cover slots for Chinese intelligence operatives overseas—all allegations which Huawei has fiercely rebutted with the exception of state subsidies, which it does acknowledge having received but to no greater a degree than many of its competitors both in China and overseas.

There have been multiple allegations that Huawei's success owed much to a corporate ethos which blurred the boundaries between competitive and unethical behaviour and that its reliance on stolen foreign intellectual property, combined with generous state subsidies, was the main reason it was able to undercut foreign competitors by as much as 30%. US Department of Justice investigators claim to be in possession of Huawei documents showing that Huawei incentivises intellectual property theft through a system of bonus payments.[11] The company has been involved in litigation with a number of US corporations including Cisco and Motorola in relation to claims of intellectual property theft. Some lawsuits have been settled without admission of liability while others are still being contested. But in the main, US and other foreign companies have been reluctant to initiate suits against Huawei for fear that this might jeopardise their access to the China market. Such fears have proved justified, with Western plaintiffs who have pursued such cases finding themselves subject to retaliatory actions by the Chinese state such as anti-trust investigations.

As to allegations that Huawei has been involved in espionage on behalf of the Chinese state the case is less clear-cut. There has been one documented case of a Huawei employee based in Warsaw being arrested for espionage, though that case has not yet come to court and, as soon as his arrest was announced, Huawei dismissed him. There is also the aforementioned case of the African Union headquarters built by a Chinese state-owned corporation and provided with telecommunications systems by Huawei. Five years after the building was completed it was discovered that data stored by the African Union was being covertly transferred on a nightly basis to a server located in Shanghai. Huawei denied any knowledge or involvement. The point has also been made that China's 2017 Intelligence Law requires all citizens and commercial organisations to assist the intelligence services and that Huawei, if asked to provide such assistance to the Chinese state, would have to comply. This has been denied by Ren Zhengfei, who has claimed he would close down the company rather than accede to such requests. But in a state where, in the words of Xi Jinping, the Party controls everything and the concept of the rule of law is consciously rejected, the proposition that Huawei might be able to resist pressure to cooperate seems implausible—though there have been documented examples of Chinese telecommunications dragging their feet and providing minimal data in response to state demands.

Whether by accident or design Huawei has become a strategic actor in the Chinese Party-state's efforts to become a world leader in advanced technologies through its expansion into overseas markets. Apart from its involvement in Europe and North America, Huawei has together with ZTE provided some 43% of telecommunications networks in the Asia-Pacific region, 34% in Latin America and 70% in Africa, the latter a largely untapped market in which Western competitors have been slow to invest. This expansion includes laying undersea fibre optic cables and building core backbone communications networks. What has been termed the Digital Silk Road has been enabled by loans from the China Development Bank and marked by China's readiness to give countries what they ask for without asking questions or attaching conditions. This is in marked contrast to a Western development approach which either seeks to attach conditionality to such projects in areas such as human rights or makes decisions for states about what they are deemed to need, an approach seen by recipients as patronising and paternalistic.

In addition to building and sometimes operating core backbone networks in the developing world, Chinese systems come with all the monitoring and surveillance capabilities that are routinely deployed in China, enabling countries such as Zimbabwe and Venezuela to use their networks for repressive purposes. Huawei and ZTE are also involved in projects to develop smart cities, capabilities that potentially confer significant benefits but which also increase the ability of governments with autocratic instincts to use such technologies for repressive purposes. The Digital Silk Road can be seen as having a wider purpose than simply buying Chinese influence. By providing key states aligned with the BRI with security capabilities comparable to its own, China hopes that these states will be better-placed to ensure levels of stability and security that will make the BRI projects possible without China having to become directly involved in security provision.

China's growing telecommunications presence around the globe is about to be significantly enhanced by the introduction of 5G technology and it is here that Huawei plays a critical role. Despite its origins as a company mired in accusations of copying and reverse engineering Western systems, Huawei has always had a focus on innovation, devoting 20% of its revenues and 40% of its workforce to research and development within China and developing a network of laboratories and collaborative relationships with universities in developed Western economies. Huawei has filed more 5G patents than any other telecommunications company, in particular in relation to mobile base station technology,[12] and has taken an active part in international negotiations to determine the technical parameters of 5G through the Third Generation Partnership Project (3GPP). It has already launched 5G services in some parts of China and has begun selling 5G phones. Huawei's main strength however is its ability to act as a systems integrator for a technology that is still heavily dependent on US inputs, especially in terms of chip technology and software. Within the USA the economics of systems integration make it an unattractive option for private sector companies in the absence of significant state subsidies—and in the case of a technology like 5G the Obama administration was obliged to conclude that the cost of such subsidies would make this option infeasible. The Western companies capable of producing end-to-end 5G networks—Nokia, Ericsson and Samsung—lack the scale that Huawei and to a lesser extent ZTE have been able to bring to bear, and in any case themselves use many Chinese-manufactured components. So, efforts by the US government to persuade allies and partners to ban Huawei from 5G networks raise the question of what realistic alternatives exist.

The US intelligence community had long harboured reservations about Huawei and the US government had refused to enter into the kind of risk-mitigation process with Huawei that exists for other foreign companies doing business in sensitive sectors of the USA, including national defence. Since 2019 it has excluded Huawei from federal telecommunications projects and has sought to persuade and pressure other states to take similar action, citing the espionage risk that reliance on a Chinese network might pose. This was a relatively unconvincing argument given the already pervasive nature of Chinese cyber espionage and was not accompanied by compelling evidence. In fact US government concerns were a complex mixture of economic, national security and geo-political, and boiled down to a conviction that telecommunications networks already critical to national security and national prosperity and about to become much more so with the advent of 5G could not be put in the hands of a company so closely linked with and susceptible to control by the Chinese state. US concerns were less about the installation of Huawei hardware but rather about the risks posed by the constant stream of software updates that would be required to keep networks functioning. US concerns were specific to it and this plus the absence of clear evidence of Huawei malfeasance made it hard for the US to persuade others. At the end of the day, this became a question of trust and judgement. As former Secretary for Homeland Security Michael Chertoff put it, "When you are dealing with core national security issues it becomes much more difficult when it comes to critical equipment. There can be very unsound geopolitical consequences."[13]

It was however not the USA but its Five Eyes ally Australia that took the first decisive move. In 2018 the Australian Signals Directorate (ASD), the country's signals intelligence agency, undertook a series of war-gaming exercises which appeared to demonstrate that in the event of a conflict with China dependence on a Huawei-controlled 5G network would have potentially serious adverse consequences.[14] For Australia, a state that has recent historical memory of an attempted Japanese invasion and which navigates uneasily between economic dependence on China and security dependence on the USA, this was far from just a theoretical exercise. And it resonated powerfully with a US Department of Defense that was concerned about the risks of having to operate over networks that were not secure and controllable. This appears to have been the tipping point that drove the US government into action. For other allies such as the UK for whom the prospect of involvement in a shooting war with China seemed a remote contingency, arguments based on this extreme scenario seemed less compelling and at the beginning of 2020 the UK government decided to allow Huawei to provide 35% of the components for the UK 5G network but with no access to the core—the intelligent systems that controlled the network. A combination of US political pressure combined with an assessment of the implications of a US ban on supplying components to Huawei led the UK government in May 2020 to reverse this decision, a move to which the Chinese government reacted with anger. The US anti-China bandwagon has now begun to roll with New Zealand, Canada, Italy, France and, in all likelihood, India taking action that will effectively exclude Huawei from their 5G networks. But this still leaves many states, including within the developed world, that are ready to incorporate Huawei systems.

For the USA, China's success in dominating the global 5G market has come to represent something of a "Sputnik moment"—a point at which long-held presumptions of technical supremacy have come under challenge. The implications of this for a global superpower cannot easily be understated: in an era where ICTs enable all facets of national life, the state that controls global ICT networks and determines the technical standards on which they will operate derives significant if not always quantifiable economic, political and geostrategic advantage. It however needs to be borne in mind firstly that 5G is still in a relatively embryonic stage and likely to evolve in unpredictable directions; and secondly that 5G is not the last word in telecommunications technology, with research into 6G already under way including within China. As Ren Zhengfei has observed, "5G is not an atomic bomb."[15] It may prove to be the case that China's advantage in 5G is less durable than at first sight appears. Huawei may have expertise across the spectrum of 5G technologies, but that expertise is thin rather than deep, whereas US companies such as Qualcomm have deep expertise in specific areas, notably the production of 5G microchips, an area of weakness for Huawei that came into stark relief when, in July 2020, the USA effectively banned it from accessing any microchips manufactured on the basis of US intellectual property. Meanwhile the USA has begun to experiment with an alternative system, Open Radio Access Network, which is driven largely by software with a basic and much reduced hardware infrastructure. The philosophical and policy issue facing the USA now is whether it should persist with its current strategy of leaving technological development to be determined by the private sector or whether it requires a national strategy for telecommunications and other advanced technologies rather than relying on the current ad hoc approach, and how practicable might be a strategy of technological decoupling given the highly integrated nature of global technology supply chains and research.

Meanwhile the USA has pursued Huawei on a number of fronts in addition to excluding it from bidding for participation in US federal projects, something Huawei is currently contesting in a Texas court. In May 2019 the US Department of Commerce added Huawei to its Entities List—originally created to constrain the activities of foreign companies engaged in the proliferation of weapons of mass destruction—meaning that thenceforth US companies would have to apply for a licence to sell products to Huawei. A similar provision had been applied to ZTE in 2018 following the discovery that ZTE had been involved in selling telecommunications equipment containing US components to Iran in breach of US sanctions. The ban on ZTE, which would have deprived it of the ability to update the Oracle database software on its mobile base stations, effectively putting it out of business, was rescinded on payment of a substantial fine and an agreement by ZTE to comprehensively restructure its board.

On 15 May 2020 the US Commerce Department introduced amendments that required all foreign companies using US-designed microchip manufacturing equipment to obtain licences in order to sell their products to Huawei or any of its affiliates.[16] The immediate impact of this move was that Huawei faced running out of the high-end Kirin microchips it needs for its latest generation of smartphones, resulting in the loss of billions of dollars in sales. The ability to design these very high-end microchips—just 7 nanometres wide, somewhere between a single blood cell and a strand of DNA—is currently beyond China's capacity and there are virtually no other suppliers who do not rely on US technology to make them. The requisite machinery, electronic design automation (EDA) tools, is owned and operated by just three companies, two US and one European (Siemens), and the latter is so dependent on US technology inputs that it is guaranteed to adhere to US Department of Commerce directives. In any case, the EDAs are the product of decades of research into chemistry and materials science and their functionality is very much dependent on accumulated intuitive knowledge which would be difficult to acquire in the short-term. A series of articles in the Chinese newspaper *Science and Technology Daily*—*Keji Ribao*—entitled "The Core Technology That Urgently Needs to Be Mastered," set out the daunting challenges China faces.[17] US actions to reduce Huawei's access to US-origin technologies constituted a major blow to the company. Without access to US advanced semiconductors Huawei will be unable to power its 5G base stations, smartphones and cloud computing services and its R&D will be curtailed. From September 2020 the company will have to stop producing the Kirin microchips that power its latest generation of smartphones and the company faces the prospect of having to reinvent itself as a manufacturer of advanced PCs and gaming applications.[18] It remains to be seen how China will react to this ban, though it will certainly result in a redoubling of efforts to circumvent the ban either through indigenous innovation, links with other foreign suppliers or both. Whether the US ban will incentivise China to advance its plans for reunification with Taiwan with a view to securing the chip-making capabilities of the Taiwan Semiconductor Manufacturing Corporation (TSMC), which is licensed to manufacture advanced microchips based on US designs, remains to be determined.

In a separate but related series of developments the US Departments of Commerce and Justice have for some years been pursuing Huawei and ZTE for perceived infractions of US sanctions against Iran and North Korea by providing them with telecommunications equipment containing US-manufactured inputs. Their investigation initially focused on ZTE, whose Chief Financial Officer was detained at Logan airport in 2016. The US authorities recovered from his laptop what they described as a "treasure trove" of documents detailing ZTE's illegal transaction with Iran.[19] As a result, in 2017 ZTE was fined US$ 892 million and in 2018 paid a further US$ 1 billion for failure to implement undertakings to discipline ZTE executives involved in these violations. Among the documents found on the ZTE laptop was one which identified Huawei (the company was referred to in the document as F7 in an apparent attempt at concealment but reference to an attempted purchase of the US company Three Leaf in 2010 left no room for doubt) as having used a front company, the Hong Kong-based Skycom, as a vehicle for doing business with

Iran. According to US investigators, Huawei's concealment of its relationship with Skycom had misled Western banks such as HSBC into making payments to Iran in breach of US sanctions. This discovery led in 2018 to the arrest of Meng Wanzhou, the Chief Finance Officer of Huawei and the daughter of Ren Zhengfei by his first wife, at Vancouver airport at the request of the US government, which sought to extradite Meng to the USA.

The response of the Chinese government to Meng's arrest made it clear that she was not just any businesswoman. In their eyes Meng was part of China's nomenklatura by virtue of her senior post in one of China's national champions—and by virtue of the fact that she possessed much information on Huawei and its relationship with the Chinese state that could be highly compromising. In addition to launching a media blitz which, without any apparent sense of irony, criticised the violation of Meng's human rights and the US "long-arm" application of its domestic laws, China promptly arrested two Canadian nationals, one a tour operator and the other a diplomat on sabbatical with a think-tank, on unspecified charges of endangering national security. Both are being held in conditions which undoubtedly do violate their human rights, including the denial of access to lawyers, restricted consular access, daily interrogations and being housed in cells with the lights always on, while Meng, on bail in Vancouver, is able to live in her own home and move around the city freely pending extradition hearings that may not, given Canada's independent judiciary, result in her being sent to the USA for trial.

The cyber domain has become a key battleground for global influence and China has made dominance of this domain a national priority. This approach forms part of a wider strategy to become a world leader in all advanced technologies by 2035. The extent and implications of this ambition will be analysed in subsequent chapters. Meanwhile another key area in which China seeks to leverage its growing technical capabilities is the realm of hard power projection as part of its declared objective of having modern armed forces capable of fighting and winning wars by 2049. The following chapter looks at China's efforts at military modernisation and the role these have played in the country's emergence as a major global power.

9

FIGHTING AND WINNING WARS

THE PEOPLE'S LIBERATION ARMY

There are two important things to understand about China's armed forces, the People's Liberation Army (PLA). The first is that they are not a national military force but are instead the armed wing of the Chinese Communist Party (CCP). What is termed "nationalisation" of the PLA—turning it into a military force that owes its loyalty to the state—is anathema to the ruling Communist Party and in 2012 General Zhang Qinsheng, PLA Deputy Chief of Staff and one of the most open-minded members of his cohort, was dismissed for having the temerity to advocate it.[1] The other is that the PLA is a military force that, if one excludes the suppression of the Democracy Movement in 1989, has not fired a shot in anger in the past forty years. Its last proper military engagement took place in 1979 when it conducted a limited incursion into Vietnam, the so-called "counter-attack in self-defence." This fact is normally cited by Western analysts to call into question the PLA's ability to actually put into practice the extensive training they undergo. But in reality, no country's military has recent experience of fighting the kind of hi-tech war between states that the PLA is being prepared to fight. And unlike their principal peer competitor, the US military, the PLA is less invested in legacy systems and the mindsets that accompany them.

The PLA's status as the armed wing of the CCP was first established by Mao Zedong at the Gutian Conference in 1929. This conference, held in the Fujian village of that name, was the ninth meeting of the CCP since its establishment in 1921 and the first following the abortive 1927 Nanchang Uprising which effectively marked the founding of what was to become the PLA. At the Gutian Conference Mao Zedong, appointed by the Comintern as political commissar, attacked what he termed the "purely military viewpoint" embodied in the proposition that military affairs took precedence over politics and that the role of what was then the Fourth Army of the Chinese Workers' and Peasants' Red Army was simply to fight. Mao asserted that the Red Army was "an armed body for carrying out the political tasks of the revolution," which included propaganda work and organisation among the masses. As the US scholar James Mulvenon has observed, the Gutian Conference was "the seminal moment where the principle of CCP control of the military was enshrined as core Party doctrine and set the tone for the Party's political work during the revolutionary era and beyond."[2]

In November 2014 Xi Jinping, who unlike his predecessor Hu Jintao had immediately assumed the chairmanship of the CCP Central Military Commission (CMC) on taking up office as CCP Secretary-General, convened an event to mark the 85th anniversary of the original Gutian Conference. The anniversary was preceded by an article in the CCP theoretical journal *Qiushi*—*Seeking Facts*—by Yu Guang which highlighted the importance of the CCP's leadership of the military and the importance of people as determinants of the outcome of conflicts. Yu's article also dwelt on the threat to China from

Western forces bent on subverting China through the promotion of universal values and constitutional democracy— "pointing the spears of Westernisation at the Chinese military in a reckless attempt to pull the Chinese military from under the Party's banner"—and championing ideas such as the conversion of the PLA into a state institution.[3]

Gutian 2.0 was attended by over 400 senior military leaders including all members of the Central Military Commission. Most if not all of them would have purchased their appointments as part of a system of pervasive corruption. Commanders of China's then seven military regions might have paid in excess of US$ 3 million for their appointments, with the expectation that they would be able to more than recoup this outlay through sales of PLA land to property developers, bribes from junior officers and even such measures as hiring out PLA song and dance troupes to perform at civilian social functions. In addition to reminding the PLA where their true loyalty lay, Xi moved quickly to address the phenomenon of corruption, with first CMC Vice-Chairmen Generals Xu Caihou and Guo Boxiong cashiered and put on trial followed later by Chief of Joint Staff General Fang Fenghui. Another general, Zhang Yang, committed suicide before he could be arrested. Under these generals the PLA had not just departed a long way from its original culture of austerity and public service but had also turned into an independent satrapy no longer fully under Party control. As a consequence, PLA actions had on more than one occasion embarrassed the CCP leadership. Examples of such behaviour included the 2007 ASAT test in which the PLA destroyed a defunct low-earth orbit satellite with a ballistic missile, a technically impressive achievement which however generated an unprecedented amount of space debris; and the 2011 visit to China of US Defence Secretary Robert Gates during which the PLA conducted a test flight of their new J-20 stealth fighter—in effect a replica of the US F-35 stealth fighter—something of which the then CCP Secretary-General Hu Jintao appeared to be unaware.[4]

The PLA: The Early Days

The CCP foundation myth makes much of its role in resisting Japanese aggression during the Sino–Japanese war. It was however Chiang Kai-shek's Nationalist forces that did the bulk of the fighting while the CCP, in its remote base area in north-west China, largely sat out the conflict while taking the opportunity to rebuild its forces, which had suffered significant attrition during the Long March. Formally speaking, the CCP was part of a Second United Front with the Nationalists into which Chiang Kai-shek had been forced after his kidnapping by the Manchurian warlord Zhang Xueliang in the 1936 Xian Incident. In fact Mao Zedong used participation in the Second United Front to weaken the Nationalists by passing details of Nationalist military dispositions to the Japanese via the Shanghai-based CCP intelligence operative Pan Hannian.[5] During the civil war that followed Imperial Japan's surrender, efforts by the Red Army to win the hearts and minds of the Chinese populace were at least as important as their actual military contribution. While the increasingly debilitated and demoralised Nationalist forces behaved towards the general population in a predatory manner, the Red Army distinguished itself by observing the guidance set out in what has become the iconic PLA marching song, "The Three Rules of Discipline and Eight Points for Attention"—*san da jilu, baxiang zhuyi*: speak politely, pay fairly for what you buy, return what you borrow, pay for what you damage, don't abuse people, don't damage crops, don't take liberties with women, don't ill-treat captives. This is not however to suggest that the PLA could be seen as analogous to the boy scouts: Mao's campaign against the Nationalists involved surrounding the cities and in the course of numerous sieges the PLA inevitably inflicted severe hardship and suffering on civilian populations including in some cases starvation.

Under China's civilian-oriented Confucian system the military had not traditionally been held in high esteem, as evidenced by the popular saying "you don't use good steel for nails and don't use good men for soldiers"—*haotie budading, haonan budangbing*. It is no exaggeration to say that the PLA has transformed that popular perception into one of esteem and affection for the military. Militarily the PLA—thinly disguised as a volunteer force—fought the USA and its allies to a standstill in Korea. And while the Vietnamese victory over French forces at Dien Bien Phu in 1954 may have owed much to the generalship of Vo Nguyen Giap, it also owed much to the skills of PLA military planners and logisticians. Domestically the PLA were routinely involved in disaster relief operations, in which they performed with distinction. During the Cultural Revolution it was the PLA that re-imposed order following a chaotic societal breakdown. And the PLA's relations with the Chinese people are deeply rooted to the extent that few individuals or organisations in China are more than two or three degrees of separation from the army. Most young Chinese receive some rudimentary form of military training and most young men are involved, at least in principle, in some form of militia activity including increasingly in the form of cyber militias. The PLA also has significant involvement in the universities sector, though by no means all those who attend or teach in PLA-affiliated universities are members of the military.

In general, the PLA observed a culture of discipline, public service and austerity until the beginning of the reform and opening-up. At this point Deng Xiaoping made it clear to the PLA that the Fourth Modernisation, that of the military, would have to await progress in the other three. The PLA were however offered a consolation prize in the form of the ability to raise revenue from arms sales working in collaboration with companies like the state arms corporation Norinco and Polytechnologies, a company set up by and for the PLA. This was the point which marked a transition towards the culture of corruption which Xi Jinping sought to address.

By the late 1980s the PLA was a long way from being a modern military. A low-tech mass mobilisation land-based force with no ambition or capacity to operate much beyond China's borders, its military doctrine was based on Mao Zedong's concept of People's War, otherwise known as Prolonged War, an essentially defensive doctrine which involved drawing an attacking force deep into China's heartland where it could be worn down and ultimately overwhelmed by guerrilla activity by both regular and irregular forces. It was a determinedly low-tech form of warfare reflecting Mao's conviction that people, not materiel, were key to determining victory or defeat—*jueding zhanzheng shengfu de zhuyao yinsu shi ren bushi wu*.[6] Relatively limited attention was paid to the PLA Navy, which was no more than a riverine and coastal defence force—in military parlance a brown-water navy. The PLA Air Force was in no better state and though China was able by the mid-1960s to develop a nuclear weapons capability, its missile holdings amounted to a minimal deterrent with no second-strike capability.

More importantly the PLA's fighting capability had atrophied as, during the Cultural Revolution, it became more and more embroiled in activities that would normally have been the preserve of civilian authorities and, inevitably, tainted by the prevailing climate of factionalism. The extent of this deterioration was demonstrated during the 1979 incursion into Vietnam. Intended to last just a few days, the operation required several weeks to achieve its military objectives against mostly second-tier provincial militias, with casualty rates far higher than anticipated. Some

officers—during the Cultural Revolution military ranks had supposedly been phased out in a spurious nod towards socialist
egalitarianism—were so old and out of condition that they were
unable to keep up with their troops in the field. Coordination
between units was chaotic, with military communications often
being reduced to flags and whistles, logistics were noticeable
largely by their absence, and the quality and reliability of Chinese
weaponry was poor. A furious Deng Xiaoping gave the PLA
high command a dressing-down—"you have grown fat and
lazy!"—dismissed them and impressed on their successors the
imperative of extensive military reform while also providing
them with a timely reminder of who was really in charge.

A more consequential reminder of how far behind the PLA
had fallen was the 1991 First Gulf War during which the US
military showcased a new generation of precision-guided conventionally armed missiles and achieved rapid air supremacy by
disabling Iraq's Soviet-supplied air defence systems. In the words
of the IISS 2020 Military Balance, "While the PLA had operated according to the doctrine of 'People's War', the Gulf War
acutely highlighted the need for technological superiority over
quantity of equipment and personnel, and the PLA's need to
enhance military-systems integration and develop joint operations."[7] This led to a Chinese version of the US Revolution in
Military Affairs, the first phase of which was "mechanisation"—
the comprehensive upgrading, modernisation and standardisation of weaponry, command systems and structures across all
service branches but with a primary focus on land-based forces.
But as China's military planners began to address the reforms
needed to bring China closer to parity with potential adversaries,
they also began looking at ways in which China could in due
course develop capabilities that would give them an edge in
future conflict scenarios.

The Taiwan Factor

This thinking coincided with the collapse of the Soviet Union which, while seen by the CCP leadership as highly unwelcome, did paradoxically enable China's military planners to move away from prioritising the defence of China's northern land borders towards a focus on the development of maritime capabilities. A key driver for this was the challenge posed by Taiwan, which for the CCP represents a vital piece of unfinished business. In 1949 Chiang Kai-shek's Nationalist government fled to Taiwan, an island off the coast of Fujian which for much of China's history had not been under effective Chinese control and which from 1895 to 1945 had been a Japanese colony. There Chiang re-established the Republic of China and pledged to retake the entire country, maintaining "representatives" of each Chinese province in Taiwan's Legislative Yuan. US support enabled Chiang's Nationalists to hold China's seat at the United Nations and to resist efforts by Mao Zedong to retake the island militarily. In 1971 the PRC took Taiwan's UN seat and the US rapprochement with the PRC begun under President Richard Nixon led to the US government de-recognising Taiwan as, in 1979, it established full diplomatic relations with Beijing. While committing itself to a "one-China policy" and repealing the Sino-American Mutual Defense Treaty that had served as an important guarantee of Taiwan's security, President Jimmy Carter's administration also passed the Taiwan Relations Act which stipulated that under US law Taiwan was to be treated as "foreign countries, nations, states, governments or similar entities"; established a substantial quasi-diplomatic presence in the form of the American Institute in Taiwan (AIT); and stipulated that "the United States will consider any effort to determine the future of Taiwan by other than peaceful means, including by boycotts or embargoes, a threat to the peace and security of the

Western Pacific and of grave concern to the United States." The Taiwan Relations Act also required the USA to provide Taiwan with "arms of a defensive character" and required the USA to maintain the capacity to resist any use of force or coercion that would jeopardise the security of Taiwan.[8]

For the CCP national reunification constitutes a significant part of its "offer" to the Chinese people. But once Mao had accepted that forcible reunification was infeasible, he moved towards an approach based on persuasion rather than coercion. This policy was further developed by Deng Xiaoping whose formula of One Country, Two Systems, the basis on which Hong Kong reverted to Chinese sovereignty in 1997, was conceived with Taiwan as the main prize. China under Deng was prepared to exercise strategic patience in relation to Taiwan, believing that in due course China's growing economic influence would exercise an irresistible pull. Talks between the two sides led to a consensus in which both maintained that there was only one China but left open the question of which China they were talking about. For China the red line was a declaration of independence by Taiwan. As Taiwan evolved in the 1990s from a regime just as autocratic as that of the PRC into a genuine multi-party democracy, the main opposition Democratic People's Party (DPP) proclaimed its ambition to do precisely that.

Since then, cross-straits relations have been characterised by ambiguity and uncertainty, with China applying a combination of carrot and stick to bring Taiwan into the greater China fold. The carrot consists of economic incentives, favourable treatment for Taiwanese investment in the PRC and the encouragement of tourism, while the stick comprises efforts to close down Taiwan's international space by such means as denying it participation in international organisations such as the World Health Organisation and penalising states which conduct high-profile exchanges with Taipei. Meanwhile Taiwan's own population has increasingly developed its own distinctive identity, with a 2019 National Chengchi University poll determining that 59.9% of respondents identified as Taiwanese, 36.5% as both Chinese and Taiwanese and only 3.6% as Chinese.[9] And the protests that erupted in June 2019 triggered by a proposed extradition bill which would enable Hong Kong residents to be extradited to mainland China have significantly discredited the One Country, Two Systems concept. China's own leaders, starting with Jiang Zemin in the late 1990s, have periodically indicated that their patience in relation to Taiwan is not unlimited and that Taiwan cannot expect to continue kicking the reunification can down the road indefinitely.[10] But China's leadership also know that an attempt to reunify Taiwan by force is not guaranteed to succeed, particularly in the face of sustained resistance. In another public opinion poll conducted in 2019, 68% of respondents declared themselves ready to defend Taiwan in the event of a Chinese attempt at forcible reunification.[11]

In 1995 a crisis erupted in the Taiwan straits when the US government allowed President Lee Teng-hui to make a visit to the USA in contravention of earlier practice whereby serving Taiwanese politicians had been denied visas. In response the PRC undertook naval exercises including a series of unarmed ballistic missile tests in the seas off Taiwan. The US reaction, which was to dispatch two carrier battle groups to the region, took the PLA by surprise and sparked the development of a new strategy that has become known as Anti-Access, Area Denial (A2AD)—though this is in fact a US term and not one used in PLA strategic documents. The aim of this strategy was to develop a suite of capabilities which would, in the event that China sought to re-unify Taiwan by force, keep US forces out of theatre long enough to ensure that they would be unable to intervene within an operationally meaningful timescale. As Professor Aaron Friedberg observes in his book *Beyond Air–Sea Battle*,

Rather than a general emphasis on modernising in all dimensions at once, the prospect of American intervention with carrier-based aircraft gave planners a very specific set of problems on which to focus. Equally important, top military leaders now had a concrete threat on which to base their requests for more resources.[12]

A further incentive to focus on some very specific military objectives was the 1999 US intervention in Kosovo where the USA was able to use sophisticated satellite and airborne radar capabilities to seek out and destroy Serbian targets using "smart bombs" and precision-guided missiles while neutralising Serbian command and control and air defence systems through a combination of electronic warfare and computer network attack.

The PLA realised that to combat what Soviet military theorists had referred to as the US Surveillance Strike Complex, it would have to undergo a process characterised by what can only be translated rather inelegantly as "informatisation"—*xinxihua*—and to use information capabilities asymmetrically to defeat a superior force—read the USA—by disabling their command and control and communications systems at the start of any conflict. The 1990s witnessed an outpouring of writings on the subject of information warfare by military thinkers such as Wang Pufeng, often referred to as the father of information warfare, who spoke of the need for China to achieve information dominance in the early stages of conflict and of the ability of information warfare to produce "soft casualties" by damaging the information capabilities of an adversary and creating military outcomes with minimal loss of life[13]—a reflection of the classical Chinese military strategist Sunzi's concept of subduing the adversary without fighting—*buzhan er qu ren zhi bing*. This has evolved into a conception of modern warfare as a confrontation between opposing operational systems in which system destruction is a major determinant of victory. It sees warfare as extending beyond the traditional domains of land, sea and air and goes beyond the kinetic to include all areas of potential adversary vulnerability—a concept articulated in the book *Unrestricted Warfare—chaoxian zhan*—published in 1999 by two PLA Air Force colonels, Qiao Liang and Wang Xiangsui—though this publication should be seen as a work of advocacy rather than something that represents formal Chinese strategy or doctrine.

In terms of military capabilities China has experienced a rapid transformation within the past two decades. Comparing national defence budgets is more art than exact science since there are no internationally agreed criteria as to what items should be included. In particular, expenditure on military R&D, much of which may be conducted by private sector corporations or universities and may be dual use in nature, is notoriously hard to account for. In China's case the problem of estimating defence expenditure is further complicated by the endemic unreliability of Chinese government statistics and by a culture of opacity. But broadly speaking it is safe to say that China's defence expenditure has since 1990 increased annually by or close to double digits while still only accounting for around 2% of GDP thanks to China's rapid economic growth.

In terms of implementing its A2AD strategy China has sought to push its defensive perimeter as far out as possible by developing a sophisticated network of reconnaissance capabilities based on a combination of over 100 satellites, Unmanned Aerial Vehicles (UAVs)—popularly referred to as drones—and over-the-horizon radars used for situational awareness but also target acquisition. In terms of offensive capabilities, the PLA has developed a comprehensive range of short, medium and long-range conventionally armed missiles that collectively have the capacity to give the USA pause for thought should it wish to come to Taiwan's aid. There are estimated to be some 1,100 short-range ballistic missiles deployed along the Chinese coast and aimed at Taiwan as well as hundreds of land, sea and air launched cruise missiles.[14] China has been able to develop substantial medium-range ballistic and cruise missile capabilities by virtue of not being included in the now-defunct Intermediate-Range Nuclear Forces (INF) Treaty. This treaty, negotiated between the USA and USSR in 1987 and which banned both parties from developing, testing or deploying land-based ballistic and cruise missiles with ranges between 500 and 5,000 kilometres, was renounced by the Trump administration in October 2018 partly because of the perception that Russia, as the successor state to the Soviet Union, had breached the terms of the treaty but also due to the realisation that it had significantly disadvantaged the USA in relation to China.

By developing its medium and long-range capabilities it seems that China is seeking to challenge the US way of war which involves projecting force out from bases that are assumed to be invulnerable to enemy action. Such bases, both within the USA and in locations such as Guam in the Western Pacific, have few if any hardened facilities, lack effective air defences and would thus be vulnerable to missile strikes and drone attacks. For China the big strategic prize would be the closure of US military bases in the first and second island chains, thus leaving China in uncontested control of the Western Pacific. Another key element of US military power projection, the carrier battle group, which requires a large number of surface and submarine vessels to protect the actual aircraft carrier, could prove equally vulnerable to attack by missiles and drone swarms. It is probably too early to conclude that the era of the aircraft carrier is over—China's own investment in this capability suggests that it still has life—but the growing prevalence of "carrier killer" systems will undoubtedly lead to a rethink about the ways in which such capabilities are deployed.[15]

Perhaps the most startling aspect of Chinese military modernisation has been China's rapid transition to becoming a major naval power with the beginnings of a genuine "blue-water" capability, by which is meant the capability to project naval power beyond its littoral. In 2012 CCP Secretary-General Hu Jintao called for China to become a maritime power, a call subsequently reiterated by Xi Jinping.[16] Between 2014 and 2018 China launched more naval vessels than the total possessed by the UK's Royal Navy. By 2018 the PLA Navy (PLAN) had a total of 300 ships, more than the US Navy. However, the PLAN still has only two aircraft carriers compared with the USA's eleven and although it has a fleet of nuclear-powered submarines the majority of vessels in the submarine fleet are diesel-powered and date back to the Soviet era. Until recently the focus of PLA naval expansion had been on littoral capabilities with a particular emphasis on missile-armed coastal patrol craft, frigates and corvettes. But recent additions to the surface fleet have included larger high-capability surface combat vessels, notably the Type 055 cruiser, which speak to blue-water aspirations. The PLAN has sought to acquire blue-water experience through participation in anti-piracy patrols off the coast of Somalia in relation to which they have acquired a naval base in Djibouti; participation in international naval exercises such as RIMPAC; and independent naval operations in the Pacific, Indian and Atlantic Oceans, the Mediterranean and Baltic Seas and the Arctic and Antarctic. An indication of the PLAN's growing reach and ambition is its 2015 evacuation of 600 Chinese and 225 foreign nationals from Aden during a period of intense fighting, an operation that would have been challenging for any navy to undertake.

An expansion of naval power has been accompanied by comparable developments in air power. The PLA Air Force (PLAAF) has since 2004 had a mandate to "integrate air and space and to be simultaneously prepared for offensive and defensive operations."[17] It has a substantial fleet of fourth generation fighter aircraft, a squadron of so-called 4.5 generation Su-35 fighters from Russia and is developing indigenous J-20 fifth generation fighters with stealth technology. Its H-6 strategic bombers are equipped with land-attack cruise missiles that offer the potential for what is termed stand-off strike capability against foreign military bases up to and including Guam. Progress on the H-20, an advanced stealth replacement for the H-6 thought to be nuclear capable, is on track. Indigenously manufactured Unmanned Aerial Vehicles (UAVs) offer a growing range of capabilities while also constituting a substantial export sector. The PLAAF manages a large and sophisticated set of air defence capabilities based on advanced Russian systems. Operationally its focus is increasingly on longer range operations over water, reflecting China's military refocusing away from land-based operations.

The final element in China's development of a world-class military arsenal is the progress it is making towards developing a credible nuclear second-strike capability, in other words the capability to retaliate in the event of a nuclear attack and hence call into question the rationale for undertaking such an attack in the first place. In the past China's nuclear deterrent has consisted of a small force of intercontinental and medium range ballistic missiles operated by what until the 2016 military reforms had been the Second Artillery, now rebranded as the Strategic Rocket Force. These missiles were liquid fuelled and kept in silos, making them slow to deploy and vulnerable to pre-emptive strike. They are however gradually being replaced by solid-fuel road-mobile missiles that can quickly be deployed and are much harder to target. In addition, China now possesses a fleet of nuclear-powered submarines able to launch ballistic missiles. Once the PLAAF acquires the new nuclear-capable H-20 bomber it will possess the "nuclear triad" of ground, sea and air launch capabilities. China appears to have no desire to match either the USA or Russia in overall nuclear holdings and maintains that it will never launch a first strike. The aim is to maintain a minimum credible deterrence capability.

An important and growing aspect of China's defence capabilities is its industrial defence sector, which has two functions: firstly, to develop advanced indigenous systems for China's national defence, but also to contribute to China's efforts to move up the industrial value chain away from a reliance on low-end manufacturing. China's indigenous defence industries are now among the most profitable on the planet and have helped China to become the seventh largest international arms supplier as of 2018, with a growing focus on sales of UAVs, precision-guided weaponry and naval vessels, the two former capabilities being ones that Western arms manufacturers are often inhibited from selling to third countries who are not close allies. A key element in developing China's defence industries is the concept of civil-military fusion, first conceived in the 1990s but given a significant boost under Xi Jinping with the aim of expanding civil sector participation in military projects not just in relation to hardware but also in education, personnel, investment, infrastructure and logistics. Achieving a high level of civil-military fusion has been identified as a strategic objective and the full resources of the Party-state have been brought to bear, with all major state-owned enterprises required to identify areas in which they will participate.

Military power is not merely a function of weaponry but is also about organisation, training and doctrine. To achieve its long-term objectives of becoming a world class military able to fight and win wars, as announced by Xi Jinping at the 19th Party Congress, the PLA needed restructuring to enable the creation of an all-arms force no longer dominated by the army and able to undertake sophisticated joint operations. As Chairman of the CMC, Xi initiated a wide-ranging military reorganisation beginning in September 2015 with an announcement that the PLA would reduce its forces by 300,000 troops, mostly from the ground forces. At the beginning of 2016 a major structural reform was announced with China's seven military regions being replaced by five theatre commands falling directly under the command of the CMC. The PLA's four General Staff departments—command, political, logistics and equipment—were replaced by fifteen groups also directly answerable to the CMC. And three new services were announced: the PLA General Command, the PLA Strategic Rocket Force and the PLA Strategic Support Force. These changes were clearly targeted at institutional inertia and stove-piping within the PLA while reducing the hitherto dominant role of the Army and bringing the PLA more directly under Party control. The changes also reflected the CCP's commitment to informatisation with the Strategic Support Force responsible for integrating cyber and space capabilities and subsuming the former signals intelligence and electronic warfare departments, the Third and Fourth Departments of the PLA respectively.

In 2017 a further reorganisation was announced with the creation of eighty-four units at a combined corps level to be commanded by officers with the rank of major-general or rear-admiral and the creation by 2020 of a joint operational command structure. Meanwhile military training exercises which in the past had been heavily scripted have been replaced with blue and red teams opposing one another without predetermined outcomes. Such exercises now also contain a considerable information component with the aim of ensuring that the PLA will be able to fight "localised wars under conditions of informatisation."

The PLA has been set a challenging agenda by the CCP leadership at the 19th Party Congress. It is expected to have "basically" achieved mechanisation by 2020 whilst continuing to make significant progress on informatisation. By 2035 it is expected to have achieved "basic" modernisation across the realms of theory, organisational structure, personnel and weaponry. By 2049 it is expected to be a world-class military capable of fighting and winning wars. In addition to informatisation it has acquired the additional challenge of "intelligentisation"—*zhinenghua*—an objective added in the 2019 Defence White Paper, the most authoritative statement of China's defence strategies. By intelligentisation is meant the applications of artificial intelligence to enhance the analysis of large data sets and to enable the automation of decision-making and potentially weapons systems. This is a process with which all advanced military forces are currently struggling, as they are with informatisation, something which has to date mainly been used to deliver tactical outcomes on the battlefield. The PLA also suffers from continuing institutional issues including corruption, a culture that privileges centralised decision-making over the encouragement of individual initiative and the problem faced by all military forces in attracting the kind of talent they will need to make an informationised environment a reality: geeks are not natural soldiers.

Nonetheless the transformation achieved by the PLA in the past twenty years has been remarkable. And while it is unlikely that the PLA will fully achieve the objectives it has been set—complete mechanisation by 2020 is now clearly an impossibility—it is likely that they will make enough progress in all of these target areas to produce overall capabilities that are good enough to deter potential aggressors. Already senior US military leaders have questioned whether they would be able to prevail against the PLA in a full-blown military conflict.[18] If indeed China is able to achieve something close to military parity with the USA this may prove to be globally stabilising if neither sees benefit in going to war. That presupposes rational decision-making and levels of self-awareness that are not always in evidence in international relations. But even if military conflict between China and the USA can be avoided, this needs to be considered in the light of a world in which great power conflict is being conducted at a level below armed conflict and increasingly plays out in the areas of economics, finance and technology. Technology in particular is at the heart of this contest and the extent to which the USA and China either compete or cooperate in the field of technology will have far-reaching implications for the global order.

10

CHINA AS HI-TECH SUPERPOWER

Shortly after assuming office in 2013 Xi Jinping gave two speeches that demonstrated his preoccupation with technology as the key to achieving the China Dream. According to Xi:

> Advanced technology is the sharp weapon of the modern state. An important reason that Western countries were able to hold sway over the world in modern times was that they held the advanced technology... Our technology still generally lags that of developed countries and we must adopt an asymmetric strategy of catching up and overtaking, bringing our own advantages to bear.[1]

The word Xi used for catching up and overtaking—*ganchao*—is a shorthand term in use since 1949 that encapsulates a consistent ambition to see China resume its historical status as a leading global power. Since making those speeches Xi has launched a series of initiatives designed to promote this objective and has made countless further speeches exhorting his countrymen to do more, faster. The overriding tone is one of positivity—*zheng nengliang*—with frequent references to the need to take advantage of a period of "global change unprecedented in the past hundred years."[2] But behind this positivity lurks a keen awareness of the consequences of failure. A *People's Daily* article of 16 January 2018 entitled "Firmly Grasp the Period of Historic Opportunity to Achieve Great Things," while radiating positivity, also reminds its readers of the consequences China suffered as a result of failing to match the West's Industrial Revolution and emphasises that China cannot again afford to miss the boat.[3]

In order to avoid falling into a middle-income trap China needs to move rapidly up the value chain away from low-end labour-intensive manufacturing. China may or may not be close to the Lewis Turning Point, the moment at which a country runs out of cheap surplus labour.[4] But there can be no doubt that wages in the Chinese manufacturing sector have risen to the point where the country is no longer competitive relative to other regional states such as Vietnam and Indonesia. As China's economy has rebalanced towards internal consumption, fewer Chinese workers are willing to spend years away from their families working in sweatshops in Shenzhen and the Yangzi valley. And even in cases where manufacturing capacity has been relocated inland to take advantage of China's remaining pools of rural labour, factory work exercises diminishing attraction as an increasingly diversified domestic economy offers more attractive alternatives.

Moreover, China is facing a demographic crunch. During the early years of the People's Republic Mao Zedong was dismissive of the New Population Theory advanced by the noted economist Ma Yinchu, which argued for state population control, believing that large reserves of manpower constituted one of China's greatest strengths.[5] By 1979 however fears of unsustainable population growth led to the imposition of a one-child policy—designed by rocket scientists who were virtually the only intellectuals then afforded any status or respect—that was revoked only in 2016. This led to a massive male–female imbalance—in some parts of the country as high as 117 males for every 100 females, reflecting strong Chinese cultural preferences for male offspring. Added to this is the current reluctance of China's urban millennials to shoulder the increasingly high costs of parenthood; and the unwillingness of educated high-earning urban women even to contemplate marriage despite heavy-handed and largely unsuccessful efforts by the Chinese state to shame them by referring to them publicly as *sheng nü*—"women left on the shelf." The net result is that the population bulge that played a major part in China's latest phase of industrialisation has run its course. Population growth dropped below replacement rate in 2016 and in 2019 China's birth-rate fell to its lowest level since 1961.[6] China now confronts the challenge of a rapidly aging population that will need to be supported by a diminishing workforce—the famous inverted pyramid whereby one worker ends up supporting two parents and four grandparents—in a state whose social security networks are still embryonic. Some Western commentators have claimed that this means China will get old before it gets rich.[7] How far this proves to be the case will to a large extent depend on the ability of the Chinese state to leverage the benefits of emerging technologies such as Artificial Intelligence and robotics.

The Chinese Party-state has drawn up a series of ambitious plans for turning the country into a global technology leader. In 2015 the Internet Plus strategy was launched with the aim of integrating China's online and real-world economies as part of an effort to move away from a reliance on exports in favour of an economy based more on domestic consumption. Internet Plus sought to promote the incorporation of the Internet, cloud computing, big data and the Internet of Things (IOT) into a range of industries including manufacturing, the services sector and agriculture while also enhancing e-government. The same year saw the launch of Made in China 2025, designed both to enhance the country's competitiveness and also to reduce its vulnerabilities to supply-chain interruptions and national security threats by increasing the proportion of indigenously manufactured components in ten "core" technology sectors to 40% by 2020 and 70% by 2025. The relevant sectors are: advanced information technologies including Artificial Intelligence (AI) and quantum computing; automated machine tools and robotics; maritime equipment and hi-tech shipping; rail transport; aerospace equipment; self-driving and new energy vehicles; power equipment; agricultural equipment; new materials; and bio-pharma and advanced medical products.

Made in China 2025 called on Chinese companies to declare new technology standards that are either compatible with or able to replace existing international standards. Influence over global standards forms a major part of China's overall technology strategy. Already three major international agencies responsible for technology standards—the International Organisation for Standardisation (ISO), the International Electrotechnical Commission (IEC) and the International Telecommunication Union (ITU)—are headed by Chinese nationals. A bid by China in 2020 to secure control of the World Intellectual Property Organisation (WIPO) was however frustrated. China now enjoys a global lead in establishing technical standards for blockchain, a technology to which the CCP Politburo dedicated an entire day's study session in October 2019,[8] the Internet of Things, 5G and biometrics. The Chinese leadership interest in blockchain has little to do with its attractions as a distributed and quintessentially democratic system that provides constant and immediate verification of transactions but is rather to do with its potential for enabling China to develop a digital currency that will reduce the country's dependence on the US dollar and hence its vulnerability to US-imposed financial sanctions.

Made in China 2025 has become a major irritant in Sino–US relations in the context of the trade war initiated in 2018 by US

President Donald Trump's decision to impose tariffs on a wide range of Chinese goods. For the USA the Made in China strategy is emblematic of a model of state capitalism fundamentally antithetical to the liberal economic model of open competition that forms the basis for international trade under the World Trade Organisation (WTO). China's initial response was to argue that the plan did not violate WTO rules by virtue of being transparent, indicative rather than mandatory, and in principle open to foreign participation. But as the trade war with the USA unfolded China's Propaganda Department issued instructions to cease referring to Made in China 2025 to avoid aggravating Sino–US tensions while also undertaking revisions with a view to permitting greater foreign participation in the project.[9]

Made in China 2025 also attracted domestic criticism with former Finance Minister Lou Jiwei—replaced in 2016 by Xi Jinping for being too outspokenly reformist—characterising the plan as "a waste of taxpayers' money." Speaking in a panel discussion at the 2019 Chinese People's Political Consultative Conference (CPPCC), an advisory body whose function and status are in some ways akin to those of the British House of Lords, Lou argued that "There was no need to talk about the year 2025 in the first place. The government wants industries to be top-notch by then, but these industries are not predictable and the government should not have thought it had the ability to predict what is not foreseeable."[10] For his temerity Lou was dismissed from his position as Chair of the National Council for Social Security—though he subsequently found a position at the State Council's Development Research Centre from which he has continued to be an outspoken critic of government policies.

The third element in Beijing's strategy for global technology supremacy is the 2017 Next Generation Artificial Intelligence Plan, which has three phases. By 2020 China should have kept pace with the world's leaders and have developed a core AI industry worth RMB 150 billion. By 2025 China should have registered important breakthroughs in AI, increased the value of its core AI industries to RMB 400 billion and developed a corpus of laws and ethical standards for AI. By 2030 China should be the world's leading AI innovation centre with a core industry worth RMB 1 trillion and AI being used in multiple domains, including social governance and national defence.[11] The plan sees the development of AI as key to China's next phase of economic and social development and also for the development of innovative national defence applications through civil-military fusion. The announcement of the plan was the trigger for provinces and municipalities to vie with each other to attract AI start-ups through the provision of dedicated development zones, tax holidays and other incentives involving sums that dwarf the investment of other developed nations. In 2018 the municipality of Tianjin announced an AI investment fund of US$ 16 billion[12] while in the same year France set up an AI development fund of just Euros 1.5 billion.

Artificial Intelligence (AI) is a term that is used very loosely to cover a wide range of capabilities, from the most basic of tasks using rules-based algorithms, such as recognising pictures of cats, through to highly sophisticated programmes that can provide accurate translation of different languages, distinguish individual human faces, voices and gaits or outplay humans in complex games such as chess and Go. What makes the more sophisticated capabilities possible is the neural network, a concept that has been around since the 1950s and which seeks to replicate the functioning of the human brain by building banks of algorithms into which are fed volumes of labelled data and which are then left to identify underlying patterns of correlation, a process known as deep learning. In the early days of AI, a lack of adequate computing power and data relegated neural networks to the fringes of AI theory but a massive growth in both over the past decade has had a transformational impact.

"Narrow" AI should not be confused with Artificial General Intelligence, the point at which machine intelligence surpasses that of humans, referred to by AI specialists as the singularity. There is in principle no reason why silicon-based intelligence should not become superior to the "wetware" that has evolved somewhat haphazardly in human skulls over millions of years and some AI enthusiasts have argued that this might happen sooner than is generally supposed. Other experts take the view that such a development is a long way off and may never happen. At present even the most sophisticated AI programmes cannot engage in the kind of working across intellectual boundaries or the use of heuristics in decision-making that are intrinsic to human beings: even Google's AlphaGo Plus, which made history by teaching itself to play Go to a level beyond anything the best humans could match—or even understand—could be brought to a standstill by simply having to play on a different-sized board from the one it trained on. What AI programmes can do is process data at volumes and speeds that far outstrip the capacity of the human brain and identify correlations not discernible by humans; and perform specific tasks such as distinguishing between benign and malignant tumours from MRI scans with greater accuracy and consistency than human experts.

Until relatively recently AI research was focused in the United Kingdom and North America. China has been a relative latecomer, with the result that its AI skills are still relatively embryonic; many of China's best AI experts are currently located either in US universities or Silicon Valley. This is recognised by the authors of the Next Generation Artificial Intelligence plan, who identify Chinese vulnerabilities that include a lack of original research and weakness in the mathematics of algorithms. The plan seeks to remedy these shortcomings through collaboration with foreign research institutes, acquisitions and investments in foreign companies and the promotion of the Thousand Talents programme, another initiative to which Chinese officials no longer publicly refer and which is designed to attract foreign talent to work in China and encourage expatriate Chinese talent to return home. Some Western scientists who have relocated to China describe enjoying laboratory facilities far superior to what they could even dream of in their home countries. The plan also promotes the use of open-source software and open access to data to optimise research outcomes.

China has often been criticised for its lack of focus on original scientific research, with even Chinese academics such as Rao Yi, Dean of life sciences at Peking University, arguing in a blog post on the social media platform *Zhishi fenzi*—"intellectuals"—that Chinese students pursued STEM studies not out of intrinsic interest but because they were seen as a route to riches, and that China had produced virtually no home-grown Nobel prize winners in contrast to small countries such as Israel and European states.[13] But as the Chinese hi-tech entrepreneur Kai-fu Lee points out, the technology of AI can be likened to the discovery of electricity. Once the breakthrough has been made—and major scientific breakthroughs are by definition rare—subsequent developments come in the form of incremental improvements and innovative applications of the basic technology.[14] This is where Chinese entrepreneurs have excelled and although their focus to date has been on the development of lucrative customer-facing products, the quantities of money being made available by the state must enhance the prospect of innovation in areas prioritised by the state.

For the Chinese Party-state AI is seen as a game-changing technology that offers the potential to overtake the West and set the agenda for the coming century through a combination of state direction plus the incentivisation of the private sector to take risks and innovate. China's major technology companies have become national champions for different aspects of AI. Baidu has been given the lead in autonomous vehicles, Alibaba in the development of smart cities, Tencent in medical imaging, iFlytek in smart voice and Sensetime in facial recognition. As mentioned in a previous chapter AI plays a key role in the surveillance technologies increasingly deployed across China and for which Xinjiang has become a test-bed. China has become a world leader in facial recognition but also in the area of natural language programming. All these technologies are designed to come together in the planned new smart, green megalopolis of Xiong'an to be built in Hebei province at an estimated cost of RMB 4 trillion—US$ 580 billion—over the next two decades, with autonomous vehicles as the default transport mode. To boost capabilities China is seeking to establish fifty new AI academies and research institutes while 196 Chinese universities now offer courses in big data and data science.

China's own car industry, though producing large volumes of vehicles, is almost entirely based on existing Western technologies and far from innovative. Electric and autonomous vehicles represent a way for China to catch up and surpass the West—and help mitigate the disastrous environmental legacy of China's dash for growth over the past thirty years. The US entrepreneur Elon Musk was able to build a $2 billion "Gigafactory" in Shanghai to manufacture the Tesla Model 3 in just over a year from scratch. Thirty percent of the components are produced in China with the intention to increase that to 80% by the middle of the decade. Musk was looking to gain early access to a market that has been incentivised by a range of central government and local subsidies for electric vehicles in the expectation that by 2025 new energy vehicles will represent 20% of the total.[15] In doing so he is up against a number of indigenous firms including BYD and SAIC, which are also involved in developing autonomous vehicles. Both Beijing and Shanghai have established autonomous vehicle testing zones amid a level of popular enthusiasm in China for such products typically much higher than in the West.[16]

As with vehicles, so with robotics. China has for some years been the world's largest market for robots, accounting in 2016 for 30% of global sales. But in terms of density of distribution China is far below the global average with just 68 units per 10,000 workers. In 2014 President Xi Jinping called for a robotics revolution to address the challenges outlined above of rising labour costs, low productivity and an aging demographic. The Chinese state is aiming for the indigenous manufacture of 100,000 robots by the end of 2020 for use in manufacturing, services including healthcare, financial services, logistics and customer services, as well as specialised robots for use in military applications and disaster relief. This will not be straightforward as China lacks a corpus of specialised and experienced workers able to programme the robots. More generally the percentage of senior technicians in China's workforce is just 5% as opposed to 40% for Japan and 50% for Germany and the relatively short shelf-life of Chinese small and medium-sized enterprises, averaging just three years, militates against the development of this skilled cadre of workers.[17] As is the case in other developed economies concerns have been expressed about the potential implications of AI and robotics for the future of employment. But such polls as have been conducted suggest that Chinese respondents are generally sanguine about these implications. This optimism may be justified by a growing realisation that while these technologies can perform tasks, they cannot necessarily do jobs other than those that involve high levels of predictably repetitious work and are best deployed alongside human beings, freeing the latter to engage in work that involves creativity and interaction with other humans.

China's aging population and weak healthcare systems have combined to provide the impetus for what amounts to a revolution in bio-pharma. A combination of government focus over three Five-Year Plans combined with a large influx of Chinese scientists trained in the West—estimated at 250,000 over the past decade—has begun to transform what was once a sclerotic sector characterised by the production of a small number of generic drugs into something far more dynamic. Regulatory changes are facilitating the import of internationally approved drugs with regulations increasingly harmonised with global standards, while Chinese start-ups are racing to develop indigenous drugs to deal with a range of medical conditions such as cancer and diabetes with significant unmet demand. China has witnessed the establishment of some 100 bio-sciences parks across China with significant investment from the state, with the aim of enabling bio-sciences to account for 4% of GDP by 2020. In 2016 China announced a US$ 9 billion Precision Medicine Initiative with the aim of mapping 100 million human genomes, while expenditure on developing biosimilar products is estimated to constitute 20% of the global market. Concerns about whether China's bio-medical sector might be susceptible to lower ethical standards than in Western liberal democracies appeared to be borne out in the case of He Jiankui, who in 2018 claimed to have created the world's first gene-edited children. But the levels of condemnation of He's actions from within China's scientific community and the alacrity with which he was tried and imprisoned suggest that China takes such ethical issues, and its own international reputation, seriously.[18] China's investment in bio-sciences demonstrated its value when Chinese scientists were able very quickly to sequence the genetic make-up of COVID-19, thereby preparing the ground for the early development of a vaccine.

The Final Frontier—with Chinese Characteristics

China has emerged as a major space-faring nation having undertaken five manned space launches under the Shenzhou—"Divine

Land," a poetic name for China—space programme begun in 1992; established two Tiangong unmanned space laboratories with two manned space dockings having taken place; and accomplished several lunar missions including the 2019 lunar space rover Chang'e 4, which made the first ever landing on the dark side of the moon.[19] China has the aim of establishing a permanent lunar research station by 2035. While space has obvious applications in the military domain, a key driver of China's space programme is economic, in particular with regard to space mining. The lunar surface is estimated to contain substantial deposits of minerals that include thorium, magnesium, platinum, titanium, silicon, aluminium and iron ore as well as water in the form of ice.[20] Asteroids too are a rich source of minerals and China's National Space Science Centre is working on ambitious plans to capture a Near Earth Asteroid, bring it back to Earth and exploit its resources. It also has ambitions to develop space-based solar power plants which, if the considerable practical obstacles can be overcome, could provide an inexhaustible supply of clean energy to the planet.

At present there is little in the way of international legislation covering outer space. The only relevant legal instrument is the 1967 Outer Space Treaty negotiated between the USA and the Soviet Union, then the world's only two spacefaring powers. This treaty bans the positioning of weapons of mass destruction in outer space and determines that no nation can claim sovereignty over outer space or celestial bodies. But it has nothing to say about how activities such as space mining might be regulated, nor does it prohibit the militarisation of space per se. Space has for some time been a contentious area in Sino–US relations, beginning with a 2011 Congressional ban on NASA having any dealings with Chinese counterparts unless these dealings "pose no risk of resulting in the transfer of technology, data, or any other information with national security or economic security implications to China or a Chinese-owned company."[21] In military terms China has long focused on US dependence on satellites for what in military shorthand is termed C4ISR—command, control, communications, computers, intelligence, surveillance and reconnaissance—and for precision-guided weaponry. China has on the one hand sought to exploit US military dependence on space-based systems by such means as developing ground-based anti-satellite capabilities involving ballistic missiles and laser weapons whilst simultaneously developing its own space-based military facilities including through the development of the Beidou global positioning system as an alternative to GPS and the creation of the PLA Strategic Support Force to integrate information and electronic warfare with space. The United States meanwhile set up a dedicated Space Force at the end of 2019 with a remit to conduct space operations. It is hard to avoid the conclusion that space has the potential to become a major zone of contestation between China and the USA.

Military Uses of AI and Autonomous Systems

The Chinese PLA have, like most other major military forces, been thinking hard about the ways in which AI and autonomous systems might alter the character of conflict. For the PLA AI in particular appears to offer a route to reduce the gap between US and Chinese military capabilities and potentially to overtake the USA. In the words of Major-General Ding Xiangrong, deputy director of the Central Military Commission's General Office, speaking at the 2018 Xiangshan Forum, "the PLA aims to narrow the gap with global advanced powers by taking advantage of the ongoing revolution...centred on information technology and intelligent technology."[22] At present this thinking takes the form of a wide-ranging and relatively open debate which encompasses all aspects of the topic including the legal and ethical implications of battlefield AI, autonomous weapons and command systems that are to varying degrees automated. The current debate in China on military AI is reminiscent of the debate that took place a decade ago on information warfare when it seemed that every other senior officer in the PLA hierarchy was writing books and articles and giving talks on the subject. This debate came to an end once the PLA had begun to develop the relevant doctrines and capabilities, and it may well be that the debate on military AI goes the same way. It also needs to be borne in mind that the PLA are accustomed to using published articles either as a means of allaying foreign concerns about particular developments or as a form of deterrence by giving the impression that particular capabilities are further advanced than is in fact the case.

Military applications of AI focus on two main areas: the development and use of autonomous weapons systems, and the use of AI in decision-making and battlespace control. Autonomous weapons systems already exist in the form of Unmanned Aerial Vehicles (UAVs), such as the US Predator drones equipped with Hellfire missiles that have been deployed in the Federally Administered Tribal Areas of Pakistan against al Qaeda and in Syria and Iraq against Islamic State; and Chinese-manufactured Wing Loong drones that have been deployed in the Libyan civil war. These systems are not fully autonomous, in the sense that the drones are programmed to "phone home" before any lethal action is undertaken, thereby maintaining the principle of always having a human in the decision-making loop; in the US case, it is the drone pilot, situated in an airbase thousands of miles from the target, who presses the trigger. There is however no technical reason why these drones could not be programmed automatically to open fire if specific criteria are met: air and ship defence systems are programmed to do just that and Israel's Harpy drones are programmed automatically to attack hostile radar installations.

Fears about the threat posed by "killer robots" has animated international action, with discussions about the banning of lethal autonomous weapons taking place in the United Nations under the Convention on Certain Conventional Weapons, thus far without success.[23] China has expressed formal support for such efforts whilst arguing for an impossibly narrow definition of such weapons and itself working to develop capabilities such as autonomous long-range unmanned submarines. Chinese military planners are betting that the US military will remain too invested in mature systems such as stealth aircraft and carrier battle groups to focus sufficiently on the development of such disruptive new systems, an approach referred to in Chinese military writings as *wandao chaoche*—making a tight turn to overtake an adversary.

Chinese military applications of AI can be expected to focus initially on enhancing existing military capabilities in areas such as logistics, weapons design—where AI can potentially enhance the performance of autonomous weapons including tanks, aircraft, submarines and missiles—and military training, where Virtual Reality can generate experiences that closely resemble actual combat situations. As China's 2019 Defence White Paper makes clear, AI can be used to enable more rapid planning and execution of military operations. In combat situations AI can be used to enhance situational awareness while potentially revealing exploitable vulnerabilities in an adversary's information systems. It can also enhance information warfare activities designed to erode the will of adversaries to resist, something that has become referred to as cognition warfare. And in a data-suffused environment where conflict is being undertaken simultaneously across multiple zones, collapsing traditional distinctions between civil and military, AI can be used to collect and analyse data and engage in automated decision-making.

Beyond these broad headings opinion appears to differ between those thinkers who see AI systems as subordinate to human decision makers and those who perceive future warfare as essentially a contest between algorithms. As a senior executive in the Chinese armaments corporation Norinco put it at the 2018 Xiangshan forum, "In future battlefields there will be no people fighting."[24] Others take a more nuanced view. While expecting that over time the PLA will make more extensive use of AI systems for data aggregation and decision-making and that such reliance may extend to areas such as machine–brain interface— *renji ronghe*—such thinkers argue that AI systems will enhance rather than replace the role of the human on the battlefield. This is particularly true in terms of using AI for decision-making to overcome human vulnerabilities including tiredness, forgetfulness and allowing thinking to become dominated by emotion.[25] The latter view accords more closely with the evolution of thinking in Western military circles. No military commander could realistically want to preside over a "Sorcerer's Apprentice" war in which AI systems compete against each other in what would inevitably become a highly escalatory environment with no human able to press the override button.

National security and military considerations have played a dominant role in the development of two other emerging technologies, quantum computing and quantum encryption. Quantum computing is based on the particle physics phenomenon of superposition: the ability of a quantum bit or Qubit to assume simultaneously the states 1 and 0. By linking Qubits through the process known as entanglement a quantum computer could in principle perform orders of magnitude more calculations than is possible with a conventional computer, offering the prospect of enormous and rapid advances in areas such as materials science and pharmacology, not to mention AI. The processing speed of quantum computers would also enable them to break all existing cryptographic systems, most of which are based on the fact that identifying the factors that make up a very long digit is near to impossible with existing computing capabilities. This risk is already driving governments and private sector organisations to consider how they can future-proof the security of existing data against retrospective decryption. Thus far quantum computing remains in essence a series of experiments in particle physics and no quantum computer has yet been developed that can perform any of the tasks of which any conventional computer is capable. Yet the potential is so great that a number of governments, notably those of the USA, China, France and the UK, are investing resources in this capability, as are many established private-sector corporations such as Microsoft, Google, IBM, Alibaba and Baidu, not to mention a growing number of start-ups.

Quantum encryption works on the principle of quantum entanglement, the phenomenon whereby pairs of photons generated simultaneously continue to interact irrespective of where in the universe they are located—what Albert Einstein referred to as "spooky action at a distance." Quantum encryption offers the prospect of potentially unbreakable encrypted communications, since any attempt to intercept a transmission encrypted using quantum key distribution collapses the quantum state of the photons used to encode the transmission, destroying the information and signalling the presence of an intruder. China's efforts to develop this technology are led by Professor Pan Jianwei of the University of Science and Technology of China (USTC), the youngest ever member of the Chinese Academy of Sciences. In 2017 Pan oversaw a successful exercise in quantum encryption when China's first quantum satellite, named after the classical philosopher Mozi—romanised as Micius—distributed quantum encryption keys to two base stations in China and Austria, enabling a secure encrypted video conference to take place between the two locations. Pan sees this experiment as a prelude to eventually establishing a global network of quantum satellites providing an alternative quantum-secured Internet. Already China has built a 2,000-kilometre fibre-optic quantum key distribution link from Beijing to Shanghai that can be used in the secure transmission of financial and other sensitive data, and is in the process of constructing a US$ 1 billion National Laboratory for Quantum Information Sciences in Hefei.[26]

For the PLA the prospect of being able to develop a secure communications network that cannot be intercepted by an adversary is dangerously appealing. Dangerously because since the advent of the nuclear age a degree of transparency between nuclear-armed states has played a critical role in maintaining strategic stability and any development that threatens this stability risks setting in train a rapid escalation potentially ending with a nuclear exchange. In practice such a situation is unlikely to occur in the foreseeable future due to the formidable challenges of developing quantum technologies at scale. The same is to varying degrees true of other quantum capabilities such as quantum radars, which may be able to defeat stealth technology, quantum remote sensors and quantum navigation systems that may eliminate dependence on GPS. Nor should it be forgotten that China is not the only state to appreciate the potential of quantum computing and encryption to achieve a step change in capabilities. Europe, which failed to exploit the potential of the Internet as the USA was able to do, is equally focused on achieving breakthroughs in this new area while within the USA work by the private sector compensates for a relative lack of federal government investment in these and other hi-tech areas.

This raises the question of how far advanced in these new technologies China is relative to the USA. Making judgements in this area is complicated by the fact that China tends to oscillate between bouts of what might be termed "techno-exuberance," during which its achievements are relentlessly highlighted by the state's propaganda apparatus, as was the case with the

Micius quantum satellite; and periods during which, in the face of US pressure, Chinese officials and academics have gone out of their way to emphasise that China lags behind the USA in most areas of science and technology and will take many years to catch up. Comparisons are also hard to make between two very different systems: on the one hand, China's state capitalist model with long-term objectives pursued through high levels of targeted state funding; and on the other a US model that is much more laissez-faire and tends to leave the private sector to make the running.

That the USA enjoys a significant advantage of incumbency in all areas of science and technology is not in serious doubt. The science behind AI and the majority of the algorithms used in AI programmes are American, as is much of the software and chip technology. China is short of expertise in algorithms, which matters, because the theoretical basis for deep learning is still incomplete and the ways in which algorithms work is not always understandable. Applying algorithms to particular deep learning projects hence requires the kind of instinctive expertise that only comes with long experience and this is in short supply: as much as 75% of China's expertise in AI is located overseas, though a growing anti-China mood within the USA is beginning to drive some of this expertise to return home. China also lacks the capacity to design and manufacture the Graphics Processing Units (GPUs) which enable large numbers of calculations to be carried out simultaneously and the Field Programmable Gate Arrays used to "train" computers, though Chinese companies such as Alibaba and Tencent have begun to produce their own AI chips.

China's main advantages consist of scale—China now produces three times as many graduates in STEM subjects as the USA—and a determined and sustained state-led effort to achieve progress in these areas, which involves a readiness to invest large sums of state capital and the ability to create an enabling environment for private sector companies. In 2018 total state funding for R&D was RMB 2 trillion (US$ 429 billion), amounting to just over 2% of GDP, and in 2017 AI start-ups received a total of RMB 383 billion (US$ 56 billion) in funding. A significant proportion of this funding is likely to be wasted on projects having little to do with AI, but an economy as big as China's can tolerate relatively high levels of waste while still achieving results. China's other main advantages are a general readiness on the part of the population to embrace new technologies and huge volumes of data generated by the totality of China's online activity which the state is able to access and share more freely than is the case in liberal democracies. Data are however of limited value if their quality is poor: the old adage "garbage in, garbage out" applies just as much to AI as it does to other aspects of computing. To be of value data have to be accurately labelled—China has been able to take advantage of cheap labour in some less-developed provinces to build a national infrastructure of data-labelling factories which ensure that China's AI industry has a supply of reliable data.[27] This has played an important role in the rapid development of facial recognition technology and is now being applied to other areas including medical imaging and autonomous vehicles.

But as with much else about China numbers do not tell the whole story. One example is in the area of technology patents. In 2019 China's National Intellectual Property Administration granted over 2.3 million patents, more than any other country. But the quality of these patents is, to put it mildly, variable. Two thirds are so-called utility model patents—sometimes referred to as second-class patents—that do not represent a significant contribution to basic innovation. And few of these patents are filed internationally, suggesting that the originators do not feel a pressing need to protect their innovations in other jurisdictions.

Meanwhile China remains a significant net importer of Intellectual Property with a total expenditure in 2018 of US$ 30 billion paid to trading partners in royalties and licensing fees.[28] And while large sums have been invested in R&D through top-down state-led initiatives, levels of R&D by China's private sector are, with notable exceptions such as Huawei, low compared with the USA and other advanced economies.

China is producing three times as many graduates annually in STEM subjects as the USA but the quality of these graduates is also variable. It is investing heavily in new university courses in areas such as AI. But the problem of "administrative dominance" identified by the CCP Central Committee as a major barrier to progress in China's higher education research culture[29] remains an issue that has arguably been made even worse by the inclusion of ever more ideological content in university courses. The growing role of ideology in the Chinese university system was starkly illustrated when in December 2019 Fudan, a "key-point" university, altered its constitution, replacing a commitment to academic independence and freedom of thought with a pledge to accept the leadership of the CCP.[30] Quantity of research papers takes precedence over quality, while plagiarism, a problem in universities around the world, is especially prevalent in Chinese higher education.

The USA represents almost a mirror-image of the Chinese case. Relatively little federal funding goes to areas such as AI and there is no articulated national strategy for developing this technology, but this is compensated for by significant expenditure by the private sector, dwarfing the sums spent in China. The USA has attracted a corpus of AI talent from around the world, including China, but its own public education system underperforms in STEM subjects and the high costs of tertiary education act as a discouragement for American students. This matters little while the USA remains open to attracting the best foreign talent. But a general bias against immigration by the Trump administration and a growing climate of distrust in relation to Chinese scholars and researchers in particular could jeopardise this talent-pool. While China is working hard to develop the concept of civil-military integration, this approach has been hard-wired into the US system since the end of World War II. Latterly some US technology companies have been more reluctant to collaborate with the US government, especially on defence-related projects. The highest-profile example of this was Google's Project Maven, a collaboration with the US Department of Defense to use AI to interpret video imagery to enhance the effectiveness of drone strikes, which was the subject of protests by several thousand Google employees—who turned out to be ethnically Chinese.[31] But while cooperation with Silicon Valley is not something the federal government can take for granted, such cooperation is still taking place and will likely only increase.

Ultimately the problem of making comparisons between the hi-tech capabilities of the USA and China is that the technologies themselves are so entangled. There is currently no such thing as a Chinese AI that could be compared with its US equivalent. The algorithms than make modern AI possible are basically American in construct and most Chinese AI specialists use essentially the same algorithms. Such algorithms are not values-neutral: they reflect the assumptions and biases of the individuals that produce them, which explains why for example Silicon Valley, populated almost exclusively by young middle-class Caucasian males, has found it so hard to develop facial recognition systems that can reliably identify non-Caucasian faces. In due course it may be that a coming generation of Chinese AI scientists not trained in the West may develop their own algorithms reflecting their own biases and preconceptions, in which case there may be significant divergences based on cultural and ideological factors. That point is some way off. Whether and how a scientific and technical bifurcation between China and the West takes place will to a significant extent depend on how relations between China and the USA evolve. This relationship looks set to define the nature of international relations in the twenty-first century and hence merits its own detailed analysis.

11

US–CHINA RELATIONS

CHRONICLE OF A DEATH FORETOLD?

On the face of it, it is hard to imagine two cultures less alike than the USA and China. The USA's creation myth is of a young vigorous country built on Enlightenment values and individual liberty, enshrined through the US Constitution and a political system of checks and balances designed to frustrate the emergence of an overmighty state. It portrays itself as a restless pioneer culture that celebrates individuality, self-reliance, inventiveness and openness. Contemporary China by contrast claims to be the heir to a 5,000-year-old continuous civilisation which places a premium on social stability, the subordination of the individual to the interests of the collective and acceptance of authoritarian power structures. As is usually the case there is some truth in these generalisations though the reality is far more complex as both societies undergo profound shifts that call into question some cherished assumptions about their respective self-images and to some degree turn them into mirror images of each other. Relations between the USA and China have never been straightforward. But China's emergence as a global economic and strategic power has exacerbated long-standing differences in ideology and values and made for an increasingly fraught relationship with implications for every country on the planet. For the twenty-first century the major strategic question is whether these differences can be successfully contained or whether, as Graham Allison suggests, they may lead to outright conflict.[1]

The USA first became involved with China in the late eighteenth century through trade initially in products such as furs and ginseng but eventually including opium (sourced from Turkey rather than Bengal, where the British East India Company exercised a monopoly). By the early nineteenth century US merchants including the philanthropist John Jacob Astor and Warren Delano, grandfather of Franklin Delano Roosevelt, were making large fortunes from the China opium trade.[2] Following the UK's conclusion of the Treaty of Nanking with the Qing government in 1842, which established five treaty ports in which trade could be freely conducted, the USA two years later concluded the Treaty of Wangxia giving US merchants similar access to what the British had negotiated—the "most-favoured nation" provision. In due course the USA acquired two foreign concessions in China: in Shanghai where it was merged into the International Concession, and Tianjin, which was eventually merged with the British concession. The USA, which did not see itself as an imperialist power, arguably adopted a more altruistic approach to China than avowedly imperialist European nations, an altruism expressed through a focus on providing educational and medical services, even though these were often accompanied by Christian missionary proselytising. But the relationship was adversely affected by an influx of Chinese migrant workers during the 1840s California gold rush, many of whom subsequently became involved in building the Pacific railway. Chinese workers came to be seen as a threat to the livelihoods of Caucasian Americans and found themselves subjected to campaigns of racist vilification and discrimination, sometimes descending into violence. The smoking of opium, the preferred Chinese method of consuming what was both a recreational drug and virtually the only then-available medication able to mitigate the symptoms of many common ailments, was banned, while opium in liquid form—laudanum—was freely advertised and even more freely consumed. In 1882 the China Exclusion Act was passed, effectively preventing ethnic Chinese from immigrating to the USA. That act remained in force until 1943.

During the Sino–Japanese War US supplies and military aid to China played an essential role in keeping China in the war on the side of the allies. This aid included the contribution made by General Claire Chennault's volunteer fighter pilots, who became known as the Flying Tigers; the supplies flown by US Army Air Corps pilots over the Himalayas to Chengdu—an incredibly dangerous route that became known as "the Hump"; and the provision of lend-lease military equipment. Once Imperial Japan had been defeated, US officials led for some eighteen months by General George Marshall worked to effect a reconciliation between Chiang Kai-shek's Nationalists and the Communists. When the latter achieved victory in the civil war, the USA moved its embassy to Taipei and continued to recognise the Nationalists, who thanks to US support were able to retain their seat at the United Nations until 1971. The Communist victory led to a witch-hunt in the USA initiated in part by Senator Joseph McCarthy who, in a speech in 1950, blamed the "loss" of China on communists in the US State Department, leading to the premature termination of some distinguished foreign service careers and the loss of a significant corpus of China expertise.[3] The anti-communist campaign also resulted in the USA losing some distinguished scientists of Chinese origin, notably Qian Xuesen. Qian, who had taken part in the Manhattan Project, was stripped of his security clearance because of suspected communist sympathies and held under house-arrest for five years before returning to China as part of a prisoner exchange. There he drew on the knowledge he had acquired in the USA to play a major role in China's nuclear and missile programmes, earning the title "Father of Chinese aerospace."[4]

The next twenty years were characterised by unremitting antagonism. China and the USA fought each other in Korea and were involved in a proxy struggle in Indo-China. Under Mao the CCP sought to foment communist revolution in Asia while the CIA engaged in destabilisation in Tibet through support for the Khampa rebellion. Such diplomatic engagement as took place was conducted largely through intermediaries in locations such as Geneva. Commercial relations were practically non-existent and China was denied access to advanced US and Western technologies, the export of which were subject to restrictions imposed by the Coordinating Committee for Multilateral Export Controls (COCOM). The gradual rapprochement begun by President Richard Nixon in 1972 brought to an end this period of outright hostility and replaced it with a period of strategic convergence, focused initially on containing Soviet military expansion through political, military and intelligence cooperation, then extending into economic engagement. But the relationship was never easy and might best be characterised by the Chinese term *tong chuang yi meng*—sharing a bed but having different dreams.

The US belief was that a policy of engagement with China would bring about a country that was more politically open and more market-oriented. Initially this approach seemed to be working as China went through a period of bold experimentation and openness to new ideas as part of its search for modernisation. However, the violent suppression of the Democracy Movement in 1989 was a forcible reminder that the CCP was not about to transmogrify into a Western-style social democratic movement, and this realisation led to a fundamental change in the relationship, further exacerbated by the Chinese leadership's alarm at the collapse of communism in Eastern Europe followed by the Soviet Union. The USA imposed wide-ranging sanctions on China, including a ban on military sales and dual-use equipment which it insisted its European allies also applied and which remains in effect. The embargo intensified the view of China's leadership that, in the words of one Chinese commentator, "the West forced on China an inequitable distribution of the benefits of science and technology...depriving China of its legitimate rights."[5]

The Chinese scholar Dr. Yan Xuetong has argued that from 1989 onwards Sino–US relations could be characterised as a pretended friendship that masked deep-rooted differences and pointed to a fundamental instability in the relationship.[6] That assessment almost certainly pays insufficient regard to the considerable efforts made by both parties to make the relationship work or to the very real achievements it delivered in effecting change, particularly economic but also systemic, in China. China's economic miracle undoubtedly owes much to the energy and talent of the Chinese people, but, although it is now inconvenient for the CCP to acknowledge this, it almost certainly owes much more to China's readiness to adopt American technologies and economic and business practices. But US and other Western policy-makers consistently overlooked or downplayed the message in all documents published by the Party-state on economic modernisation, which made it abundantly clear that its primary purpose was to strengthen the role of the CCP.

Sino–US engagement was punctuated by a succession of incidents that hinted at this more deep-rooted instability. These included the sending of two US carrier battle groups to the Taiwan Straits in 1995 in response to Chinese efforts to intimidate Taiwan; the bombing of the Chinese embassy in Belgrade during the 1999 Kosovo campaign, a consequence of US military incompetence but believed by the Chinese government to be deliberate; the 2001 incident in which a Chinese fighter jet crashed into a US Navy Orion EP-3 surveillance aircraft off the coast of Hainan, resulting in the death of the PLA pilot and the temporary incarceration of the US crew; continued US support for and arms sales to Taiwan; meetings by US politicians with high-profile critics of China such as the Dalai Lama; and persistent public US government criticism of China's human rights record. The Taiwan Straits crisis led both countries to conduct a reappraisal of the relationship in the interests of avoiding a further catastrophic deterioration. The best they could come up with was to categorise each other as neither enemy nor friend— *feidi feiyou*.[7] A more telling indication of the nature of the relationship was the absence of summitry between the two countries from 1989 to 1997.

Understandably enough both sides saw benefit in papering over the cracks and accentuating the positive in the relationship. Economically both appeared to be benefitting from China's evolution into the workshop of the world, selling cheap consumer goods to the USA then investing the proceeds in US Treasury bonds, leading to a relationship that might be characterised, to paraphrase the Cold War strategic concept, as one of mutually assured dependence. Ironically it was this Chinese willingness to invest in the USA that enabled the US government to fund what became the "forever wars" in Afghanistan and Iraq without having to raise taxation to a level that might have led US taxpayers to call into question the utility of such undertakings. The USA supported China's entry to the World Trade Organisation as a developing nation, which exempted it from many of the obligations required of a developed economy. The two states found common cause on some key international issues, including climate change and the de-nuclearisation of the Korean Peninsula. And in the aftermath of the 2008 financial crisis both pledged, albeit in China's case through gritted teeth, to work together to restore global financial stability. When President Barack Obama broke with precedent by visiting China in the first year of his presidency, he and Hu Jintao formally agreed to respect each other's "core interests"—without however agreeing on what those core interests actually were.

But beneath the veneer of positivity it was becoming harder to overlook the fault-lines in the relationship. China remained resistant to US pressure to contribute more to international public goods in a way commensurate with its growing economic and strategic influence. The annual Shangri-La Dialogue held each year in Singapore to bring together the defence ministers from around the Asia-Pacific region became a forum in which successive US defence secretaries and their Chinese counterparts publicly locked horns over a wide range of issues. These included China's failure to condemn North Korea's acts of aggression that included the sinking of a South Korean submarine, China's efforts to exercise control over the South and East China Seas, and US insistence on conducting freedom-of-navigation exercises in what China regarded as its territorial waters. By 2012 Henry Kissinger, architect of the US rapprochement with China, felt moved to observe that "enough material exists in China's quasi-official press and research institutes to lend support to the theory that relations are heading for confrontation rather than cooperation."[8]

The Obama administration, while striving to accentuate the positive in the relationship, also sought increasingly to push back against what it saw as unacceptable Chinese behaviour. This included publicising and protesting about a 2009 incident in which a number of Chinese fishing vessels had sought to expel an unarmed US Navy surveillance vessel from China's Exclusive Economic Zone. In February 2013 the US Department of Justice unveiled indictments against five PLA officers from the Shanghai-based Unit 61398 who had been involved in a

pervasive and long-running campaign of cyber espionage targeting US private sector corporations. This set the scene for raising
the issue of cyber espionage at the June 2013 Sunnylands
Summit with Xi Jinping. At that point China's leadership may
well have been genuinely unsighted about the extent of such
espionage and the impact it was beginning to have on Sino–US
relations, which may explain why Xi did not offer a substantive
response to US concerns. Two years later, in the run-up to Xi
Jinping's state visit to the USA, the Obama administration got
China's attention by threatening to take legal action against
Chinese corporations including Chinalco, Baosteel and China
State Nuclear Power Technology Corporation that were deemed
to have been the beneficiaries of stolen US technology.[9] This
threat led to frantic negotiations in advance of Xi's visit, led on
the Chinese side by Meng Jianzhu, head of the CCP's Central
Political and Legal Committee, the organisation that oversees
the Chinese intelligence community. At the end of the state visit
the two leaders announced that they would not "conduct or
knowingly support cyber-enabled theft of intellectual property,
including trade secrets or other confidential business information for commercial advantage."[10]

Throughout Obama's term in office US officials had been pri-
vately warning Chinese counterparts about the consequences of
failure to address concerns about China's anti-competitive policies and mercantilist approach to international trade. During the
latter part of the Obama administration the Office of the US
Trade Representative (USTR) had begun attempts to build a
coalition of like-minded states to take collective action within
the World Trade Organisation (WTO) against Chinese behaviours that included intellectual property theft, the forced transfer
of technologies as a condition of entry to Chinese markets, a
failure to live up to promises to open Chinese markets in areas
such as insurance and financial services and large-scale subsidies

to Chinese industries significantly in excess of what the WTO permitted. In the view of the USTR the WTO had not been configured to accommodate a state capitalist economy the size of China's and unless this situation was addressed the organisation risked becoming unfit for purpose. Meanwhile negotiations were concluded in 2016 on the Trans-Pacific Partnership (TPP), a trade agreement between the USA and major states of the Asia-Pacific region that did not deliberately seek to exclude China but which would have required it to sign up to commitments at odds with its state capitalist model. The TPP would have acted as a significant constraint on China's behaviour but in one of his first acts on assuming office President Donald Trump withdrew the USA from the treaty.

Trump's election in 2016 produced a seismic shift in Sino–US relations. During his presidential campaign Trump had sought to appeal to blue-collar communities that had suffered dispropor-tionately from the de-industrialisation resulting from US manu-facturers moving their operations to China (the consequences of this process are visible to anyone taking the train from New York to Washington as it trundles past mile after mile of abandoned industrial plant and adjacent residential communities that have been hollowed out). Trump, who himself had a mercantilist, zero-sum approach to foreign trade whereby any gain for another state was seen as a loss for the USA, committed himself to addressing the US–China trade deficit as part of his plan to "make America great again" and also pledged to take action against what he referred to as China's manipulation of its cur-rency to make its exports more competitive.

Given what he had said about China while a candidate, the newly elected President Trump's initial engagement with China seemed surprisingly emollient. He was at pains to reassure China of the US commitment to the One-China policy, the basis on which bilateral relations had been established. China meanwhile was able to build relations with the Trump inner cabinet of Jared Kushner and Ivanka Trump and patent applications for the Trump organisation that had long been pending in the Chinese legal system were resolved in Trump's favour, leading a senior Chinese official to observe that "it seems we have bribed the US President." Early encounters between Trump and Xi Jinping appeared to go well and during his November 2017 state visit Trump appeared to endorse China's economic and trade policies—"I don't blame China."[11] But by that point US Trade Representative Robert Lighthizer had already initiated a Section 301 investigation into China's trade practices. And at the end of 2017 the Trump administration's first National Security Strategy stated that the world had entered an era characterised by the re-emergence of great-power competition and highlighted China as the USA's main strategic threat, a threat which manifested itself primarily in the economic domain.[12] In June 2018 Trump announced the imposition of 25% tariffs on US$ 50 billion of Chinese imports, with the threat of more to come. It became apparent that this decision was not merely about trade but went to much deeper issues of ideology, values and the exercise of geo-political power. If confirmation was needed on this point it was provided by US vice-president Mike Pence in a speech at the Hudson Institute in October 2018 in the course of which he set out a long litany of objectionable Chinese behaviours including covert efforts to influence US domestic politics—without providing substantiating detail.

It was clear that China had been blindsided by the unpredictable behaviour of the Trump administration. Few of their established interlocutors had the access necessary to offer insights and the US business community, once a reliable advocate for good Sino–US relations, had become disillusioned by the growing difficulties of doing business in China and was quietly supportive of Trump's actions, which they saw as long overdue. China's initial reaction was calm and measured, amounting to little more than imposing countervailing tariffs, primarily on US agricultural produce in the belief that pressure on the US farm lobby might produce concessions. China's state media meanwhile produced articles focusing on the benefits of the global trading system and arguing that trade wars never produced winners. The importance China accorded to globalisation had been amply demonstrated at the beginning of the year when, in a remarkable example of role reversal, Xi Jinping had attended the World Economic Forum in Davos, where he presented China as the pre-eminent champion of globalisation at a venue from which his US counterpart was conspicuously absent.[13]

In December 2018 China agreed to enter into negotiations. The Chinese negotiating team was led by vice-premier Liu He, a respected economist who however had no experience of trade negotiations. The US team, made up largely of lawyers with deep expertise in international trade negotiations—Lighthizer had cut his teeth in the negotiations leading to the 1985 Plaza Accord, which had led to a significant devaluation of the Japanese yen against the dollar—reflected the very different approaches towards China within the Trump administration. The three main US constituencies in relation to China could be character-ised as the "economic rebalancers," led by Trump and US Trade Representative Robert Lighthizer, who prioritised economic relations with China over security issues, supported the use of non-traditional policy tools, principally economic, to gain advan-tage and did not advocate for economic decoupling with China; macroeconomic pragmatists, led by Treasury Secretary Steven Mnuchin who, while broadly supportive of the Trump position, were more cautious and concerned to maintain economic and financial stability; and national security hawks led by Vice President Mike Pence, Commerce Secretary Wilbur Ross and Trump's trade advisor Peter Navarro, an academic and author of books with titles such as *Death by China*. The national security hawks argued for greater efforts to erect permanent barriers around technology and security-related investments, a robust military posture in the Asia-Pacific region and a partial economic decoupling with China.[14] The US Congress, an entity which China had always struggled to understand or engage with effectively, adopted a rare bipartisan consensus on the need to get tough on China by passing a bill that significantly tightened the criteria for referring potential foreign investments and take-overs of US companies to the Committee on Foreign Investment (CFIUS) in the USA in order to protect what the USA's 2017 National Security Strategy termed the country's national-security innovation base, i.e. emerging technologies on which the USA would depend for its future prosperity and security.

The Trump approach to dealing with China on trade could best be described as retorsion, a legal term referring to the recognised right of states who perceive themselves to have been the victim of internationally wrongful acts to apply measures such as economic sanctions and trade tariffs to compel the perpetrator to return to internationally accepted norms of behaviour. As the negotiations progressed it became clear that US expectations were far-reaching. They demanded that China acknowledge culpability for multiple cases of intellectual property theft and make detailed and verifiable undertakings to desist from further such behaviour, including making extensive changes to China's laws; bringing state subsidies into line with WTO provisions; taking measures to address the issue of forced technology transfer as a condition for access to Chinese markets (China had for the first time admitted in the negotiations that it was engaging in this practice); and agreeing to the establishment of a bilateral commission to review China's performance in these areas on pain of tariffs being re-applied in the event of non-compliance. In essence the USA appeared to be demanding that China dismantle its model of state capitalism. In response China did little more than offer to buy more US products and repeat commitments to open up its markets which had been made but not honoured previously, to be achieved through China's preferred mechanism of administrative rather than, as the USA insisted, legal instruments. The extent of the gap between the two sides became apparent in May 2019 when a draft agreement negotiated with Liu He was returned with all the provisions China found contentious struck out. In response the USA increased from 10 to 25% percent the tariffs it had additionally imposed on China earlier in the negotiating process and published the details of what they thought had been agreed, much to China's discomfiture.

The trade war initiated by the Trump administration had the effect of bringing to the surface underlying concerns within China's intellectual elite about the direction the country had taken under Xi Jinping. There was a widespread perception that the trade war was a self-inflicted injury brought about by China's inappropriately assertive approach towards the USA at a time when China was still heavily dependent on US trade, technology and investment and was simply not ready to challenge the global hegemon. Critics argued that China's best option was to adopt a lower international profile, reach a quick accommodation with the USA that took account of legitimate US concerns, and focus on further reform and opening-up of China's markets. The extent to which this criticism was a cause for concern can be seen from the rash of editorials and opinion pieces in the official Chinese media in the middle of 2019 excoriating such attitudes as coming from people who "worshipped the USA, fawned on the USA or lived in terror of the USA."[15] In early June 2019 the CCP theoretical journal *Qiushi—Seeking Facts*—published a lengthy article with the characteristically snappy headline "Clearly understand the essence, clearly address the main issue, struggle to the end: aspects of the Sino–US trade friction [sic] that need to be clarified." This article sought to repudiate US claims that China had reneged on earlier points of agreement—which it clearly had—while castigating the USA for a zero-sum approach that made it unable to accept gains by other states and sought, in the words of the German economist Friedrich List, to "deny others the ladder to her greatness." The article ended with the words "China doesn't want to fight but isn't afraid to fight and, if need be, certainly will fight"—*zhongguo buyuan da, bupa da, biyao shi bude bu da*.[16]

But neither Xi Jinping nor Donald Trump actually wanted a fight and a so-called Phase One deal was finally signed by President Trump and Liu He in January 2020. Neither side published the full details of the agreement, which according to the US government ran to eighty-six pages. On the face of it Trump appeared to have got the better of the deal and it is hence unsurprising that China's state-controlled media were sparing in reporting the detail of the agreement. But China's concerns were as much about presentation as substance. China, with a population of 1.4 billion, has just 9% of the world's arable land. Twenty per cent of that land is polluted with heavy metals and China is facing acute water stress in the north of the country where much of its wheat is produced. China has to import significant quantities of food—and water in the form of agrarian products that are water-dependent—from somewhere. Arguably the biggest losers in this deal were countries such as Brazil and Australia to which China had turned as alternatives to the US farming sector, a consideration Beijing sought belatedly and rather unconvincingly to address. In terms of financial services China had already bought enough time for its domestic financial sector to develop to the point where US competitors were unlikely to be able to make significant inroads, at least in the retail sector. And while China would have wished to avoid having a formal resolution mechanism, if only on the grounds that this might appear to China's highly nationalistic populace as a humiliating climbdown, the government would have some confidence that it could kick this can down the road. More importantly the USA made no progress in its main strategic objective, which was to get China to abandon its state capitalist model.

The Phase One agreement amounted to no more than a tactical pause, and the entire trade dispute was in any case just a symptom of a much wider malaise. Within the USA, the perception had increasingly taken hold that US policy towards China had been a failure.[17] Engagement with China, far from producing a more liberal society integrated into the global order, had enabled the emergence of a more authoritarian and ideologically hostile regime that sought to challenge this order. One strain of thinking held that the USA had been "played" by a regime which had sought to lull the USA into a false sense of security while secretly pursuing a strategy aimed at replacing it as global hegemon by 2049.[18] Attitudes had hardened within the US foreign policy community, including some distinguished sinologists who had become comprehensively disenchanted with China's shift towards a more ideological and authoritarian approach. Other elements of the US policy community, including paradoxically President Trump himself, were less invested in this hostile approach. Trump vacillated over the extent to which the USA should deny Huawei and ZTE access to US technology, and expressed himself reluctant to limit sales by GE of aero engines to the PRC, also for commercial reasons.[19] The net result was a lack of policy clarity best summed up by former US Treasury Secretary Henry "Hank" Paulson, who observed that "we have a China attitude, not a China policy."[20] In essence every department of the US government, having digested the message that it was open season on China, began pursuing its own particular grievances without any overarching coordination.

The harder line on China translated into a reduction in the number of Chinese students coming to the USA for tertiary education amid a tightening of visa rules and concerns about espionage and intellectual property theft. In 2017–18, 360,000 Chinese students enrolled in US universities but amid greater uncertainty and a more hostile atmosphere many Chinese students began considering alternatives such as the UK, Canada and Australia. In 2018 the US government reduced from five years to one the duration of visas for graduate students wishing to study aviation, robotics and advanced manufacturing and made it harder for foreign students—not just Chinese—to work in the USA after graduation. As a consequence, a growing number of such graduates returned to China where they are known as "sea turtles"—*hai gui*, a play on words that sound the same but, written differently, mean "return from abroad." A growing climate of suspicion gripped US university science and technology departments as their links with Chinese institutions were subjected to greater scrutiny, including by the FBI, which arrested and prosecuted a number of US-based Chinese but also US academics for espionage.[21] Bio-science and healthcare became a key battleground. In the words of one analyst, "Since the National Institutes of Health (NIH) launched a campaign to root out foreign influence in federally funded research in August 2018, universities in the U.S. have investigated nearly 200 scientists. Many of these are well-funded and established researchers who are ethnically Chinese."[22] Some ended up in federal courts charged with stealing trade secrets.

Chinese inward investment in the USA was also hit hard by a combination of closer US government scrutiny of planned Chinese purchases of and mergers with US corporations under the revised CFIUS legislation, and a Chinese government crackdown on capital flight. From a high point of US$ 46 billion in 2016, Chinese investment in the USA fell to just US$ 1.8 billion in the first five months of 2018. This figure included significant divestiture in the US market by major Chinese corporations such as Wanda, Anbang and HNA. By contrast, US investment into China increased by 1.5% in 2019 despite President Trump "ordering" US companies to divest from China and return manufacturing to the USA. The focus of such investment was on manufacturing for the China market rather than for exports, in order to avoid the impact of US tariffs.[23] Against that, major US technology manufacturers such as Apple, Hewlett Packard and Dell took steps to diversify production away from China, a trend that intensified as the novel coronavirus COVID-19 illustrated the risks inherent in having China as a single point of failure in global supply chains. US and other foreign corporations confronted the need to weigh the attractions of a market the size of China's against the growing complexities and uncertainties of doing business in an environment that was becoming ever more politicised and ideological, while in the USA Chinese corporations were increasingly viewed with suspicion as agents of a hostile state. Those Chinese companies that had listed on US stock markets found themselves under pressure to open their books to US regulators and rather than do so began decamping for Hong Kong.

COVID-19: The Last Straw

What sent US–China relations into freefall was the outbreak of the COVID-19 coronavirus that appeared in the city of Wuhan at the end of 2019. As with other similar viruses COVID-19 appears to have originated in bats, though how it crossed the species gap to infect humans is still and may always remain unclear. The outbreak of the virus coincided with the preparations for the Spring Festival, China's most important national celebration, during which millions of Chinese return to their home provinces and, increasingly, travel overseas. Steeped in a bureaucratic culture that does not incentivise officials to report bad news, Wuhan's officials sought to suppress news of the outbreak. By the time China's central government had discovered the truth, informed the World Health Organisation and imposed a lockdown on 23 January 2020, millions of citizens had already left Wuhan and the disease, which Chinese officials initially denied could be transmitted between humans, was on the way to becoming a global pandemic with grave implications for public health and even graver implications for the global economy, as countries shut down to contain the spread of the virus. According to the World Bank's June 2020 Global Economic Prospects:

> The baseline forecast envisions a 5.2 percent contraction in global GDP in 2020...the deepest global recession in decades, despite the extraordinary efforts of governments to counter the downturn with fiscal and monetary policy support. Over the longer horizon, the deep recessions triggered by the pandemic are expected to leave lasting scars through lower investment, an erosion of human capital through lost work and schooling, and fragmentation of global trade and supply linkages.[24]

For China, the coronavirus initially looked as if it might become Xi Jinping's Chernobyl moment, the point at which the inadequacies of the regime could no longer be concealed or explained away. But after its initial failings, the Chinese state quickly rallied and through a process of lockdowns and quarantines that were brutal but effective managed to contain the virus by the end of March 2020. In the event it was the USA whose system revealed significant shortcomings that could no longer be concealed. The Trump administration, concerned that a lockdown would adversely affect a buoyant economy which formed the centrepiece of Trump's re-election campaign, played down the severity of the outbreak until 13 March, when it could no longer be ignored. In contrast to previous pandemics, during which the USA exercised effective global leadership, the USA not only failed to do so but oversaw a chaotic and uncoordinated response within the USA itself resulting in 5.5 million confirmed cases and close to 175,000 deaths by mid-August 2020.

As the USA appeared to flounder, China was quick to take the opportunity to burnish an international reputation severely tarnished by the early failures that had allowed the virus to spread. This involved familiar Chinese propaganda mechanisms in which China sought to emphasise the strengths of its system and to compare these unfavourably with what it was quick to portray as the stumbling, belated and uncoordinated responses of Western liberal democracies. Typical of this approach was a statement by Chinese foreign minister Wang Yi that "China's signature strength, efficiency and speed in this fight have been widely acclaimed...and the institutional advantage of China's governance is there for all to see."[25] As China emerged from the first phase of the pandemic it engaged in an extensive programme of "mask diplomacy," sending, with much fanfare, consignments of masks, protective clothing, testing equipment, ventilators and medical teams to other afflicted countries including Italy and Spain— then pressing the recipients to express effusive public gratitude for China's largesse. There was also a significant negative element to China's global messaging. This involved the coordinated use of tweets from Ministry of Foreign Affairs "wolf warrior" spokesman Zhao Lijian, amplified by Chinese embassy Twitter accounts, to spread disinformation about the origins of the virus. The narratives put out included the suggestion that members of a US Army team which had taken part in a military games contest in Wuhan in October 2019 had brought the virus to China, and that it may have originated in a US military laboratory.

China's behaviour infuriated the Trump administration. The Republican party, fearing that Trump's poor performance in handling the coronavirus might cost him the election, doubled down on a policy of blaming China for not taking early action to control the virus. Trump and Secretary of State Mike Pompeo took to referring to COVID-19 as the China virus, the Wuhan virus and "kung flu," and claimed that the virus had escaped from the Wuhan Institute of Virology, though no evidence was produced to support this contention. Although US intelligence estimates indicated that local officials had concealed the outbreak from the central government for some weeks, the Trump administration persisted in arguing that China's belated response, a function of a system in which secrecy and opacity were endemic, made it responsible for the economic damage the USA had suffered. It was suggested that China should be held to account both through an independent international investigation into the origins of the virus and by seeking financial reparation for the economic dislocation it had caused. US politicians and lawyers made a series of recommendations that included stripping China of its sovereign immunity, suing the Chinese Communist Party rather than the Chinese state, and even refusing to honour interest payments on Chinese holdings of US Treasuries ostensibly in recompense of pre-1949 debts that the PRC government had refused to honour.[26]

By the late summer of 2020 the Trump administration had launched a barrage of anti-China initiatives. In late May 2020 the White House published a "United States of America Strategic Approach to the People's Republic of China" document which set out in detail US concerns about China and made clear its intention to orchestrate a comprehensive global pushback. The two countries became embroiled in a media war, with China expelling journalists from the *Wall Street Journal* and the USA retaliating by reducing the number of Chinese journalists operating in the USA and requiring Chinese media organisations to register as foreign agents. The US government demanded the closure of the Chinese consulate in Houston, with China responding by closing the US consulate in Chongqing. Chinese and Hong Kong government officials and organisations deemed responsible for human rights abuses in Xinjiang and Hong Kong were made the subject of financial sanctions and Hong Kong's trading privileges with the USA were revoked. This included the Xinjiang Production and Construction Corps, an economic and paramilitary organisation which plays a major role in Xinjiang's administration and economy. After a prolonged period of studied neutrality, the US government finally declared China's territorial claims in the South China Sea to have no legal basis.

The US government also launched an all-out assault on China's technology companies, banning federal agencies from buying equipment or services from major corporations including Huawei, ZTE and the video surveillance national champions Hikvision and Dahua, and tightening restrictions on the sale of advanced microprocessors to Huawei to the degree that called into question the survival of its 5G ambitions. An executive order was issued which would have the effect of preventing any US citizen or company from transacting business with ByteDance or Tencent, in effect sounding the death-knell for ByteDance's hugely successful US-based video streaming service TikTok and calling into question the future within the USA of Tencent's WeChat messaging service used by hundreds of thousands of Chinese nationals overseas—resulting in both companies initiating legal action against the US government. The pressure on China technology was further exacerbated by the Clean Network initiative launched by Pompeo in August 2020, which was effectively a recipe for excluding China from US networks entirely, combined with an invitation to other liberal democracies to pursue the same course.

It became increasingly clear that the hawks in the Trump administration were promoting an explicitly ideological agenda and seeking to put US–China relations beyond the point where a possible Democrat administration could reverse the downward trend. Secretary of State Pompeo delivered a speech at the Nixon Library on 23 July 2020 in which he characterised engagement with China as a failure, sought to draw a distinction between the Chinese people and the Chinese Communist Party and called for an internationally coordinated effort to change China's behaviours.[27] In practice however there was little need for the Republicans to inoculate US–China relations against the possibility of a return to the status quo ante. It became evident that a Biden administration would be just as hard on China but might be more focused and effective in areas such as building an international coalition to orchestrate an anti-China pushback.

The rising level of anti-Chinese sentiment led the Chinese Ministry of State Security's think-tank, the Chinese Institutes for Contemporary International Relations (CICIR), to produce a report that, according to Western journalists informally briefed on its contents, stated that "Beijing faces a rising wave of hostility in the wake of the coronavirus outbreak that could tip relations with the USA into confrontation."[28] And as the US government piled on the pressure China was careful to avoid escalatory responses. In late July and August China began to rein in its "wolf warrior" diplomats while signalling that it was seeking to shore up the collapsing relationship. On 6 August Chinese foreign minister Wang Yi gave an interview to the state news agency Xinhua. Couched as a response to Pompeo's earlier speech, Wang Yi rejected US criticisms, stating that China wanted to restart a dialogue with Washington and "put in place a clear-cut framework" for the relationship. He also made clear that the USA must "abandon its fantasy of remodelling China to US needs." A more nuanced speech by China's ambassador to Washington, Cui Tiankai, reflected the difficulty China faced in dealing with a US administration that seemed bent on pushing the relationship over the brink.[29]

But it was clear by then that there could be no going back. Too much had been said and done that could not be unsaid or undone. As the veteran commentator on Sino–US relations Professor Wang Jisi observed, bilateral ties were at their worst level since formal ties were first established in the 1970s and bilateral economic and technological decoupling were "already irreversible."[30] The USA and China now seem to be on an irreversible track towards divergence and decoupling. What this means for both countries and for the wider world will be looked at in the final chapter.

12

THE GREAT DECOUPLING

The story of China for the past 170 years has been the story of a search for a modern identity. In the mid-nineteenth century China went practically overnight from being a major civilisational power to an indigent outlier, pilloried in the West as the "sick man of Asia"—a meme that was to resurface with unfortunate consequences when the COVID-19 pandemic struck in 2020. Since then the country has been on a relentless quest to recover its previous status and self-esteem. It has largely achieved the first objective. China is now the world's second-largest economy and may well soon become the largest, with all the geo-political leverage that status confers. It has become a major military power, with the ability not just to defend the homeland but increasingly to project military force beyond its borders should it need or wish to do so. And it is well on the way to becoming a major global centre for science and technology innovation, giving the lie to complacent and racist Western assumptions that this would be beyond its capabilities.

But it has not yet achieved the second objective. China's new-found pre-eminence has been universally recognised but by no means unconditionally accepted, and this lack of acceptance has translated into an almost adolescent prickliness that makes it harder for states to acquiesce to China's aspirations for such acceptance. Until recently it was still unclear what China wanted to do with its growing power. Consequently, many Western policy-makers and analysts were able to use China as a backcloth on which to project their own ideas and preconceptions of what the country was and might become. Much of the wishful thinking this engendered has, or should have, been dispelled by China's unambiguously assertive and self-interested behaviour and the clear messaging about China's desire to see the world order reshaped in ways favourable to its interests. It could be argued that Xi Jinping's strategic mistake was to reveal his hand too early, thereby giving states which for either ideological reasons or reasons of realpolitik found the Chinese vision objectionable time to orchestrate a response. But this would be to overlook the reality that China's leadership is caught up in a dynamic that they themselves cannot fully control. Neither the West nor China itself expected the country to develop economically and technically at the speed it has.

The way China's current leadership views its relations with the wider world seems to embody some stark contradictions. On the one hand their behaviour seems driven by a conviction that the country has only a narrow window of opportunity to cement a globally pre-eminent position before declining economic growth, an aging population and the drag factor caused by the negative externalities associated with rapid industrialisation—pollution, water stress, ill-health—put this objective out of reach. On the other is the conviction that history is on China's side, a product of both Marxist historical determinism and a belief in the inherent superiority of Chinese culture and civilisation. Similarly, China seeks to cement its role as a trading nation and exponent of globalisation whilst simultaneously keeping unwelcome foreign cultural and political influence at bay and pursuing policies of industrial and technological self-sufficiency exemplified by the Made in China 2025 strategy. And while China aspires, thus far with limited success, to exercise soft power, it is clear that it will not be deterred by adverse reactions or push back from pursuing its strategic objectives, having apparently concluded that like it or not, the world will have to get used to dealing with China on China's terms. The fact that many within China's political elite have expressed concerns about what they see as inappropriate Chinese hubris and overreach is unlikely to make much difference to how the CCP pursues the China Dream, an aspiration broadly shared by the majority of Chinese people. The CCP's focus on maintaining domestic legitimacy through nationalistic grandstanding appears to have foreclosed on the possibility of a foreign policy based on prudence and restraint. Xi Jinping has talked of future Sino–US relations as being characterised by a combination of "entanglement and struggle"—*chandou*.

This is not the first time the USA has faced such a challenge. In the early phase of the Cold War the USA perceived the risk of the USSR overtaking it in science and technology, the so-called "Sputnik moment." Inter alia this led to a significant effort to increase the US nuclear arsenal to address what proved to be a non-existent "missile gap." It was not until the 1980s that the USA felt comfortable in assessing that the Soviet Union's apparent strength as measured by military capabilities was significantly undermined by its poor economic performance and doctrinal rigidity. In the 1980s a perceived threat from Japan to US industrial and economic pre-eminence led to another extreme response as US academics and opinion-formers filled the shelves of US bookstores with jeremiads about an imminent Japanese economic takeover of America. The USA was able to use its leverage to address this problem through the Plaza Accord in which Japan was compelled to revalue its currency against the US dollar, eliminating much of the advantage it had exploited and buying time for US corporations to catch up with Japanese innovation in areas including the automotive and electronics industries. It is less obvious how the USA will be able to achieve its aim of containing China. But there can be no doubting the extreme nature of the US response to China's perceived challenge.

By any reasonable criteria the USA enjoys advantages that China can only dream of in terms of a low population; ample arable land; abundant natural resources including, critically, water; economic and financial pre-eminence by virtue of the US dollar's role as the global reserve currency; a geography that offers a high degree of physical security; a system of global alliances that collectively represents a significant extension of US geo-political reach; and continuing soft-power appeal. Global elites, including that of China, still want to have their children educated in the USA and their wealth invested there. None see China as a credible alternative. Despite concerns about the risk of being overtaken by China, the USA still enjoys global pre-eminence in science and technology. And while the US federal government can often seem lumbering and bureaucratic, the governments of individual US states and municipalities have often shown themselves to be agile and innovative. Most US vulnerabilities are arguably self-inflicted: ideologically polarised party politics leading to legislative gridlock; a continuing toxic legacy of racial discrimination; insufficient investment in infra-structure and human capital, in particular in education and healthcare; economic and social inequality; and a system that has arguably ceded too much power to the private sector at the expense of effective government. Externally the USA has ceded space in the international arena that China has been quick to occupy while demonstrating an increasingly ambivalent approach towards the alliance relationships that help give it global reach. All these shortcomings are fixable. None can be laid at China's door. But if they are not fixed, US and by extension Western economic and technological decline could prove to be a chronicle of a death foretold.

China's emergence as a powerful modern state with a different ideology and values and a long-term strategy pursued through a centralised, state-driven all-of-nation approach has raised serious questions about how fit for purpose the Western liberal democratic order is in the twenty-first century. The COVID-19 pandemic has highlighted these questions in ways that would seem to play into China's narrative—though it needs to be pointed out that liberal democracies have proven capable of the same rapid levels of mobilisation as China and, as in the case of Taiwan, were able to achieve good outcomes without resorting to authoritarian methods. The COVID-19 challenge makes a powerful case for a rebalancing of the relationship between the private sector and the state. China's rise has also raised the question of whether modern ICTs may prove to have been the missing ingredient, in terms of both delivering economic performance and social control, that condemned previous authoritarian regimes such as the Soviet Union to chronic inefficiency and eventual failure. It is only now that Western liberal democracies have begun seriously to address the challenges of coexisting with such a powerful competitor, or even formally to designate it as such. Nor is there any unanimity in how to deal with China, as evidenced by considerable disparities of approach within the European Union. In the USA on the other hand a greater degree of consensus has emerged, not just within the political class but increasingly within the population as a whole, that China's rise must be contained and that this will involve a parting of the ways—the Great Decoupling.

The stage is set for a contest that will define the geo-politics of the twenty-first century. It is a contest that will be fought in the realms of trade, economics, finance and technological competition but always with the potential to turn kinetic. It looks set to involve a significant rewriting of global rules and a turn away from full globalisation towards a regime based more on regional trading arrangements. The US instinct is now to dis-engage from China and go its own way, reducing dependence on China trade, repatriating as much China-based manufacture as possible, excluding China from US markets and the US banking system and denying it access to hi-tech components. And if speeches by US Deputy National Security Advisor Matt Pottinger and Secretary of State Pompeo are to be taken at face value, it will also involve ideological confrontation that Beijing will interpret as aimed at regime change. The impact of such policies will not be felt overnight. What will matter will be their cumu-lative impact over time.

The question therefore is not whether the Great Decoupling is happening; it has already begun. Rather the issue is how far and how fast this process will go and what wider impact it will have. It is likely to be complex and uncertain, driven by factors that pull in opposing directions: economic, commercial, cul-tural and geo-political, with the latter likely to be decisive. And there is as yet little in the way of settled thinking on how it might unfold.

The Great Decoupling coincides with what might be described as the peaking of the phase of globalisation that began following the end of the Cold War and in which China has played such an important part. Experts continue to disagree on how much China's emergence onto the world economic stage contributed to the de-industrialisation of the West generally and the USA in particular. The figures for the USA are not in dispute: between 1999 and 2010 the US lost between 5 and 6 million manufactur-ing jobs, amounting to roughly a third of the total. But econo-mists have tended to ascribe this loss of jobs to increased auto-mation and other advances in industrial production techniques rather than to the impact of China. Recent studies by academics such as Susan Houseman of the Upjohn Institute however suggest that China's accession to the WTO was a major game changer and that assumptions that the US manufacturing sector thereafter remained in rude health were based on statistical analysis distorted by the disproportionate emphasis given to added value in the IT sector.[1] An additional discovery, by MIT professor David Autor, was that US manufacturing companies most exposed to Chinese competition were compelled to skimp on research and development, leading to a decline in innovation as evidenced by a drop in patents filed and productivity.[2]

Meanwhile COVID-19 has highlighted the implications of a global economy based on complex entanglement between states in which products were manufactured in multiple locations but with high levels of specialisation that made some states single points of failure in the global supply chain. At its apogee, it was a system that saw inventory, in words that Apple CEO Tim Cook may or may not have used, as "fundamentally evil," and operated on a basis of just-in-time delivery, build to order and lean operation. The result was efficiency at the expense of resilience, something which the markets had no mechanism for pricing. Moreover, supply chain complexity was such that virtually no manufacturer or retailer had full visibility of all the links in the chain and it was hence inevitable that the crisis would reveal hitherto unknown dependencies and vulnerabilities. China's salience as a potential single point of failure in global supply chains was highlighted in a May 2020 report by the Henry Jackson Society. The report identified varying degrees of strategic dependence by the states making up the Five Eyes intelligence alliance—the USA, the UK, Canada, Australia and New Zealand—on 831 categories of Chinese imports, with strategic dependence defined as when a country is dependent on China for over 50% of goods, is a net importer of those goods and where

China controls over 30% of the global market for the good. Categories of such goods include consumer electronics like laptops and mobile phones and pharmaceutical ingredients for antibiotics, anti-virals and pain killers.[3]

Unwinding the complexities of a system that has evolved organically over forty years will be hugely problematic and it is unlikely that anything close to a complete reversal of globalisation could ever take place. No country, not even those with economies as large of those of the USA and China, can realistically hope to achieve total self-sufficiency. But the private sector has already begun to react to market signals in different ways depending on their relationship with China. Some low-end manufacturing has already migrated to cheaper locations, a reflection of both rising Chinese labour costs and a more restrictive environment for Western companies. At the hi-tech end of the spectrum Apple, Dell and Hewlett Packard had all begun to diversify production away from China. This process might be accelerated if states make good on a determination to offer financial incentives to companies to repatriate manufacture, something the Japanese government has already done and something members of the Trump administration have spoken of doing. A decision to move manufacture away from China is relatively straightforward for production that is labour intensive, and in principle straightforward for hi-tech manufactures reliant on automation, though the costs involved will not be trivial. But manufacturers invested in producing for the Chinese domestic market may at some point face a binary choice: go deeply local or retreat to the country in which they are incorporated.[4]

At one point during the trade war with China President Trump speculated that he might order US companies to withdraw from China altogether. The legal basis for doing so would be contentious and would certainly be the subject of legal challenge. And it would almost certainly not deliver one of Trump's stated objectives, of repatriating a million manufacturing jobs from China to the USA. But if the US government were to pursue a strategy of forced decoupling the implications for the US hi-tech sector would be especially severe and would have worldwide implications. Deutsche Bank technology strategist Apjit Walia has calculated that a total technology decoupling from China could take at a minimum between five and eight years to effect and cost US$ 3.5 trillion. This figure is calculated on the basis of a loss of Chinese domestic demand, the costs of relocating supply chain from China and the increased operating costs of divergence into two competing sets of technical standards.[5]

To look in greater detail at the three components, in 2018 twenty US corporations listed in the Standard and Poor 500 index, all but three of them in the hi-tech sector, registered US$ 150 billion in sales in China. Apple alone accounted for US$ 44 billion, representing 20% of its total sales. Moreover US hi-tech corporations derive significant revenue from sales of inputs for manufactured goods that are then re-exported. Walia calculates that as averaging US$ 400 billion, all of which could be at risk in the event of a total technology decoupling. Firms seeking to move manufacture from China will look instead to other low-cost countries in Asia, but China offers a unique combination of infrastructure, clustered networks and a skilled labour force on a scale that other countries will struggle to match without significant investment in infrastructure and training. The most significant aspect of a total technology decoupling would be a bifurcation of technology standards and the challenges and costs of ensuring interoperability between rival systems. Forced decoupling would have significant implications for the US hi-tech sectors as it faced a perfect storm of reduced profits, higher costs and hence fewer resources to devote to R&D, leading in turn to a decline in innovation. The implications would be significant for third countries, who could come under pressure to align themselves technologically with either the USA or China as the UK was compelled to do in relation to 5G. In the worst case the consequence could be a general slow-down in the pace of global innovation.

It is not yet apparent that this extreme outcome will come to pass. The USA appears as yet to have evolved no clear strategy for decoupling. This is an issue on which Donald Trump has to date been ambivalent and inconsistent beyond talking of repatriating manufacturing jobs to the USA and denying federal contracts to US firms that outsource jobs to China. The Democrats have yet to publish detailed policy prescriptions. But a report produced in November 2019 for the National Bureau of Asian Research by former US congressman Charles Boustany and Professor Aaron Friedberg of Princeton University has looked in detail at the various options facing the USA and offers recommendations on how the US government should conduct economic relations with China in the light of recent developments. The report, entitled "Partial Disengagement," considers four scenarios for US–China economic relations. The first is that the two countries operate open liberal economies, an unlikely outcome given China's commitment to its hybrid economic model but one which the report's authors argue the USA should continue to press for. The second is the status quo, with the US maintaining an open and China a partly closed economy, an undesirable outcome precisely because of the distortions and imbalances that have made relations so problematic to date. The third scenario is partial disengagement, in which the economies of both states are partly closed to each other, and the fourth is termed Cold War, where in effect the USA and China close off their economies from each other. This latter option might prove more damaging to China in the long term but also poses risks for the USA if it is unable to carry like-minded states with it. In the words of the report's authors:

> If in its efforts to compel others to go along with it Washington were to impair relations with its major allies and trading partners, as well as with other countries, the United States might end up isolating itself, damaging its prospects for future growth, reducing its relative power and diminishing rather than enhancing its security.[6]

The report plumps for partial disengagement and makes four key recommendations: achieve a ceasefire in the current tariff war; strengthen defensive measures to reduce vulnerabilities to surveillance, sabotage or disruption and to slow diffusion of critical technologies to China; invest in innovation, technology and education; and strengthen trade and investment relationships, cooperation and information sharing with close allies. It also makes a powerful argument for the US government to address the question of solvency given that the measures recommended in the report would require significant investment. It should not be forgotten, however, that the report was produced before the COVID-19 epidemic led to a massive increase in federal expenditure to preserve livelihoods and prevent an economic collapse. The question arises as to what might happen if the USA proves unable to address its own shortcomings and instead focuses on constraining China's technology ambitions.

It is hard to predict exactly how a technology decoupling might play out, not least because the relevant technologies do not evolve in a predictably linear fashion. But it is possible to draw some broad conclusions about the likely impact of a technical de-coupling that results in two distinct spheres, one—the USA—driven by free market principles and the other—China—state-directed and mercantilist. For the USA the risks of such a development hinge on reduced global sales, a drop in profitability and the costs of replicating either in the USA or in trusted third countries manufacturing capacity that already exists. All of which translates into fewer resources to invest in a future generation of products and services, especially in areas which take time to commercialise such as quantum computing. Added to that is a reduction in the global exchange of ideas that contributes much to innovation and the ability to leverage some of the best of China's talents in areas such as AI. It does not require a giant leap of imagination to see how this process could become a vicious cycle in which the USA progressively loses its leading innovative edge. Just as happened with the British Asquith government in the early years of World War I the USA is having to learn that a laissez-faire approach is no match for an adversary mobilised on an all-of-nation basis. To maintain its edge the USA may have to rediscover the kind of industrial strategies that led to success in the past, as happened with the military-industrial complex, the space programme and even the Internet. That will not prove easy given the extent to which Washington and Silicon Valley have gone their separate ways. But first and foremost, US policy-makers will need to internalise the reality that continued US science and technical dominance is not a foregone conclusion. The USA could be eclipsed by a China that is devoting enormous and sustained focus and resources to displacing it as the global science and technology leader. Avoiding this outcome will be costly and require commitment and determination.

China equally is not immune to the damaging effects of a global decoupling, a fact registered by many Chinese commentators, some of whom fear that a process of de-sinicisation—*qu zhongguo hua*—could in the worst case presage a return to the isolation that has proven so counter-productive in the past.[7] It remains to be seen whether in key areas of technology China has yet achieved lift-off in terms of developing a culture of innovation in foundational science and a technology base that is self-standing. It is easy enough to focus on the current shortcomings in the Chinese systems and make a case as to why China is not yet ready to disentangle from the USA and that by doing so now risks coming to grief. But it is hard to overstate just how ready China's population is to embrace technology, irrespective of the obvious downsides, as a way of achieving self-empowerment and global standing. And it would be highly unwise for Western policy-makers to base their strategies on a presumption of Chinese failure.

There is now much talk of the USA and China becoming embroiled in a new Cold War. But this analogy is not an apposite or appropriate characterisation. A better analogy might be the relationship between Britain and Imperial Germany in 1914 that involved strategic rivalry but also an entanglement so deep that commentators at the time believed it would make war between them inconceivable. In the event it did not. The resulting conflict brought globalisation to an end and ushered in a period of economic autarky and a vacuum in global leadership that was to have profound consequences for the planet. Whether that will be the case with the USA and China is impossible to determine. But the odds of conflict appear to be shortening as decoupling takes them further apart, reduces contact and mutual understanding and generates a climate of distrust in which each side's behaviour is interpreted in worst case terms and where each side is incentivised to maximise espionage and covert efforts to undermine the other. There are numerous ways in which conflict might start driven by miscalculation and inadvertent escalation. But when it comes to China there is one particular ingredient not present in the relationship between Britain and Germany which might prove decisive.

Until recently, Western policy-makers either overlooked or gave insufficient attention to the psychological implications of the humiliation China had suffered at the hands of the West. That lack of awareness has now come home to roost. In retrospect the experience of Imperial Japan should have given pause for thought. Not long after China was forcibly opened up to the

West, Japan was subjected to the same experience at the hands of the US Navy. Its response was very different from that of China. In the face of overwhelming US military and technological superiority, Japan's ruling samurai class put down their swords, donned business suits and rapidly turned their country into a modern industrialised economy—in the process compounding China's humiliation as it witnessed a former client state accomplishing what it could not. Yet despite this apparently successful and relatively painless transition to modernity, in the course of which Japan was able to preserve its distinctive national culture, the psychological impact of having its doors forced open proved profound. It gave rise to what psychologists would once have termed an inferiority complex that manifested itself in militarism and colonial expansion. This put the country on a collision course with the USA, with results too well known to need rehearsing. That China might experience a similar trajectory should come as no surprise. As the Chinese saying has it, when a gentleman seeks revenge, ten years is not too long to wait—*junzi baochou, shi nian bu chang.*

NOTES

INTRODUCTION

1. John Perry Barlow, "A Declaration of the Independence of Cyberspace," Electronic Frontier Foundation, https://www.eff.org/cyberspace-independence

2. International Telecommunications Union "Final Report", March 1994, http://vlib.iue.it/history/internet/algorespeech.html

3. Shoshana Zuboff, *The Age of Surveillance Capitalism: The Fight for a Human Future at the New Frontier of Power*, New York: PublicAffairs, 2019.

4. "Clinton Says Trade Deal and Internet Will Reform China," *Tech Law Journal*, 9 March 2000, http://www.techlawjournal.com/trade/20000 309.htm

1. CHINA'S INTELLECTUAL AND SCIENTIFIC TRADITIONS

1. Full text: "China's new party chief Xi Jinping's speech," *BBC*, 15 November 2011, https://www.bbc.co.uk/news/world-asia-china-20338586

2. For a brief and accessible account of China's traditions of science and technology, see Robert Temple, *The Genius of China: 3,000 Years of Science, Discovery and Invention*, Rochester, Vermont: Inner Traditions, 2007.

3. Chonglan Fu and Wenming Cao, *An Urban History of China*, Palgrave MacMillan, 2019.

4. Wang Yuan-kang, "Managing Regional Hegemony in Historical Asia: The Case of Early Ming China," *Chinese Journal of International Politics*, Vol. 5 Issue 2, Summer 2012, pp. 129–153.

5. Joseph Needham, *The Great Titration: Science and Society in East and West*, Allen and Unwin, 1969, p. 190.

6. Louis Gallagher (ed.), *China in the Sixteenth Century: The Journals of Matteo Ricci*, Random House, 1953, p. 30.

7. Needham, *Science and Civilization in China Vol. 4*, cited in Jonathan D. Spence, *Chinese Roundabout*, Norton, 1992, p. 143.

8. Carlo Rovelli, *Reality Is Not What It Seems*, Penguin Random House, 2016, pp. 7–10.

9. Fang Lizhi and Zhou Youyuan, "Concepts of Space and Time in Ancient China and in Modern Cosmology," *Journal of Dialectics of Nature* II(4), 1980, pp. 30–33.

10. *Analects* 12.11.

11. Needham, op. cit. note 5.

12. Mark Elvin, *The Retreat of the Elephants: An Environmental History*, Yale University Press, 2004, p. 388.

13. Jonathan D. Spence, *The Chan's Great Continent: China in Western Minds*, Norton, 1999, p. 33.

14. Elvin, op. cit. p. 7.

15. Philip A. Kuhn, *Soulstealers: The Chinese Sorcery Scare of 1768*, Harvard University Press, 1990, p. 32.

16. Charles C. Mann, *1493: Uncovering the New World Columbus Created*, Vintage Books, 2011, pp. 228–9.

2. CHINA MEETS THE WEST

1. Emperor Qian Long's Letter to King George III, 1793, http://academics.wellesley.edu/Polisci/wj/China/208/READINGS/qianlong.html

2. For a detailed account of the Taiping rebellion, see Jonathan Spence, *God's Chinese Son: The Taiping Heavenly Kingdom of Hong Xiuquan*, Harper Collins, 1996.

3. Benjamin Schwartz, *In Search of Wealth and Power: Yen Fu and the West*, Harvard University Press, 1964.

4. Orville Schell and John Delury, *Wealth and Power: China's Long March to the Twenty-First Century*, Penguin Random House, 2013.

5. Carl Crow, *Handbook for China*, Kelly and Walsh (1933), reprinted by Oxford University Press, 1984.

6. Jay Taylor, *The Generalissimo: Chiang Kai-shek and the Struggle for Modern China*, Harvard University Press, 2009, p. 169.

7. "Economic Relations Of Communist China With the USSR Since 1950," CIA Economic Intelligence Report, CIA RR/59–16 May 1959, https://www.cia.gov/library/readingroom/docs/CIA-RDP79R011 41A001400040002-9.pdf

8. Frank Dikotter, *Mao's Great Famine*, Bloomsbury Publishing, 2010, p. 105.

9. Frank Dikotter, *The Tragedy of Liberation: A History of the Chinese Revolution 1945–57*, Bloomsbury Publishing, 2013.

10. *Mao's Great Famine*, p. xi.

11. Hu Danian, "Organized criticism of Einstein and relativity in China, 1949–1989," *Historical Studies in the Physical and Biological Sciences*, Vol. 34 Issue 2, 2004, pp. 311–338.

3. CHINA GOES DIGITAL

1. Evan Osnos, "To Get Rich Is Glorious," *The New Yorker*, 7 December 2009, https://www.newyorker.com/news/evan-osnos/to-get-rich-is-glorious

2. Jeff Ding (trans), "The Sour Past of Chinese Chips," *China AI Newsletter 56*, https://chinai.substack.com/p/chinai-56-the-sour-past-of-china

3. Alvin Toffler, *The Third Wave*, Pan Books, 1981, p. 152.

4. Jiang Zemin, *On the Development of China's Information Technology Industry*, Central Party Literature Press, Beijing, 2010.

5. Edgar Snow, *Red Star Over China*, Random House, 1938.

6. Kai-fu Lee, *AI Superpowers: China, Silicon Valley and the New World Order*, Houghton Mifflin Harcourt, 2018, pp. 24–5.

7. Kuang Xianming, "What Are the Real Problems of China's Growth?" *China Today*, 13 November 2014, www.china.org.cn/opinion/2014-8/15/content_33250619.htm

8. Mo Yanlin and Cheng Mengfan, "Regulator Finds Nothing to Laugh About With Joke-sharing App," *Caixin*, 11 April 2018, https://www.caixinglobal.com/2018-04-11/regulator-finds-nothing-to-laugh-about-with-joke-sharing-app-101233132.html

9. Computer Information Network and Internet Security, Protection and Management Regulations 1997, Ministry of Public Security, http://www.lehmanlaw.com/resource-centre/laws-and-regulations/information-technology/computer-information-network-and-internet-security-protecion-and-management-regulations-1997.html

10. "Twitter's Hong Kong Archives: Chinese Commercial Bots at Work," *DFRLab*, 4 September 2019, https://medium.com/dfrlab/twitters-hong-kong-archives-chinese-commercial-bots-at-work-f4c7ae8eea64

11. Anthony Tao, "'Find the Thing You Love and Stick With It': Xi Jinping and the Perfect Meme," *SupChina*, 26 February 2018, https://supchina.com/2018/02/26/find-the-thing-you-love-and-stick-with-it-xi-jinping-winnie-the-pooh/

12. US–China Economic and Security Review Commission 2010 Report to Congress, November 2010, pp. 222–3, http://uscc.gov/sites/default/files/annual_reports/2010-Report-to-Congress.pdf

4. CHINA'S LEADERSHIP: VERSION 3.0

1. Gordon Barrass and Nigel Inkster, "Xi Jinping: The Strategist Behind the Dream," *Survival* Volume 60 Number 1, February–March 2018.

2. Pin He and Wenguang Huang, *A Death in the Lucky Holiday Hotel: Murder, Money and an Epic Power Struggle in China*, New York: PublicAffairs, 2013, p. 92.

3. Katsuji Nakazawa, "Xi Jinping bids adieu to his fellow princelings," *Nikkei*, 27 November 2017, https://asia.nikkei.com/Editor-s-Picks/China-up-close/Xi-Jinping-bids-adieu-to-his-fellow-princelings2

4. Tanner Greer, "Xi Jinping in Translation: China's Guiding Ideology," *Palladium*, 31 May 2019, https://palladiummag.com/2019/05/31/xi-jinping-in-translation-chinas-guiding-ideology/

5. For a detailed account of the challenges faced by CCP officials in managing China's economic miracle, see Richard McGregor, *The Party*, Allen Lane, pp. 34–70.

6. Document 9: A ChinaFile Translation, 8 November 2013, https://www.chinafile.com/document-9-chinafile-translation

7. See Timothy Cheek, David Ownby and Joshua A. Fogel (ed), *Voices from the Chinese Century*, Columbia University Press, 2020. Also, "The Rise

of China's Statist Intellectuals: Law, Sovereignty and 'Repoliticization'," *The China Journal*, 11 April 2019, https://doi.org/10.1086/702687

8. Yi Wang, "Meet the mastermind behind Xi Jinping's power," *The Washington Post*, 6 November 2017, https://www.washingtonpost.com/news/theworldpost/wp/2017/11/06/wang-huning/

9. Sun Zhongyi, "Draw on Cultural Self-Confidence to Unleash Spiritual Mobilisation," *Jiefangjun Bao*.

10. Chris Johnson, "Xi's Signature Governance Innovation: the Rise of Leading Small Groups," 17 October 2017, https://www.csis.org/analysis/xis-signature-governance-innovation-rise-leading-small-groups

11. David Bandurski, "Lu Wei: The Internet Must Have Brakes," *China Media Project*, 11 September 2014, http://chinamediaproject.org/2014/09/11/lu-wei-the-internet-must-have-brakes/

12. "China media: Cyber power," *BBC*, 28 February 2014, https://www.bbc.co.uk/news/world-asia-china-26379813

13. *Global Cybersecurity Index (GCI) 2018*, Geneva: ITU Publications, 2018, https://www.itu.int/dms_pub/itu-d/opb/str/D-STR-GCI.01-2018-PDF-E.pdf, p. 62.

14. Cybersecurity Law of the People's Republic of China (English Translation), https://www.newamerica.org/cybersecurity-initiative/digichina/blog/translation-cybersecurity-law-peoples-republic-china/

15. "President Xi says China faces major science, technology 'bottleneck'," *China Daily*, 1 June 2016, http://www.chinadaily.com.cn/china/2016-06/01/content_25561863.htm

5. CHINA, THE TECHNO-SECURITY STATE

1. Geoffrey Parker, *Global Crisis*, Yale University Press, 2013, pp. 115–151.

2. Lucy Hornby, "Falun Gong fights on 10 years after Chinese ban," *Reuters*, 23 April 2009, https://www.reuters.com/article/us-china-falun-gong-idUSTRE53M1TE20090423

3. Sun Liping, "China's Challenge: Social Disorder," *Economic Observer*, 9 May 2011, http://www.eeo.com.cn/ens/feature/2011/05/09/200868.shtml

4. Edward Wong, "Xi Jinping's News Alert: Chinese Media Must Serve the Party," *New York Times*, 22 February 2016, https://www.nytimes.com/2016/02/23/world/asia/china-media-policy-xi-jinping.html

5. Joseph Stalin, Speech at the home of Maxim Gorky, 26 October 1932.

6. Wanning Sun, "Chinese propaganda goes tech-savvy to reach a new generation," *The Conversation*, 11 August 2019, http://theconversation.com/chinese-propaganda-goes-tech-savvy-to-reach-a-new-generation-119642

7. Emily Baum, *The Invention of Madness: State, Society and the Insane in Modern China*, University of Chicago Press, 2018.

8. The name Skynet (in Chinese Tianwang) comes from a phrase in the Daoist classical text Laozi. The phrase—*tian wang huihui, shu er bulou*—literally translates as "Heaven's net has wide meshes but though loose, nothing escapes it," implying that Heaven is permissive but brooks no infractions. It has come to mean "there is no escaping the long arm of the law."

9. Josh Rudolph, "Sharper Eyes: Surveilling the Surveillers (Part 1)," *China Digital Times*, 9 September 2019, https://chinadigitaltimes.net/2019/09/sharper-eyes-surveilling-the-surveillers-part-1/

10. Alexa Olsen, "China's Vast, Strange and Powerful Farming Militia Turns 60," *Foreign Policy*, 8 October 2014, https://foreignpolicy.com/2014/10/08/chinas-vast-strange-and-powerful-farming-militia-turns-60/

11. See for example the 30 August 2018 report of the United Nations Committee on the Elimination of Racial Discrimination (https://tbinternet.ohchr.org/Treaties/CERD/Shared%20Documents/CHN/CERD_C_CHN_CO_14-17_32237_E.pdf) and Adrian Zenz, "Coercive Internment: Evidence for Chinese Documents about the Nature and Extent of Xinjiang's 'Vocational Training Internment Camps'," *Journal of Political Risk* Vol. 7 no. 7, July 2019, http://www.jpolrisk.com/brainwashing-police-guards-and-coercive-internment-evidence-from-chinese-government-documents-about-the-nature-and-extent-of-xinjiangs-vocational-training-internment-camps/

12. Lindsay Gorman and Matt Schrader, "U.S. Firms Are Helping Build China's Orwellian State," *Foreign Policy*, 19 March 2019, https://foreignpolicy.com/2019/03/19/962492-orwell-china-socialcredit-surveillance/

13. "Hands off the Quran or face Muslim outrage, MAPIM warns China," *New Straits Times*, 26 December 2019, https://www.nst.com.my/news/

nation/2019/12/550929/hands-quran-or-face-muslim-outrage-mapim-warns-china

14. Chris Buckley and Austin Ramzy, "Inside China's Push to Turn Muslim Minorities Into an Army of Workers," *New York Times*, 30 December 2019, https://www.nytimes.com/2019/12/30/world/asia/china-xinjiang-muslims-labor.html

15. Yuan Yang, "Xinjiang security crackdown sparks Han Chinese exodus," *Financial Times*, 22 December 2019, https://www.ft.com/content/fa6bd0b0-1d87-11ea-9186-7348c2f183af

16. "State Council Notice on Issuing the Plan for Establishing a Social Credit System—*Guowuyuan guanyu yinfa shehui xinyong tixi jianshe guihua yaogang (2014–2020) de tongzhi*," issued 14 June 2014, http://www.gov.cn/zhengce/content/2014-06/27/content_8913.htm

17. "The apps of China's social credit system," *Trivium China*, 14 October 2019, http://ub.triviumchina.com/2019/10/long-read-the-apps-of-chinas-social-credit-system/

18. Samantha Hoffman, "Engineering global consent: the Chinese Communist Party's data-driven power expansion," for *ASPI*, 2019, https://www.aspi.org.au/report/engineering-global-consent-chinese-communist-partys-data-driven-power-expansion

19. Larry Diamond, "Chinese Communism and the '70-Year' Itch," *The Atlantic*, 29 October 2013, https://www.theatlantic.com/china/archive/2013/10/chinese-communism-and-the-70-year-itch/280960/

20. Edward Cunningham, Tony Saich and Jesse Turiel, "Understanding CCP Resilience: Surveying Chinese Public Opinion Through Time," Harvard Kennedy School Ash Center for Democratic Governance and Innovation, July 2020, https://ash.harvard.edu/files/ash/files/final_policy_brief_7.6.2020.pdf

6. CHINA, THE INTELLIGENCE STATE

1. For a good general account of Chinese Communist intelligence activity before Liberation, see Dr. David Ian Chambers, "Edging in from the Cold: The Past and Present State of Chinese Intelligence Historiography," *Studies in Intelligence*, Vol. 56 No. 3, September 2012, https://www.cia.gov/library/center-for-the-study-of-intelligence/csi-publications/

csi-studies/studies/vol.-56-no.-3/pdfs/Chambers-Chinese%20 Intel%20Historiography.pdf

2. "Espionage: A Spy's Grisly Solution," *Time*, 3 March 1986. The defector in question was Yu Qiangsheng, a senior officer in the Beijing State Security Bureau's counter-espionage division and brother of Yu Zhengsheng, who served on the Politburo Standing Committee from 2012 to 2017.

3. Chambers, op. cit.

4. Intelligence Resource Program, Federation of American Scientists, https://fas.org/irp/world/china/mss/index.html

5. Evan A. Feigenbaum, *China's Techno-warriors: National Security and Strategic Competition from the Nuclear to the Information Age*, Stanford University Press, 2000, pp. 141–66.

6. David Wise, *Tiger Trap: America's Secret Spy War with China*, Boston: Houghton Mifflin Harcourt, 2011, p. 10.

7. Nigel Inkster, *China's Cyber Power*, Routledge for IISS, 2016, pp. 58–9.

8. John Kehoe, "How Chinese hacking felled telecommunication giant Nortel," *Financial Review*, 28 May 2018, https://www.afr.com/technology/how-chinese-hacking-felled-telecommunication-giant-nortel-20140526-iux6a

9. Siobhan Gorman, "Chinese Hackers Suspected In Long-Term Nortel Breach," *Wall Street Journal*, 14 February 2012, https://www.wsj.com/articles/SB10001424052970203363504577187502201577054

10. Tim Harford, "Killed for spying: the story of the first factory," *BBC*, 10 July 2019, https://www.bbc.co.uk/news/business-48533696

11. Peter Mattis, "The Dragon's Eyes and Ears: Chinese Intelligence at the Crossroads," *The National Interest*, 20 January 2015, https://nationalinterest.org/feature/the-dragons-eyes-ears-chinese-intelligence-the-crossroads-12062

12. Sean Lyngaas, "Meet APT41, The Chinese hackers Moonlighting for Personal Gain," *Cyberscoop*, 7 August 2019, https://www.cyberscoop.com/apt41-fireeye-china/

13. https://www.c-span.org/video/?474729-1/assistant-ag-john-demers-countering-chinese-espionage

14. Much MSS operational activity is undertaken not at headquarters level but rather by the State Security Bureaux (SSBs) that exist in every

province and directly administered municipality. The priority targets of the SSBs tend to align with their historic overseas linkages. Thus, for the Shanghai SSB the priority target is the USA. The Jiangsu SSB is focused on Northern Europe, the Qingdao SSB against Japan and Korea, the Fujian SSB against Taiwan, the Guangzhou SSB against Hong Kong and Southeast Asia and the Beijing SSB against Russia and Eastern Europe. These priorities do not however constitute hard and fast demarcation lines.

15. Anderson Cooper, "How a Former CIA Officer Was Caught Betraying His Country," *CBS*, 23 December 2018, https://www.cbsnews.com/news/chinese-spy-how-a-former-cia-officer-was-caught-betraying-his-country-60-minutes-2019-08-11/

16. Karen Leigh, "How China's Spies Became Key Players in the Trade War," *Bloomberg*, 3 January 2019, https://www.bloomberg.com/news/articles/2019-01-03/how-china-s-spies-became-key-players-in-the-trade-war-quicktake

17. Steven Feldstein, "The Global Expansion of AI Surveillance," Carnegie Endowment for International Peace, 17 September 2019, https://carnegieendowment.org/2019/09/17/global-expansion-of-ai-surveillance-pub-79847

18. Aislinn Lang, "China 'planted bugs' while building African Union H.Q.," *The Times*, 1 February 2018, https://www.thetimes.co.uk/article/china-planted-bugs-while-building-african-union-hq-wqgw5ff7q

19. Christopher Andrew, *For the President's Eyes Only: Secret Intelligence and the American Presidency from Washington to Bush*, New York: Harper Collins, 1995, p. 501.

20. Adam Segal, "China and the Power Grid: Hacking and Getting Hacked," Council on Foreign Relations, 3 December 2014, https://www.cfr.org/blog/china-and-power-grid-hacking-and-getting-hacked

21. See Ioanna Iordanou, *Venice's Secret Service: Organising Intelligence in the Renaissance*, Oxford University Press, 2019.

7. A WORLD ORDER WITH CHINESE CHARACTERISTICS

1. Homer H. Dubs, *A Roman City in China*, Cambridge University Press, 1957.

2. Edward H. Schafer, *The Golden Peaches of Samarkand: A Study of Tang Exotics*, University of California Press, 1963, p. 58.

3. Christopher A. Ford, *The Mind of Empire: China's History and Modern Foreign Relations*, University Press of Kentucky, 2010, pp. 83–4.

4. Mark Mancall, "The Ch'ing Tribute System: An Interpretive Essay," in J. K. Fairbank (ed.), *The Chinese World Order*, Harvard University Press, p. 63.

5. Ford, op. cit. pp. 92–100.

6. Hiram Maxim, *Li Hongzhang's Scrapbook*, Watts and Co., 2013.

7. The full 24-character strategy translates as: observe calmly; secure our position; deal with issues calmly; hide our capacities and bide our time; maintain a low profile; never take a leadership position; accomplish some achievements.

8. "China's Position Paper on the New Security Concept," http://www.china-un.ch/eng/cjjk/cjjblc/cjlc/t85397.htm

9. "The Great Decoupling: How China is Losing Its Appeal as an Export Platform and Depressing Its Consumers," *Enodo Entangled*, 31 October 2019.

10. "The NICE decade: ten years of stability," *This Is Money*, 4 May 2007.

11. Cui Liru, "China's 'Period of Historic Opportunities'," *China–US Focus*, 1 February 2018, https://www.chinausfocus.com/foreign-policy/chinas-period-of-historic-opportunities

12. The nine-dash line first emerged in 1948. It was based on an atlas published in 1936 by the self-taught Beijing Normal University geography professor Bai Meichu. The South China Sea portrayed in Bai's atlas bore little relation to geographical reality, with many shoals and reefs portrayed as actual islands.

13. Liang Haoguang and Zhao Yangjun, *The Theoretical System of Belt and Road Initiative*, Springer, 2019.

14. Zhao Tingyang, "A Political World Philosophy in terms of All-under-heaven (*Tian-xia*)," Sage, Vol 56 Issue 1, February 2009, https://journals.sagepub.com/doi/10.1177/0392192109102149

15. Nadege Rolland, "Beijing's Vision for a Reshaped International Order," *Jamestown Foundation China Brief*, Vol. 18 Issue 3, https://jamestown.org/program/beijings-vision-reshaped-international-order/

16. Gordon G. Chang, "Beijing's View of the World," Hoover Institution, 9 May 2017, https://www.hoover.org/research/beijings-view-world

17. The Kindleberger Trap refers to a book by the MIT economist Charles Kindleberger entitled *The World in Depression 1929–1939*. Kindleberger argues that the failure of the USA effectively to exercise the hegemonic role it had by default inherited from the UK following World War I resulted in a period of instability that led to the rise of Hitler and culminated in World War II.

18. "President Xi urges new media outlet to 'tell China stories well'," *Global Times*, 31 December 2016, http://www.globaltimes.cn/content/10265 92.shtml

19. Introducing *The Communist*, Selected Works of Mao Zedong, 4 October 1939, https://www.marxists.org/reference/archive/mao/selected-works/volume-2/mswv2_20.htm

20. "Daryl Morey backtracks after Hong Kong tweet causes Chinese backlash," *BBC*, 7 October 2019, https://www.bbc.co.uk/news/business-49956385

8. PROJECTING DIGITAL POWER

1. Johann Wolfgang Kleinwaechter and Virgilio A. F. Almeida, *The Internet Governance Ecosystem and the Rainforest*, Aarhus University, 2015, https://pure.au.dk/portal/en/publications/the-internet-governance-ecosystem

2. *Evolution of the Cyber Domain: The Implications for National and Global Security*, IISS Strategic Dossier, Routledge, 2015, pp. 103–113.

3. UN Disarmament Committee, "Letter dated 23 September 1998 from the Permanent Representative of the Russian Federation to the United Nations Addressed to the Secretary-General," A/C.1/53/3, 30 September 1998.

4. UN General Assembly, "Developments in the Field of Information and Communications in the Context of International Security: Report of the Secretary-General", A/62/98, 2 July 2007, pp. 7–8.

5. http://www.fmprc.gov.cn/mfa_eng/wjbxw/t1162458.shtml

6. Madhumita Murgia and Anna Gross, "Inside China's controversial mission to reinvent the internet," *Financial Times*, 28 March 2020.

7. Gordon Corera, "Long-term security risks from Huawei," *BBC News*, 28 March 2019, https://www.bbc.co.uk/news/technology-47732139

8. Elliott Zaagman, "Huawei's Problem of Being Too 'Chinese'," *SupChina*, 24 January 2019, https://supchina.com/2019/01/24/huaweis-problem-of-being-too-chinese/

9. Michael Evans, "CIA warning over Huawei." *The Times*, 20 April 2019, https://www.thetimes.co.uk/article/cia-warning-over-huawei-rz6x-c8kzk

10. Comments unofficially attributed to Pottinger at the January 2020 Raisina Dialogue, reported in the subscriber newsletter *Sinocism* on 22 January 2020.

11. Adrian Morrow and Robert Fife, "U.S. alleges Meng Wanzhou part of 10-year conspiracy by Huawei to skirt sanctions," *The Globe and Mail*, 28 January 2019, https://www.theglobeandmail.com/world/us-politics/article-us-alleges-meng-wanzhou-part-of-10-year-conspiracy-by-huawei-to/

12. "Breakingviews—China's Huawei holds a 5G trump card," *Reuters*, 27 July 2020 https://www.reuters.com/article/us-huawei-tech-5g-security-breakingviews-idUSKCN24S09Y

13. Kate Fazzini, "Why there's been a decade-long disconnect between Huawei and the US, and it's unlikely to be fixed soon," *CNBC*, 16 May 2019, https://www.cnbc.com/2019/05/16/why-huaweis-problems-with-the-us-government-have-been-so-bad.html

14. Cassell Bryan-Low and Colin Packham, "How Australia led the U.S. in its global war against Huawei," *The Sydney Morning Herald*, 22 May 2019, https://www.smh.com.au/world/asia/how-australia-led-the-us-in-its-global-war-against-huawei-20190522-p51pv8.html

15. "Huawei founder Ren Zhengfei says 5G is not an atomic bomb," *CBS News*, 21 February 2019, www.cbsnews.com/news/huawei-founder-ren-zhengfei-5g-is-not-an-atomic-bomb/

16. "US–China tensions rise as Trump administration moves to cut Huawei off from global chip suppliers," *CNBC*, 15 May 2020, https://www.cnbc.com/2020/05/15/us-china-tensions-rise-as-trump-administration-moves-to-cut-huawei-off-from-global-chip-suppliers.html

17. "*Jidai gongkede hexin jishu*," *Keji Ribao*, 5 July 2018, http://www.stdaily.com/zhuanti01/kjrbzl/hxjs.shtml

18. Raj Narayan, "Forced out of 5G race, Huawei now eyes PCs, smart screens," *TechRadar*, 18 August 2020, https://www.techradar.com/news/forced-out-of-5g-race-huawei-now-eyes-pcs-smart-screens

19. "US Probe of China's Huawei includes bank fraud accusations," *Reuters*, 7 December 2018 on *SABC News*, http://www.sabcnews.com/sabc-news/us-probe-of-chinas-huawei-includes-bank-fraud-accusations/

9. FIGHTING AND WINNING WARS: THE PEOPLE'S LIBERATION ARMY

1. Franz-Stefan Gady, "Interview: Ben Lowsen on Chinese PLA Ground Forces," *The Diplomat*, 8 April 2020, https://thediplomat.com/2020/04/interview-ben-lowsen-on-chinese-pla-ground-forces

2. James Mulvenon, "Hotel Gutian: We Haven't Had That Spirit Here Since 1929," *China Leadership Monitor* No. 46, http://www.hoover.org/research/hotel-gutian-we-havent-had-spirit-here-1929/

3. Yu Guang, "Looking at casting the military soul from the contemporary values of the Gutian Conference," *Qiushi*, 31 July 2014, No. 15.

4. Katherine Hille and Daniel Dombey, "Beijing faces PLA 'disconnect', warns Gates," *Financial Times*, 14 January 2011, https://www.ft.com/content/5571d5ac-2000-11e0-a6fb-00144feab49a

5. Homare Endo, "Mao Zedong: the Man Who Conspired with the Japanese," https://u.osu.edu/mclc/2016/07/02/truth-of-mao-zedongs-collusion-with-the-japanese-army-1/

6. *On Protracted War*, Mao Zedong's Selected Works Volume II, May 1958, pp. 143–4.

7. The Military Balance 2020, International Institute for Strategic Studies.

8. Taiwan Relations Act, Public Law 96–8 22 U.S.C. 3301 et seq. https://www.ait.org.tw/our-relationship/policy-history/key-u-s-foreign-policy-documents-region/taiwan-relations-act/

9. Brendan Taylor, *Dangerous Decade: Taiwan's Security and Crisis Management*, Routledge for IISS, 2019, p. 19.

10. Liu Zhen, "Taiwan running out of time to discuss peaceful reunification, says former Chinese general," 22 December 2019, https://www.scmp.com/news/china/politics/article/3043108/taiwan-running-out-time-discuss-peaceful-reunification-says

11. Taylor, op. cit. p. 19.
12. Aaron L. Friedberg, *Beyond Air-Sea Battle: The Debate Over US Military Strategy in Asia*, Routledge for IISS, 2014, p. 18.
13. Wang Pufeng, "The Challenge of Information Warfare," *China Military Science*, Spring 1995, http://fas.org/irp/world/china/docs/iw_mg_wang.htm
14. Sebastian Roblin, "How China Could Destroy Taiwan's Air Force: A Massive Missile Attack?", *The National Interest*, 24 August 2019, https://nationalinterest.org/blog/buzz/how-china-could-destroy-taiwans-air-force-massive-missile-attack-75861
15. Kyle Mizokami, "As It Begins Its Second Century, Is the Aircraft Carrier Obsolete?," *Popular Mechanics*, 5 November 2018, https://www.popularmechanics.com/military/navy-ships/a24409627/aircraft-carrier-obsolete/
16. "How is China modernising its navy?" *China Power*, 17 December 2018, https://chinapower.csis.org/china-naval-modernization/
17. *PLA Aerospace Power: a Primer on Trends in China's Military Air, Space and Missile Forces*, China Aerospace Studies Institute, p. 2, https://www.airuniversity.af.edu/Portals/10/CASI/documents/Research/PLAAF/CASI_Primer%202017.pdf
18. Kathy Gilsinan, "How the U.S. Could Lose a War With China," *The Atlantic*, 25 July 2019, https://www.theatlantic.com/politics/archive/2019/07/china-us-war/594793

10. CHINA AS HI-TECH SUPERPOWER

1. Chris Buckley and Paul Mozur, "What Keeps Xi Jinping Awake at Night," *New York Times*, 11 May 2018, https://www.other-news.info/2018/05/what-keeps-xi-jinping-awake-at-night/
2. "China's Xi Urges Self-Reliance Amid 'Change Unseen in 100 Years'," *Bloomberg News*, 31 December 2018, https://www.bloomberg.com/news/articles/2018-12-31/china-s-xi-urges-self-reliance-amid-change-unseen-in-100-years?sref=EgYNCHYw
3. "China should 'grasp historic opportunity'," *People's Daily*, http://en.people.cn/n3/2018/0116/c90000-9315653.html
4. Douglas Bulloch "China Is Running Out Of Cheap Rural Labour And It's Because of Failed Reforms," *Forbes*, 3 March 2017, https://www.

forbes.com/sites/douglasbulloch/2017/03/03/china-is-running-out-of-cheap-rural-labor-and-its-because-of-failed-reforms/#2f70ff7125c6

5. Bian Yufang, *Ma Yinchu: the Third Model of Thinker*, China Youth Press.

6. Sidney Leng, "China's birth rate falls to near 60-year low, with 2019 producing fewest babies since 1961," *South China Morning Post*, 15 January 2020, https://scmp.com/economy/china-economy/article/3046481/chinas-birth-rate-falls-near-60-year-low-2019-producing

7. "Aging Tigers, hidden dragons," *Deloitte, Voice of Asia*, Third Edition, September 2017, https://www2.deloitte.com/us/en/insights/economy/voice-of-asia/sept-2017/demographics-ageing-tigers-hidden-dragons.htm

8. "China embraces blockchain as next frontier for digital future," *Xinhua*, 7 November 2019, http://www.xinhuanet.com/english/2019-11/07/c_138536845.htm

9. David J. Lynch and Danielle Paquette, "China to revise plan for global technology dominance," *The Washington Post*, 12 December 2018, https://www.washingtonpost.com/business/economy/china-to-revise-global-technology-dominance-plan/2018/12/12/6942cb78-fe22-11e8-83c0-b06139e540e5_story.html

10. "China's tech strategy all talk, no action and a waste of taxpayers' money says its former finance minister Lou Jiwei," https://scmp.com/news/china/diplomacy/article/2189046/chinas-tech-strategy-all-talk-no-action-and-waste-taxpayers

11. Elsa Kania, "China's Artificial Intelligence Revolution," *The Diplomat*, 27 July 2017, https://thediplomat.com/2017/07/chinas-artificial-intelligence-revolution/

12. "China's city of Tianjin to set up $16 billion artificial intelligence fund," *Reuters*, 17 May 2018, https://www.reuters.com/article/us-china-ai-tianjin-idUSKCN1II0DD

13. Rao Yi, Bai Lu and Xie Yu, "Pragmatism/practicalism has prevailed in the ethnic Chinese community for a long time," *Zhishi fenzi*, 5 January 2016, translated by Jeffrey Ding in the subscription service China AI.

14. Kai-fu Lee, *AI Super-powers: China, Silicon Valley, and the New World Order*, Houghton Mifflin Harcourt, 2018, pp. 13–19.

15. Laura Kolodny, "Tesla is betting big on China and here's what Elon Musk had to say about it," *CNBC*, 31 January 2019, https://finance. yahoo.com/news/tesla-betting-big-china-apos-234508493.html

16. Zigor Aldama, "China's self-driving vehicles on track to take global leadership position ahead of the US," *South China Morning Post*, 22 April 2018, https://www.scmp.com/magazines/post-magazine/long-reads/article/2142449/chinas-self-driving-vehicles-track-take-global

17. Wei Pang, "*Zhongguo gaojigong quekou gaoda liangqianwan, daguo zhizao shui lai zao,*" *Zhiqizhineng*, 11 December 2019.

18. Ian Sample, "Chinese scientist who edited babies' genes jailed for three years," *The Guardian*, 31 December 2019, https://www.theguardian. com/world/2019/dec/30/gene-editing-chinese-scientist-he-jiankui-jailed-three-years

19. The name Chang'e derives from a Chinese legend. Chang'e was the beautiful wife of Yi the Divine Archer who shot down nine of the ten suns that threatened to burn up the earth. Having stolen the herb of immortality given to Yi by the Jade Emperor, Chang'e fled to the moon to escape her husband's wrath and has remained there ever since. This myth forms the basis of the Mid-Autumn Festival which takes place on the 15th day of the 8th lunar month.

20. Namrata Goswamy, "China's Get-Rich Space Program," *The Diplomat*, 28 February 2019, https://thediplomat.com/2019/02/chinas-get-rich-space-program/

21. US Public Law 112–55, SEC.539.

22. Gregory Allen, "Understanding China's AI Strategy: Clues to Chinese Strategic Thinking on Artificial Intelligence and National Security," Center for a New American Security, 6 February 2019, https://www. cnas.org/publications/reports/understanding-chinas-ai-strategy

23. Janosch Delcker, "How Killer Robots Overran the UN," *Politico*, 12 February 2019, https://www.politico.eu/article/killer-robots-over-ran-united-nations-lethal-autonomous-weapons-systems/

24. Allen, op. cit.

25. Bill Gertz, "China in Race to Overtake US Military in AI Warfare," *The National Interest*, 30 May 2018, https://nationalinterest.org/blog/the-buzz/china-race-overtake-us-military-ai-warfare-26035

26. Martin Giles, "The man turning China into a quantum superpower," *MIT Technology Review*, 19 December 2018, https://www.technologyreview.com/s/612596/the-man-turning-china-into-a-quantum-superpower/

27. "A new trinity," *The Economist*, 4 January 2020.

28. Mingda Qiu, "A Larger But Not Leaner Fat Tech Dragon," published in *China's Uneven High-Tech Drive* (Scott Kennedy ed.), February 2020, *CSIS*, https://www.csis.org/analysis/chinas-uneven-high-tech-drive-implications-united-states

29. Greg Austin, *Cyber Policy in China*, Cambridge Polity, 2014, p. 113.

30. Jane Li, "A top Chinese university stripped 'freedom of thought' from its charter," *Quartz*, 18 December 2019.

31. Scott Shane and Daisuke Wakabayashi, "'The Business of War': Google Employees Protest Work for the Pentagon," *New York Times*, 4 April 2018, https://www.nytimes.com/2018/04/04/technology/google-letter-ceo-pentagon-project.html

11. US–CHINA RELATIONS: CHRONICLE OF A DEATH FORETOLD?

1. Graham Allison, *Destined for War: Can America and China Escape Thucydides' Trap?* Scribe, 2017.

2. Jacques M. Downs, "American Merchants and the China Opium Trade, 1800–1840," *The Business History Review* Vol. 42 No. 4, pp. 418–442.

3. David Oshinsky, *A Conspiracy So Immense: The World of Joe McCarthy*, Oxford: Oxford University Press, 2005 p. 109.

4. Evan Osnos, "The Two Lives of Qian Xuesen," *The New Yorker*, 3 November 2009, https://www.newyorker.com/news/evan-osnos/the-two-lives-of-qian-xuesen

5. Keji Ribao, "International S and T Cooperation and the Sharing of Intellectual Property," 13 May 1996.

6. Yan Xuetong, "The Instability of China–US Relations," *The Chinese Journal of International Politics* Vol. 3 Issue 3, Autumn 2010, https://academic.oup.com/cjip/article/3/3/263/418406

7. Yan Xuetong, op. cit.

8. "The Future of US-China Relations," *Foreign Affairs* Vol. 91 No. 2, March–April 2012.

9. Hannah Kuchler, "China Still Hacking US Companies, Cyber Group Warns," *Financial Times*, 19 October 2015, https://www.ft.com/content/8b07a73a-7679-11e5-a95a-27d368e1ddf7

10. White House "Fact Sheet: President Xi Jinping's State Visit to the United States," 25 September 2015.

11. "Trump China Visit: US President Strikes Warmer Tone With Xi Jinping," *BBC News*, 9 November 2017, https://www.bbc.co.uk/news/world-asia-china-41924228

12. "National Security Strategy of the United States of America December State Visit to the United States," 2017, https://www.whitehouse.gov/wp-content/uploads/2017/12/NSS-Final-12-18-2017-0905-2.pdf

13. President Xi's speech to Davos in full, https://www.weforum.org/agenda/2017/01/full-text-of-xi-jinping-keynote-at-the-world-economic-forum

14. "A New US Consensus on China?" *IISS Strategic Survey 2019*, pp. 393–4.

15. Shen Yi, *Yingde zhongmei jingmao moca xuyao jiuzheng san zhong cuowu renzhi* ("Three errors of perception that need to be corrected if we are to achieve victory in the Sino–US trade dispute"), *Guangming Ribao*, 20 May 2019, https://www.thepaper.cn/newsDetail_forward_3487242

16. https://www.sohu.com/a/255898706_164508

17. James Curran, "How America's Foreign Policy Establishment Got China Wrong," *The National Interest*, 17 December 2018, https://nationalinterest.org/feature/how-america's-foreign-policy-establishment-got-china-wrong-39012

18. Michael Pillsbury, *The Hundred-Year Marathon: China's Secret Strategy to Replace America as the Global Superpower*, Henry Holt and Company, 2015.

19. Matt Egan, "GE dodges bullet in Trump's battle with China," *CNN Business*, 20 February 2020, https://www.msn.com/en-us/money/companies/ge-dodges-a-bullet-in-trumps-battle-with-china/ar-BB10as5M

20. Greg Ip, "Has America's China Backlash Gone Too Far?" *Wall Street Journal*, 28 August 2019, https://www.wsj.com/articles/has-americas-china-backlash-gone-too-far-11566990232

21. J. Michael Waller, "Harvard professor's arrest shows Chinese spying

via US universities," Center for Security Policy, 30 January 2020, https://www.centerforsecuritypolicy.org/2020/01/30/harvard-china-spy/

22. Luz Ding, "Chinese scientists in America face special scrutiny. Why?" *SupChina*, 25 March 2020, https://signal.supchina.com/chinese-scientists-in-america-face-special-scrutiny-why/

23. Tom Hancock, "US investment in China rises despite trade war, says consultancy," *Financial Times*, 27 August 2019, https://www.ft.com/content/cabf76d4-c5a1-11e9-a8e9-296ca66511c9

24. "The Global Economic Outlook During the COVID-19 Pandemic: A Changed World," World Bank, 8 June 2020, https://www.worldbank.org/en/news/feature/2020/06/08/the-global-economic-outlook-during-the-covid-19-pandemic-a-changed-world

25. "Resolutely Defeating the COVID-19 Outbreak and Promoting the Building of a Community with a Shared Future for Mankind," http://en.cidca.gov.cn/2020-03/02/c_461664.htm

26. Jonathan Garber, "GOP senator calls on China to repay $1.6 trillion of century-old debt," *Fox Business*, 13 August 2020, https://www.foxbusiness.com/markets/sen-mcsally-introduces-bill-calling-on-china-to-repay-1-6t-of-century-old-debt

27. For the full speech, see https://www.nixonfoundation.org/2020/07/event-recap-secretary-pompeo-nixon-library-2/

28. "Exclusive: Internal Chinese report warns Beijing faces Tiananmen-like global backlash over virus," *Reuters*, 4 May 2020, https://www.reuters.com/article/us-health-coronavirus-china-sentiment-ex-idUSKBN22G19C

29. Keynote Speech by Ambassador Cui Tiankai at the Webinar with the Brookings Institution, http://www.china-embassy.org/eng/zmgxss/t1807578.htm

30. Jamil Anderlini, "Why China is losing the coronavirus narrative," *Financial Times*, 20 April 2020, https://www.ft.com/content/8d7842fa-8082-11ea-82f6-150830b3b99a

12. THE GREAT DECOUPLING

1. Gwynn Guilford, "The epic mistake about manufacturing that's cost Americans millions of jobs," *Quartz*, 3 May 2018, https://qz.com/

1269172/the-epic-mistake-about-manufacturing-thats-cost-americans-millions-of-jobs/

2. Jeffry Bartash, "How Chinese imports may have curbed American ingenuity," *MarketWatch*, 22 March 2017, https://www.marketwatch.com/story/how-chinese-imports-may-have-curbed-american-ingenuity-2017-03-22

3. James Rogers, Andrew Foxall, Matthew Henderson and Sam Armstrong, "Breaking the China Supply Chain: How the 'Five Eyes' can Decouple from Strategic Dependency," Henry Jackson Society, 14 May 2020, https://henryjacksonsociety.org/publications/breaking-the-china-supply-chain-how-the-five-eyes-can-decouple-from-strategic-dependency/

4. Michael Witt, "Prepare for the US and China to Decouple," *Harvard Business Review*, 26 June 2020, https://hbr.org/2020/06/prepare-for-the-u-s-and-china-to-decouple

5. Matthew Barnard and Apjit Walia, "The $3.5 Trillion Tech Cold War Fallout," Deutsche Bank, 28 July 2020 https://www.dbresearch.com/servlet/reweb2.ReWEB?rwnode=RPS_EN-PROD$HIDDEN_GLOBAL_SEARCH&rwsite=RPS_EN-PROD&rwobj=ReDisplay.Start.class&document=PROD0000000000510609

6. Charles W. Boustany Jr. and Aaron L. Friedberg, "Partial Disengagement: A New U.S. Strategy for Economic Competition with China," The National Bureau of Asian Research Special Report N. 82, November 2019, https://www.nbr.org/publication/partial-disengagement-a-new-u-s-strategy-for-economic-competition-with-china/

7. Orange Wang, "Coronavirus: China risks being left out of new global economic order, China's former trade chief warns," *South China Morning Post*, 11 May 2020, https://www.scmp.com/economy/china-economy/article/3083874/coronavirus-china-risks-being-left-out-new-global-economic

INDEX

Abkhazia, 6
Academie Royale des Sciences, 29
active measures, 6
Addis Ababa, Ethiopia, 125
Afghanistan, 99, 136, 222
African Union, 124–5, 163
Age of Exploration, 12, 19, 20
aging population, 195, 242
agriculture, 16
    imports, 230
    mediaeval revolution, 30
    Maoist period (1949–76), 47,
        48–9
    New World revolution, 31–2
    Reform and Opening Up
        (1978–2005), 51
Ai Sixiang, 142
AI Superpowers (Lee), 58
Air Defence Identification Zone,
    139
aircraft carriers, 185–6, 207
alchemy, 26
algorithms, 198, 199, 208, 211,
    214

Alibaba, 9, 60, 103, 104, 201, 209,
    211
Allison, Graham, 11, 134, 218
AlphaGo Plus, 199
America Against Itself (Wang), 76
American Institute in Taiwan
    (AIT), 180
Anbang, 233
Andaman Sea, 114
Android, 84
Annan, Kofi, 64, 137
anquan kekong, 84
Ant Financial, 104–5
Anti-Access, Area Denial
    (A2AD), 182, 184
Anti-Rightist Campaign (1957–9),
    48
anti-vaccination propaganda, 4
Apple, 57, 83, 233, 247, 248, 249
APT 41 hacking group, 120
Aristotle, 22
ARPANET, 3, 57
Art of War, The (Sunzi), 110, 183
art, 93

Artificial Intelligence (AI), 2, 115, 124, 159, 195, 197–201, 205–15, 252
artillery, 17–18
ASAT test (2007), 175
Asia-Pacific Economic Cooperation Forum (APEC), 134–5
Asian Infrastructure Investment Bank (AIIB), 145
Asquith, Herbert Henry, 252
al-Assad, Bashar, 137
Association of Southeast Asian Nations (ASEAN), 134, 142
asteroids, 204
Astor, John Jacob, 218
astronomy, 18, 23, 24
Athens, 24
Australia, 119, 125, 147, 148, 166–7, 230, 232, 247
authoritarianism, 54, 217, 231, 245
    intelligence agencies and, 126
    Internet and, 5, 8, 67, 158
    neo-authoritarianism, 75–6
    techno-security state and, 106
automation, 112
    manufacturing, 3, 159, 202, 246, 248
    vehicles, 3, 201
    weapons systems, 206–7
Autor, David, 247
Awareness Week for National Cyber Security, 81

B1/B2 strategic bomber, 113

ba da jingang, 83
Bacon, Francis, 15
Baidu, 9, 61, 200–201, 209
ballistic missiles, 184–5, 205
Balzac and the Little Chinese Seamstress, 50
Bank of England, 136
banking, 61
baojia system, 97
Baosteel, 224
barbarians, 19, 34, 35, 87, 130
Barlow, John Perry, 2, 5
Battle of Carrhae (53 BCE), 129
Battle of Dien Bien Phu (1954), 177
beggars, 31, 61
behavioural surplus, 4
Beidou, 205
Beijing
    Civil War (1927–49), 44
    Falungong protests (1999), 89
    Macartney Mission (1793), 33, 34
    May Fourth protests (1919), 40–41, 54, 132
    Ming capital (1402–1644), 20
    National Museum, 140
    Olympic Games (2008), 93, 135
    Socialist Youth Corps, 43
    Tiananmen Square massacre (1989), 54, 89, 133–4, 173, 220
Beijing Bicycle, 90
Bejucal, Cuba, 114
Belgrade embassy bombing (1999), 221

Belt and Road Initiative (BRI), 99, 140, 143–6, 164
Berlin Wall, fall of (1989), 2, 54, 221
Beyond Air–Sea Battle (Friedberg), 182
Biden, Joseph, 238
Big Bang Theory, 49
Big Vs, 65
bin Laden, Osama, 99
Bingfa (Sunzi), 110, 183
bio-pharma, 202–3
bio-technology, 112
biometrics, 100, 196
Bo Xilai, 71–2
Bo Yibo, 70
Board of Rites, 24
bolixin, 148
Borneo, 139
Borodin, Mikhail, 44
Boursicot, Bernard, 111, 114
Boustany, Charles, 250
Boxer Rebellion (1899–1901), 37
Brahe, Tycho, 23
brain washing, 96
Brazil, 230
Brecht, Bertolt, 22–3
British Broadcasting Corporation (BBC), 147
British Empire, 33, 143
    Cable and Wireless, 145
    East India Company, 33, 218
    Hong Kong (1841–1997), 132
    Indian colonies (1793–1947), 10, 36
Macartney Mission (1793), 33
Malaya (1826–1957), 111
    opium trade, 33, 35, 218
    Opium Wars, 30, 34
    tea in, 10
British Telecom (BT), 160
'Brother Watch', 64
Buck, Pearl, 88
Buddhism, 89, 130
Buenos Aires, Argentina, 2
Bund, Shanghai, 41–2
Bush, George Walker, 100
BYD, 201
Bytedance, 62, 237
Byzantine Empire (395–1453), 10, 117

C4ISR, 205
Cable and Wireless, 145
California, United States, 160
California Gold Rush (1848–1855), 32, 218
Canada, 116, 119, 147, 167, 171, 232, 247
cao ni ma, 67
capital flight, 232
Capital Gazette, 43
Carnegie Endowment for International Peace 124
Caroline Islands, 139
carrier killer systems, 185
Carter, James 'Jimmy', 180
cartography, 18
cassava, 31
cavalry warfare, 17

Central Intelligence Agency
(CIA), 46, 111, 120, 123, 124
Central Liaison Department, 111
Central Military Commission, 70,
73, 119, 174, 175, 188–9, 205
Century of National Humiliation
(1839–1949), 35, 64, 119, 132,
253
'Chabuduo Xiansheng' (Hu), 39
Chang Heng, 18
Chang'an, 17, 129
Chang'e 4 (2019), 204
Changsha, Hunan, 44
Chaoxian Zhan (Qiao and Wang),
184
chariot warfare, 17
Chen Duxiu, 43
Chen Yun, 70
Chengdu, Sichuan, 71, 219
Chennault, Claire, 219
Chertoff, Michael, 166
Chiang Kai-shek, 44, 95, 110,
132, 176, 180
child pornography, 4
Chin, Larry Wu-Tai, 111
China Academic Network, 54
China Cybersecurity, 83
China Daily, 147
China Development Bank, 164
China Dream, 15, 74, 76, 140,
193, 243
China Global Television Network,
147
China of the Thousand Talents,
121, 199–200

China State Construction
Engineering Corporation, 125
China State Nuclear Power
Technology Corporation, 224
China Through the Ages, 92
China–Pakistan Economic
Corridor (CPEC), 145
Chinalco, 224
ChinaSoft, 83
Chinese Academy of Science, 53
Chinese Communist Party, 43–4
Anti-Rightist Campaign
(1957–9), 48
Central Committee, 76
Central Liaison Department,
111
Central Military Commission,
70, 73, 119, 174, 175, 188–9,
205
Central Party Research Office,
76
Civil War (1927–49), 44–6, 90,
94, 110, 111, 176–7, 219
corruption, 64, 71, 72–4, 91, 92
Cultural Revolution (1966–76),
49–52, 69, 93, 111, 177,
178–9
Cybersecurity Law (2016),
81–2
Document Number Nine
(2013), 74, 83
espionage, 7, 10, 89, 94,
109–27
founding of (1921), 43–4
Four Modernisations (1978),
51–2, 177

Great Leap Forward (1958–62), 48–9, 51
Gutian Conference (1929), 174
Hundred Flowers Campaign (1956), 48
Internet, control of, 5, 61, 62–7
Investigation Department, 111
Japanese War (1937–45), 45, 111, 176, 219
KMT, alliance with (1923–7), 44
legitimacy, 54–5, 71, 90, 95
Long March (1934–5), 45, 176
Mao Zedong Thought, 45–6
National Intelligence Law (2017), 125
Overseas Chinese Affairs Office, 110–11
Politburo Standing Committee, 70, 76
Political and Legal Committee, 73, 120, 224
Propaganda Department, 78, 79, 97, 146, 197
Reform and Opening Up (1978–2005), 51–2, 69, 74, 75, 112
religion, views on, 88–9
Second United Front (1937–41), 176
Secretariat, 76
Social Affairs Department, 111
Soviet split (1956–66), 47, 133
techno-security state, 85, 87–107

Tiananmen Square massacre (1989), 54, 89, 133–4, 173, 220
unitary state narrative, 15–16
United Front Work Department, 110, 146, 147
Xi Jinping Thought, 74–5
Yan'an period (1935–47), 45–6, 93
Youth League, 70
Chinese Exclusion Act (1882), 32, 219
Chinese People's Political Consultative Conference (CPPCC), 197
chinoiserie, 30, 131
Chongqing, 20–21, 71, 237
Choyleva, Diana, 135
Christianity
  cosmology, 22
  crackdown on, 100
  Feng Yuxiang, 38
  Jesuits, 21, 23
  Reformation (c. 1517–1648), 29
  science and, 22, 29
  Taiping Rebellion (1850–64), 36–7
Chung Hwa Book Company, 43
Cisco, 57, 83, 117, 163
Citizen Cloud project, 103
City Brain project, 103
civil service examinations, 27, 28, 36, 37, 40
civil society, 75

Civil War (1927–49), 44, 45, 90, 110, 111, 176–7
civil-military integration, 188, 214
Cixi, Empress Dowager, 37
Claiborne, Candace, 123
classical Chinese, 39, 40, 183
Clean Network initiative (2020), 237
climate change, 141
Clinton, William 'Bill', 2, 5
clocks, 21–2
coal, 143
Cold War
    China–US, 250, 253
    Soviet–US, 5, 10, 134, 154, 222, 243, 246
colour revolutions, 137
Comintern, 44
Commercial Press, 43
Committee on Foreign Investment (CFIUS), 228, 232
common law, 109
community of common destiny, 140–43
compasses, 15, 19
Computer Network Emergency Response Team (CNCERT), 81
Confucianism, 20, 24–5, 26–8, 35, 36, 77
    civil service examinations, 27, 28, 36, 40
    cosmology, 23
    Great Unity, 77
    hierarchy, 25, 26, 77, 130
    military and, 177

neo-Confucianism, 44
patriarchal culture, 39
Self-Strengthening Movement (1861–95), 36, 38
    settled populations and, 31
    tian xia, 130, 141
    xiaokang shehui, 74, 140
Confucius, 24–6, 27, 141
Cook, Tim, 247
Coordinating Committee for Multilateral Export Controls, 119, 220
cosmology, 23–5, 49
cotton, 31
counterfeiting, 61, 82, 104
COVID-19 pandemic (2019–20), 35, 203, 233–9, 241, 245, 251
Croatia, 80
crossbows, 17
Crowdstrike, 83
cryptography, 208
CSIS, 121
Cuba, 114, 155
Cui Tiankai, 238
Cultural Revolution (1966–76), 49–52, 69, 93, 111, 177, 178–9
currency, 12, 61, 196, 225, 227, 243–4
Cyber Administration of China (CAC), 78, 80
Cyber Security Evaluation Centre, UK, 161
Cyber Security Index China, 80
cyber security, 80–85
Cybersecurity Association of China, 81

Cybersecurity Law (2016), 81–2
cyberwarfare, 7–8, 117–18, 154–7

dafang, 72
Dahua, 237
Dalai Lama, 222
dang'an, 90
danwei, 52
Daodejing, 25
Daoism, 25–6
Darwin, Charles, 38, 95
Days of Radiance (Hao), 93
De Rerum Natura (Lucretius), 25
De' Conti Niccolò, 19
Death by China (Navarro), 228
Debt Default Checker, 105–6
'Declaration of the Independence
    of Cyberspace' (Barlow), 2, 5
Defence White Paper (2019), 189,
    207
Delano, Warren, 218
Dell, 233, 248
Demers, John, 121
Democracy Movement (1978–89),
    54, 70, 89, 133–4, 173, 220
Democratic People's Party (DPP),
    181
Democritus of Abdera, 22
demographics, 32, 194–5, 242
Deng Xiaoping, 51, 70, 112,
    133–4
    Cultural Revolution (1966–76),
        51
    Four Modernisations (1978),
        51–2, 177

'hide and bide' strategy, 134,
    139
Plan 863 (1986), 112
Special Economic Zones, 69
Taiwan, relations with, 181
Tiananmen Square massacre
    (1989), 54, 133–4
Toffler, reading of, 53
Vietnam War (1979), 179
Denmark, 80
Deobandism, 36
Department of Commerce, US,
    151, 168, 169, 170
Department of Defense, US, 123,
    167, 214
Department of Justice, US, 162,
    170, 223
Department of State, US, 123,
    124, 219
Derbyshire, England, 117
Deutsche Bank, 249
diabetes, 18
dialects, 55–6
diaosi, 91
diaspora, 147
dictionaries, 56
digital currency, 61, 196
Digital Silk Road, 164
Dikotter, Frank, 48
Ding Xiangrong, 205
discourse power, 146
distributed denial of service
    (DDoS), 6
Divine Right of Kings, 95
Djibouti, 186

Document Number Nine (2013), 74, 83
Doll's House, A (Ibsen), 39
Domain Name System (DNS), 151
dot-com boom (1995–2000), 4
Dream of Ding Village, 93
drones, 184, 187, 206, 214
Dubs, Homer, 129

East China Sea, 139, 223
East India Company, 33, 218
East Turkestan Islamic Movement (ETIM), 99–100
eBay, 59
economic revolutions, 30–31
education
  civil service examinations, 27, 28, 30, 36, 37, 40
  Cultural Revolution (1966–76), 49–50, 51, 52
  ideology, role of, 213
  overseas, 37, 53, 58, 148, 232
  Patriotic Education Campaign, 64, 97
  STEM subjects, 6, 200, 211, 213
Egypt, 80
Eight Guardian Warriors, 83
Eight Immortals, 70
Einstein, Albert, 50, 209
electoral democracy, 74, 75, 175, 181
electric vehicles, 201
electronic design automation (EDA), 169

elite capture, 147
Elvin, Mark, 29, 30
energy, 112, 143
Enlightenment (c. 1637–1789), 30, 217
Entities List, US, 102, 168
Epicureanism, 25
Epoch Times, 89
Ericsson, 165
espionage, 7, 10, 89, 94, 109–27, 163, 166, 223–4, 232
Estonia, 6
Ethiopia, 125
European Union (EU), 152, 160, 210, 245
Evolution and Ethics (Huxley), 38
Experian, 105

F-35 stealth fighters, 176
Facebook, 63, 65
facial recognition software, 98, 102, 201, 214
facts, 29
Falungong, 88–9, 114
Fan Girls, 65
Fang Fenghui, 175
Fang Lizhi, 23
fanquan nu, 65
Federal Bureau of Investigation (FBI), 113–14, 232
Federally Administered Tribal Areas, Pakistan, 99, 206
Feng Yuxiang, 38
fiancé hiring, 60
Field Programmable Gate Arrays, 211

fifth-generation telecommunications (5G), 8, 158, 159, 165–8, 170, 196, 237, 250
Fifty-Cent Party, 65–6
film, 93, 147
fingerspitzgefuehl, 122
FireEye, 120
fireworks, 17
first island chain, 139, 185
Five-Eyes, 6, 119, 166, 247
Five-Year Plans, 116, 202
Flying Tigers, 219
food imports, 230
Foreign Broadcast Information Service, 111
Four Books and Five Classics, 27
'Four Comprehensives' (2014), 82
'Four Modernisations' (1978), 51–2, 177
Foxconn, 92
France, 29, 40, 137, 167, 177, 198, 209
Free Tibet, 114
freedom of expression, 4, 156
Friedberg, Aaron, 182, 250
Fudan University, Shanghai, 43, 213
Fujian, 19, 70, 98, 105, 174
fur trade, 218
Future Shock (Toffler), 53
Fuzhou, Fujian, 105

G77, 152, 153
Galilei, Galileo, 22–3
ganchao, 48, 193

Gang of Four, 51
Gao Yu, 74
Gates, Robert, 175
GCHQ, 161
gene editing, 203
Geng Biao, 69
geoheliocentric model, 23
George III, King of the United Kingdom, 34
George, Henry, 39
Georgia, 6, 137
Germany, 40, 75, 80, 132, 202, 253
Ghost Net, 114
ginseng, 218
glass heart, 148–9
global financial crisis (2007–8), 135–6, 222
Global Information Infrastructure (GII), 2–3
global positioning systems, 205
Global War on Terror, 100, 136
globalisation, 141, 227, 242, 246, 248
Go (game), 198, 199
Golden Shield Project, 5, 63
Google, 63, 83, 84, 151, 199, 209, 214
Gore, Albert 'Al', 2–3
Governance of China, The (Xi), 74–5
Graphics Processing Units (GPUs), 211
grass-mud horses, 67
Great Coco Island, Myanmar, 114

Great Firewall of China, 5, 63
Great Leap Forward (1958–62),
   48–9, 51
great powers, 12, 137, 141, 143,
   191
Great Unity, 77
Great Wall of China, 88
Greece, 22, 24, 145
Green Gang, 37
Green Revolution (2009), 137
grey zone operations, 7, 109
grid management system, 97
groundnuts, 31
Gruzenberg, Mikhail, 44
Gu Kailai, 72
Guam, 139, 185
guanggun jie, 60
Guangming Daily, 90
Guangxu, Qing Emperor, 37
Guangzhou, Guangdong, 33, 44,
   103
Gui Minhai, 125
Guizhou, 32
Gulf War
   First (1990–91), 136, 179
   Second (2003–11), 137, 222
gun boat diplomacy, 132
gunpowder, 15, 17
Guo Boxiong, 73, 175
Guomindang, 21
   Civil War (1927–49), 44, 45,
      90, 110, 111, 176–7, 219
   espionage, 110, 111
   Hollywood, relations with, 132
   Japanese War (1937–45), 45,
      176, 219

mental hygiene (*xinli weisheng*),
   95–6
Second United Front (1937–
   41), 176
South China Sea policy, 138
Taiwan, retreat to (1949), 45,
   110, 180
United Nations and, 180
Gutian Conference (1929), 174
Gwadar, Pakistan, 145

H-20 strategic bombers, 187
H-6 strategic bombers, 187
hacking, 4, 83, 115, 120, 121
hai gui, 232
Hainan Island Incident (2001),
   125–6, 222
Hambantota, Sri Lanka, 144
Han dynasty
   Eastern (25–220 CE), 17, 18,
      27, 88, 129
   Western (206 BCE–9 CE), 17,
      26, 27, 129
Handbook for China, 42
Hangzhou, Zhejiang, 103
Hanyu pinyin, 57
Harmonious Society, 76
Harpy drones, 206
Harvard Kennedy School, 107
He Jiankui, 203
He Shang, 54
healthcare, 18, 40, 50, 103, 202–3
Hebei, 70
Hefei, Anhui, 210
heliocentric model, 23

Hellfire missiles, 206
hemp, 30
Henry Jackson Society, 247
Hewlett Packard, 233, 248
hexie, 67
Heywood, Neil, 72
hide and bide strategy, 134, 139
Hikvision, 102, 237
Hiram Maxim, 132
historical determinism, 138, 242
historical nihilism, 74
HNA, 233
Hoffman, Samantha, 106
Hollywood, 94, 132
Holy Roman Empire (800–1806),
    131
Homeland Security, 166
Hong Kong
    airlines and, 106, 148
    BAT in, 61
    British colony (1841–1997),
        132
    COVID-19 pandemic (2019–
        20), 233, 237
    Extradition Law protests
        (2019–20), 65, 126, 149, 182
    Gui Minhai rendition (2015),
        125
    Occupy movement (2014), 66
    One Country, Two Systems,
        181, 182
    South China Morning Post, 147
    Special Economic Zones and,
        52
Hong Xiuquan, 36–7

Hongmen, 37
Hongwu, Ming Emperor, 20, 88
hostile foreign forces, 85, 94, 138
Houseman, Susan, 247
Houston Rockets, 149
Houston, Texas, 121, 236
HSBC, 171
Hu Angang, 75
Hu Jintao, 70–71, 76, 134, 174,
    176, 186, 223
Hu Shi, 39
hu xuan nu, 130
Hu Yaobang, 54
Huainanzi, 26
Huangdi Neijing, 18
Huawei, 8, 58, 116, 124, 145,
    157–71, 213, 231, 237, 250
huayuquan, 146
Hudson Institute, 226
Hui people, 99, 100
hukou, 90
human intelligence (HUMINT),
    110, 121, 122
human rights, 106, 115, 156, 222,
    237
Hundred Flowers Campaign
    (1956), 48
Huxley, Thomas, 38
IBM, 83, 160, 209
Ibn Battuta, 19
Ibn Taymiyyah, 35–6
Ibsen, Henrik, 39
iFlytek, 102, 201
immortality, 26
immunology, 18

Imperial examinations, 27, 28, 36, 37, 40
In the Name of the People, 74
India, 10, 36, 130, 145, 167
Indonesia, 111, 139, 194
industrial espionage, 115–22, 224
Industrial Revolution (c. 1760–1840), 9, 12, 28–9, 35, 117, 194
inferiority complex, 254
information warfare, 5, 6–7, 154–5
informatisation, 55, 58, 78, 183, 189, 190
Intel, 83
Intellectual Property (IP), 82, 115–22, 162, 168, 213, 224–5, 228, 232
intelligentisation, 189
Intermediate-Range Nuclear Forces Treaty (1987), 185
International Electrotechnical Commission (IEC), 196
International Organisation for Standardisation (ISO), 196
International Telecommunications Union (ITU), 80, 153, 157–8, 196
Internet, 2–8, 55–67, 78–85, 151–72, 195
   cafés (*wang ba*), 59
   censorship, 5, 62, 66–7, 79, 92, 158
   criminality on, 4, 7, 80, 82
   cyberwarfare, 7–8, 117–18, 154–7

   dating services, 59
   Domain Name System (DNS), 151
   espionage, 7, 10, 89, 114
   governance, 151–4
   fiancé hiring, 60
   food delivery, 59
   gaming, 59
   information warfare, 5, 6–7, 154
   Internet of Things, 159, 195, 196
   language and, 55–7
   malware, 6
   nationalism and, 64–5, 94
   New Internet Protocol, 157–8
   payment systems, 60–61
   pornography, 4, 59
   quantum technology, 208–10
   security, 78–85, 154–8
   shopping, 59
   sovereignty, 5, 9, 79–80, 155–6
   surveillance capitalism, 4–5
   terms for, 55
   video streaming, 60
Internet Corporation for Assigned Names and Numbers (ICANN), 151, 153–4
Internet Engineering Task Force (IETF), 152
Internet Governance Forum, 152
Internet of Things, 159, 195, 196
Internet Plus initiative, 60, 81, 195
Investigation Department (ID/CCP), 111

investigative reporting, 92
Iran, 7, 123, 137, 170–71
Iraq, 136, 137, 179, 206
iron, 16
Islam, 99–103
Islamic State, 206
Islamic world, 22, 23, 35–6
Israel, 200, 206
Italy, 80, 167, 235
Ivanov, Igor, 154

J-20 stealth fighters, 175–6, 187
Jabhat Fatah al-Sham, 100
Japan
 Chinese nationalism and, 64–5,
  93
 Chinese War, First (1894–95),
  37
 Chinese War, Second (1937–
  45), 20–21, 45, 111, 132,
  176, 219
 cyberwarfare, 119, 121
 first island chain and, 139
 industrial espionage, 117, 119,
  121
 Korea colony (1910–45), 46
 modernity in, 40
 Manchukuo (1932–45), 46
 Mukden Incident (1931), 46
 Pacific War (1941–5), 166
 Perry Expedition (1853–54),
  253–4
 piracy, 20
 Plaza Accord (1985), 227,
  243–4

 robotics in, 202
 Taiwan colony (1895–45), 46,
  180
 UNSC affair (2005), 64–5
 Versailles Treaty (1919), 40,
  132
jaywalking, 98
al-Jazeera, 147
Jesuits, 21, 23, 131
jian ai, 26
Jiang Qing, 93
Jiang Shigong, 75, 142
Jiang Zemin, 53, 71, 76, 160, 182
Jiangsu, 70, 121
Jiangxi, 45
Jiaoliang Wusheng, 154
Joint Intelligence Committee,
 UK, 125
Journey to the West, The, 130
Ju Dou, 93
Judaism, 101
Jurchen, 18
just-in-time delivery, 247

Kaifeng, Henan, 101
Kang Sheng, 111
Kangxi Dictionary (1716), 56
Kazakhs, 99
Keji Ribao, 169
KGB (Komitet Gosudarstvennoy
 Bezopasnosti), 126
Khitan, 18
Khrushchev, Nikita, 47, 133, 147
kidnapping, 125
Kindleberger Trap, 143

King, Mervyn, 136
Kirin microchips, 169
Kissinger, Henry, 223
'Kong Yiji' (Lu Xun), 40
Kong Zhongni, 24–5
Korean War (1950–53), 133, 177, 220
Korla, Xinjiang, 114
Kosovo War (1998–9), 183, 221
Kryuchkov, Vladimir, 126
Kuhn, Philip, 31–2
Kushan Empire (30–375), 129
Kushner, Jared, 226

lacquer, 16
landlords, 47
lang wenhua, 161
language, 55–7
lasers, 112
laudanum, 219
Law of Armed Conflict (LOAC), 109, 156, 157
Leading Small Groups (LSGs), 77–8
Leben des Galilei (Brecht), 22–3
Lee Kai-fu, 58, 200
Lee Teng-hui, 182
Legalism, 25
Leibniz, Gottfried, 30
Leninism, 10, 45, 49, 50, 71, 72, 76, 82, 94, 110
Lenovo, 53–4
Leung, Katherine, 113–14
Lewis Turning Point, 194
Li Baoding, 155

Li Dazhao, 43
Li Hongzhang, 132
Li Keqiang, 81
Li Peng, 71
Li Xiannian, 70
Liangjiahe, Shaanxi, 50, 69
liberalism, 39, 75
Liberation Army Daily, 77
Libya, 137, 206
Life of Galileo, The (Brecht), 22–3
Lighthizer, Robert, 226, 227
LinkedIn, 123
Linyi, Shandong, 98
List, Friedrich, 230
listening stations, 114
literacy, 30, 50, 56
literature, 93
Little Ice Age (c. 1550–1850), 87
little pinks, 65
Liu He, 227, 229, 230
Liujia, Fujian, 19
Liverpool, Merseyside, 42
loans, 61
Lombe, John, 117
Long March (1934–5), 45, 176
Lou Jiwei, 197
Lu Gwei-djen, 20
Lu Wei, 78–80
Lu Xun, 39–40
Lucretius, 25
luoti ganbu, 73
Luoyang, 17

M. Butterfly, 111
Ma Yinchu, 194

Ma, Jack, 60
Macao, 106, 132
Macartney Mission (1793), 33–4
MacKinnon, Rebecca, 67
Made in China 2025 strategy, 84,
    120, 122, 195–7, 243
magnetic compasses, 15, 19
maize, 31
Malaya (1826–1957), 111
Malaysia, 101, 102, 145
Mallory, Kevin, 123
Malthus, Thomas, 32
malware, 6
Mancall, Mark, 130
Manchukuo (1932–45), 46
Manchuria, 37, 46
Manchus, 18, 32, 87
Mandate of Heaven, 24, 25, 130,
    141
Mandiant, 83
Manhattan Project (1942–6),
    219–20
manufacturing, 57–8, 188, 194,
    225, 233, 246–51
    automation, 3, 159, 202, 246,
    248
Mao Dun, 42
Mao Zedong, 43, 45, 133
    Anti-Rightist Campaign
    (1957–9), 48
    Civil War (1927–49), 45–6, 176
    Cultural Revolution (1966–76),
    49–50, 51, 52, 69, 93, 111
    Forum on Art and Literature,
    93

Great Leap Forward (1958–62),
    48–9
Gutian Conference (1929), 174
Hundred Flowers Campaign
    (1956), 48
Peking University librarian
    (1918–19), 43–4
People's War, 178
population control, views on,
    194
Second United Front (1937–41),
    176
Soviet split (1956–66), 47, 133
statues of, 100
Taiwan, relations with, 180,
    181
Three Worlds theory, 133
Yan'an period (1935–47), 45–6,
    93
written language, views on, 56
Mao's Great Famine (Dikotter), 48
Mariana Islands, 139
maritime technology, 18–19, 136,
    139, 178, 186
Marshall, George, 219
Marxism–Leninism, 10, 43, 45,
    49, 50, 71, 72, 76, 82, 138, 242
Massachusetts Institute of
    Technology (MIT), 247
mathematics, 18
May Fourth Movement (1919–
    21), 40–41, 54, 132
McCarthy, Joseph, 219
McKinsey, 160
Me Too, 67

medicine, 18, 40, 202–3
'Medicine' (Lu Xun), 40
Megvii Technology, 102
Meiguo fandui Meiguo (Wang), 76
Mencius, 27, 141
Meng Jianzhu, 224
Meng Wanzhou, 171
Mengzi, 27, 141
mental hygiene, 95–6
mercantilism, 224, 225, 251
Methodism, 38
Mexico, 107, 132
Micius, 26–7
Micius satellite, 27, 209, 211
Microsoft, 57, 83, 151, 209
middle-income trap, 71, 119, 194
Midnight (Mao Dun), 42
military technologies, 113
millenarianism, 77
Ming dynasty (1368–1644),
    19–20, 21–2, 23, 30, 36, 88,
    131
mini-Ice Age (c. 1550–1850), 87
Ministry of Foreign Affairs, 78,
    235
Ministry of Industry and
    Information Technology, 78
Ministry of Public Security, 62,
    64, 65, 78, 80, 111, 112
Ministry of Science and
    Technology, 58
Ministry of State Security, 112,
    114, 120, 121, 238
Mnuchin, Steven, 227
Mohamed, Mahathir, 101

Mongol Empire (1206–1368), 18,
    35–6, 130
Mongols, 18, 20
moon, 204
Motorola, 117, 163
Mozi, 26–7, 209
Mukden Incident (1931), 46
Mulvenon, James, 174
Musk, Elon, 201
Myanmar, 114

'naked officials', 73
Nanfang Zhoumo, 92
Nanjing, 20, 105
National Aeronautics and Space
    Administration (NASA), 204
National Basketball Association
    (NBA), 149
National Bureau of Asian
    Research, 250
National Council for Social
    Security, 197
National Development Reform
    Commission, 105
National I tutes of Health (NIH),
    232
National Information Security
    Standardisation Technical
    Committee, 81
National Intellectual Property
    Administration, 212
National Intelligence Council,
    US, 125
National Intelligence Law (2017),
    125, 127, 163

National Laboratory for Quantum
  Information Sciences, 210
National Museum, Beijing, 140
National Security Agency, US,
  81, 118, 156
National Security Council, 77
National Security Law (2014), 81
National Security Strategy, 226,
  228
National Security Week, 94
National Space Science Centre,
  204
nationalism, 64–5, 91, 146
  art and, 94
  glass heart, 148–9
Nationalist Party, see Guomindang
Navarro, Peter, 227–8
Nazi Germany (1933–45), 75
Needham, Joseph, 20–21, 22, 26,
  28
Neihan Duanzi, 62
neo-authoritarianism, 75–6
neo-Confucianism, 44
neo-Maoism, 75
neologisms, 56
neural networks, 198
New Army, 37
New Culture Movement (c.
  1915–19), 39–40
New Internet Protocol, 157
new materials, 112
New Population Theory, 194
New Zealand, 119, 147, 148, 167,
  247
Newton, Isaac, 26

Next Generation Artificial
  Intelligence Plan, 197–201
NICE decade (1998–2008), 136
nine-dash line, 138
Nixon, Richard, 133, 180, 220
Nobel Prize, 206
Nokia, 165
Non-Aligned Movement, 133
non-official cover officers (NOCs),
  112
Norinco, 178, 208
North China Daily News, 43
North China Herald, 43
North Korea, 7, 135, 170, 222,
  223
Northern Expedition (1926–7),
  44
nuclear weapons, 46–7, 99, 113,
  178, 187, 219–20, 243
Nye, Joseph, 143

Obama, Barack, 66, 119, 136,
  138, 165, 223, 224
Occupy Hong Kong (2014), 66
Office of National Intelligence,
  Australia, 125
Office of Personnel Management
  (OPM), 124
Office of the US Trade
  Representative, 224
Olympic Games, 93, 135
One Country, Two Systems, 181
one-child policy (1979–2015),
  194
One-China policy, 225

Open Radio Access Network, 168
Operation Fox Hunt (2014–), 74
operations short of war, 7
opium, 33, 35, 38, 218, 219
Opium Wars
First (1839–42), 30, 34
Second (1856–60), 34
Oracle, 83, 169
Ou Yanghai zhi Ge (Jin), 93
Outer Space Treaty (1967), 204
Overseas Chinese Affairs Office,
110–11

paedophilia, 4
Pakistan, 99, 145, 206
Pan Hannian, 176
Pan Jianwei, 209
paper, 15
Parthian Empire (247 BCE–224
CE), 129
Partial Disengagement, 250
Partido Revolucionario
Institucional (PRI), 107
Patriotic Education Campaign,
64, 97
Paulson, Henry 'Hank', 231
peaceful evolution, 85, 154
peaceful rise, 134
Peking Socialist Youth Corps, 43
Peking University, 43, 200
Pence, Michael, 226, 227
Peng Zhen, 70
People's Daily, 92, 194
People's Liberation Army (PLA),
136, 146, 173–91

Air Force, 178, 186–7
Anti-Access, Area Denial
(A2AD), 182, 184
Artificial Intelligence, 205–8
ASAT test (2007), 175
business activity, 52, 178
Civil War (1927–49), 44–6,
176–7
civil-military integration, 188,
214
corruption, 73, 120, 175, 178
Cultural Revolution (1966–76),
177, 178–9
cyberwarfare, 177, 189
Defence White Paper (2019),
189, 207
gaming, use of, 59
General Command, 189
General Staff, Second Department, (2/PLA), 112, 189
General Staff, Third Department, (3/PLA), 114, 119,
120, 189
Gutian Conference (1929), 174
Huawei and, 160, 162
Korean War (1950–53), 133,
177
missiles 184–5, 205
modernisation, 136, 177, 184,
188–90
Navy, 136, 139, 178, 186
People's War, 178, 179
quantum technology, 210
restructuring, 188–90
san da jilu, baxiang zhuyi, 176

Silent Contest (2013), 154

Strategic Rocket Force, 187, 189

Strategic Support Force, 189, 205

Taiwan, relations with, 180–82, 184

Tiananmen Square massacre (1989), 54, 173

Unit 61398 indictments (2013), 223–4

Vietnam War (1979), 52, 173, 178–9

People's Republic of China (1949–)

Anti-Rightist Campaign (1957–9), 48

Belt and Road Initiative (2013–), 99, 140, 143–6, 164

China Dream (2012–), 15, 74, 76, 140, 193, 243

community of common destiny, 140–43

COVID-19 pandemic (2019–20), 35, 203, 233–9, 241, 245

Cultural Revolution (1966–76), 49–52, 69, 93, 111, 177, 178–9

Cybersecurity Law (2016), 81–2

Defence White Paper (2019), 189, 207

Democracy Movement (1978–89), 54, 70, 89, 133–4, 173, 220

East China Sea policy, 139, 223

espionage, 7, 10, 89, 94, 109–27, 163, 223–4, 232

Falungong, 88–9, 114

foundation of (1949), 45, 133

Four Modernisations (1978), 51–2, 177

global financial crisis (2007–8), 135–6, 222

Great Leap Forward (1958–62), 48, 51

Hainan Island Incident (2001), 125–6, 222

Hundred Flowers Campaign (1956), 48

Korean War (1950–53), 133, 177

Made in China 2025 strategy, 84, 120, 122, 195–7, 243

National Intelligence Law (2017), 125

one-child policy (1979–2015), 194

Olympic Games (2008), 93, 135

population, 194–5, 242

pre-1949 debts, 236

Reform and Opening Up (1978–2005), 51–2, 69, 74, 75, 112

South China Sea policy, 138–9, 142, 223, 237

Soviet assistance (1949–60), 46–7

Soviet split (1956–66), 47, 133

Taiwan Strait Crises (1954–5, 1958), 180

techno-security state, 85,
   87–107
Tiananmen Square massacre
   (1989), 54, 89, 133–4, 173,
   220
UN accession (1971), 180
Vietnam War (1979), 52, 173,
   178–9
WTO accession (2001), 60,
   134, 222, 247
Xinjiang, 98–103, 144, 201,
   237
People's Three Principles, 44
People's War, 178, 179
Permanent Court of Arbitration,
   138
Perrault, Claude, 29
Personal Information Security
   Specifications (2018), 82
Phase One deal (2020), 230
Philippines, 138, 139
Piedmont, 117
pinyin, 57
piracy, 20, 186
Piraeus, Greece, 145
Plan 863 (1986), 112
Plato, 22
Plaza Accord (1985), 227
poison gas, 17
pollution, 59, 60, 143, 230, 242
Polo, Marco, 19
Polytechnologies, 178
Pompeo, Michael, 236, 238, 246
population, 32, 194–5, 242
porcelain, 16, 31, 33

pornography, 4, 59
Portugal, 31
potatoes, 31
Pottinger, Matthew, 162, 246
Precision Medicine Initiative, 203
Predator drones, 206
princelings, 70
Princeton University, 250
printing, 15
Project Maven, 214
Prolonged War, 178, 179
Propaganda Department, 78, 79,
   97, 146, 197
property rights, 29
protests, 91–2
psychiatry, 95–6
Puyi, Qing Emperor, 37, 46

Qadhafi, Muamar, 137
al-Qaeda, 99–100
Qian Xuesen, 219
Qianlong, Qing Emperor, 32
Qiao Liang, 184
Qin dynasty (221–206 BCE), 25
Qin Shi Huang, 25
Qing dynasty (1644–1912), 23,
   32, 33–7
   Boxer Rebellion (1899–1901),
      37
   foreign concessions, 34–5, 40,
      41, 43, 132, 218
   gun boat diplomacy, 132
   Japanese War (1894–95), 37
   Kangxi Dictionary (1716), 56
   Macartney Mission (1793),
      33–4

Malthusian dilemma, 32
Opium War, First (1839–42), 30, 34
Opium War, Second (1856–60), 34
Self-Strengthening Movement (1861–95), 36, 38
Taiping Rebellion (1850–64), 36–7
Treaty of Nanking (1842), 218
Treaty of Nerchinsk (1687), 131
Treaty of Wangxia (1844), 218
treaty ports, 41, 218
Xinhai Revolution (1911–12), 37
White Lotus Rebellion (1794–1804), 88
Qitai, Xinjiang, 114
Qiushi, 174, 229
Qualcomm, 83, 168
quality of life, 91
quantum technology, 27, 208–10, 211, 252
queues, 32
Quran, 102

racial identity, 15, 39, 74
Radio Free Europe, 154
Raise High the Red Lantern, 93
Rao Yi, 200
Rape of Nanjing (1937–8), 20
Red Sorghum, 93
Red Star Over China (Snow), 45
Red Turban Rebellions (1351–1368), 88

Reform and Opening Up (1978–2005), 51–2, 69, 74, 75, 112
Reformation (c. 1517–1648), 29
Ren Zhengfei, 159, 161, 163, 168, 171
renminbi, 12, 135, 225
Republic of China (1912–49), 38–46
  Civil War (1927–49), 44–6, 90, 94, 110, 111, 176–7, 180
  Communist Party founding of (1921), 43–4
  espionage, 110, 111
  foreign concessions, 40–43, 132
  Hollywood, relations with, 132
  Japanese War (1937–45), 20–21, 45, 111, 132, 176, 219
  Long March (1934–5), 45, 176
  May Fourth Movement (1919–21), 40–41, 54, 132
  mental hygiene (*xinli weisheng*), 95–6
  Mukden Incident (1931), 46
  New Culture Movement (c. 1915–21), 39–40
  Northern Expedition (1926–7), 44
  Second United Front (1937–41), 176
  South China Sea policy, 138
  Versailles Treaty (1919), 40–41, 132
  World War I (1914–18), 40
  Xi'an Incident (1936), 94, 176

Responsibility to Protect, 137
retorsion, 228
Retreat of the Elephants, The
(Elvin), 29
Revolution in Military Affairs,
136, 179
Ricci, Matteo, 21–2, 23, 30, 131
rice rabbit, 67
rice, 30
RIMPAC (Rim of the Pacific
Exercise), 186
river crabs, 67
River Elegy, 54
robotics, 195, 196, 202
Roman Empire (27 BCE–476
CE), 129
Romance of Three Kingdoms, 45
Roosevelt, Franklin Delano, 218
Rose Revolution (2003), 137
Ross, Wilbur, 227
Royal Navy, 186
rule by law, 82
rule of law, 74, 75, 76, 82, 163
Rulin Waishi (Wu), 28
Russian Empire (1721–1917), 42,
43, 46, 131
Russian Federation (1991–)
cybersecurity, 153, 154, 155,
156
cyberwarfare, 5–6, 8, 115
Georgian War (2008), 6
INF Treaty expiration (2019),
185
Shanghai Cooperation Organ-
isation (SCO), 135

Su-35 fighters, 186–7
Russian Revolution (1917), 42, 43

sabotage, 7
Safe Cities initiative, 98
saibo, 55
SAIC, 201
samizdat, 154
Samsung, 165
Sandia National Laboratories, 115
sang wenhua, 91
Sanguo Yanyi, 45
sanmin zhuyi, 44
Sanshiliu Ji, 110
Santiago de Cuba, 114
satellites, 6, 27, 153, 175, 183,
205, 209–10, 211
Saudi Arabia, 7, 99
SCADA (Supervisory Control
and Data Acquisition), 123
Schmitt, Carl, 75
Science and Technology Daily, 169
scientific method, 29–30
Scientific Outlook on
Development, 76
sea turtles, 232
Second Artillery, 187
second island chain, 139, 185
Second United Front (1937–41),
176
Seeking Facts, 174, 229
seismology, 18
self-criticism, 46, 96
Self-Strengthening Movement
(1861–95), 36, 38

semiconductor industry, 52
SenseTime Group, 102, 201
Serve the People, 93
Sesame Credit, 104–5
Shaanxi, 45, 50, 69
Shandong, 40, 98, 132
Shang dynasty (c. 1600–1046
   BCE), 17, 141
Shang Shu, 141
Shanghai, 41–4, 70, 80, 93, 123
   African Union data in, 125,
      163
   American Concession (1848–
      63), 218
   Citizen Cloud project, 103
   French Concession (1849–
      1943), 41, 44
   International Settlement
      (1863–1941), 41, 218
   3/PLA, 114, 119, 120
   universities, 43
Shanghai Cooperation
   Organisation (SCO), 135
Shangri-La Dialogue, 223
Shanxi, 38
Shaoshan, Hunan, 50
Shaoxing, Zhejiang, 39
Sharp Eyes Project, 98
Shen Bao, 43
sheng nü, 195
Shenzhen, Guangdong, 98, 159,
   194
Shenzhou space programme,
   203–4
Shi Beipu, 111

Shields, Brian, 116
Shuihu Zhuan, 88
Shun Emperor, 141
Siberia, 131
Sichuan, 34
   earthquake (2008), 92
'sick man of Asia', 35, 241
Siemens, 169
signals intelligence (SIGINT),
   110, 114, 148
Silent Contest, 154
Silicon Valley, 5, 58, 199, 214,
   252
Silk Road, 129
silk, 10, 31, 33
silver, 20, 33, 35
Singles Day, 60
Sino–American Mutual Defense
   Treaty (1954), 180
Sino–Japanese War
   First (1894–95), 37
   Second (1937–45), 20–21, 45,
      111, 132, 176
Sino–Vietnamese War (1979), 52,
   173, 178–9
Sishu Wujing, 27
Six-Party Talks (2003–9), 135
sixth-generation telecommunica-
   tions (6G), 168
Skycom, 170
Skynet project, 97–8
smallpox, 18
smart cities, 103, 164, 201
smartphones, 59, 169, 170
Smith, Adam, 5

Snow, Edgar, 45, 56
Snowden, Edward, 81, 118, 156
Social Affairs Department, 111
Social Credit schemes, 103–6, 148
Social Darwinism, 38, 95
social media, 4, 61, 62–7, 94, 137, 148
soft power, 143, 147, 243, 244
Somalia, 186
Song dynasty (960–1279), 22, 97
Song of Ou Yanghai, The (Jin), 93
Song Renqiong, 70
'Sorcerer's Apprentice' war, 208
Soulstealers (Kuhn), 31–2
South China Morning Post, 147
South China Sea, 138–9, 142, 223
South Korea, 117, 223
Southern Weekly, 92
Soviet Union (1922–91), 2, 45, 46–7, 99
    Chernobyl disaster (1986), 234
    collapse (1991), 6, 54, 107, 154, 180, 221, 245
    global revolution, 91
    industry, focus on, 48
    information warfare, 154
    Intermediate-Range Nuclear Forces Treaty (1987), 185
    KGB, 126
    Khrushchev's secret speech (1956), 47, 133
    KMT, relations with, 44
    literature in, 93
    Outer Space Treaty (1967), 204
    SIGINT on, 114

Sino-Soviet split (1956–66), 47, 133
Sputnik 1 launch (1957), 167, 243
STEM subjects in, 6
technological assistance (1949–60), 46–7
World War II (1939–45), 132–3
Space Force, US, 205
space, 112, 203–5
Spain, 29, 235
Special Economic Zones, 52, 69
Spencer, Herbert, 38
Spring and Autumn period (777–476 BCE), 110, 130
Spring Festival, 60, 233
Sputnik 1 satellite, 167, 243
Sri Lanka, 144
St John's University, Shanghai, 43
Stalin, Joseph, 44, 45, 93, 133
Standard and Poor 500 index, 249
State Council, 197
state-owned enterprises (SOEs), 61, 115
stealth aircraft, 175–6, 187, 207
steel production, 49
STEM subjects, 6, 200, 211, 213
stirrups, 17
Story of Qiu Ju, The, 93
Strategic Rocket Force, 187, 189
Strategic Support Force, 189, 205
Study of Sociology, The (Spencer), 38
Stuxnet attack (2010), 123
Su-35 fighters, 186–7

submarines, 113, 186
Sukarno, 111
Sun Yat-sen, 37, 44
Sunni Islam, 99
Sunnylands summit (2013), 66, 224
Sunzi, 110, 183
surveillance capitalism, 4–5
Sweden, 160
Symantec, 83
Syria, 35, 100, 137, 206

Taiping Rebellion (1850–64), 36–7
Taiwan, 148, 180–82, 184
  airlines and, 106, 148
  COVID-19 pandemic (2019–20), 245
  espionage, 110
  first island chain, 139
  Foxconn, 92
  Guomindang withdrawal to (1949), 45, 110, 180
  identity in, 182
  Japanese occupation (1895–45), 46, 180
  One Country, Two Systems, 181, 182
  reunification prospects, 170, 181–2
  United States, relations with, 180–82, 221, 222
Taiwan Relations Act (1979), 180–81
Taiwan Semiconductor

  Manufacturing Corporation (TSMC), 170
Taiwan Strait Crisis
  First (1954–5), 180
  Second (1958), 180
  Third (1995–6), 181, 221, 222
Tallinn, Estonia, 6
Tang dynasty (618–907 CE), 17, 129–30
tea, 10, 30, 33
techno-security state, 85, 87–107
telecommunications, 58
  Belt and Road Initiative and, 145–6
  espionage and, 124–5, 163, 166
  fifth generation (5G), 8, 158, 159, 165–8, 170, 196, 237, 250
  International Telecommunication Union (ITU), 80, 153, 157–8, 196
  IP theft, 116–17
  sixth generation (6G), 168
Telegraph, 147
Tencent, 9, 61, 201, 211, 237
terrorism, 63, 81, 100, 136, 141, 156
Tesla, 201
Texas, United States, 160, 168
Thailand, 125
Third Generation Partnership Project (3GPP), 165
Third Wave, The (Toffler), 53
Thirty-Six Stratagems, The, 110
thought reform, 46, 96

Thousand Talents programme, 121, 199–200
Three Leaf, 170
Three Represents, 76
Three Worlds theory, 133
Thucydides Trap, 11, 134, 253
tian xia, 130, 141
Tiananmen Square massacre (1989), 54, 89, 133–4, 173
Tiangong space laboratories, 204
Tianjin
  AI investment fund (2018), 198
  American Concession (1860–1902), 218
  explosions (2015), 64
  World Economic Forum (2014), 79
Tibet, 18, 100, 114, 135, 220, 222
tibi wangzi, 57
Tiger Trap (Wise), 113
TikTok, 62, 237
Titan Rain, 115
Toffler, Alvin, 53
Tongmenghui, 37
Torch programme, 58
Trans-Pacific Partnership (TPP), 225
Treaty of Nanking (1842), 218
Treaty of Nerchinsk (1687), 131
Treaty of Versailles (1919), 40–41, 43, 132
Treaty of Wangxia (1844), 218
tribute system, 19, 34, 130–31
Trivium, 105
Trotsky, Leon, 106

Trump, Donald, 197, 214, 225–38, 248–9, 250
Trump, Ivanka, 226
Tsinghua University, 69
tuberculosis, 40
Tungusic peoples, 87
Turkey, 80, 218
Turkic peoples, 87, 130
Twitter, 61, 63, 65, 148
Type 055 cruiser, 186

Uighur Human Rights Policy Act (2020), 101
Uighurs, 99–103
unitary state, 15–16
United Front Work Department, 110, 146, 147
United Kingdom
  AI research in, 199
  Cable and Wireless, 145
  Cyber Security Evaluation Centre, UK, 161
  East India Company, 33, 218
  Five-Eyes, 6, 119, 166, 247
  GCHQ, 161
  hegemonic model, 143
  House of Lords, 197
  Huawei in, 9, 160, 161, 167, 250
  Indian colonies (1793–1947), 10, 36
  Industrial Revolution (c. 1760–1840), 28–9, 117
  industrial espionage, 10, 117
  Li Hongzhang in, 132

Libya intervention (2011), 137
Malayan colonies (1826–1957), 111
opium trade, 33, 35, 218
Opium Wars, 30, 34
quantum computing in, 209
Royal Navy, 186
Sino–Japanese war (1937–45), 20–21
students in, 232
tea in, 10
Treaty of Nanking (1842), 218
World War I (1914–18), 252, 253
United Nations (UN)
Belt and Road Initiative and, 143
Charter (1945), 109
General Assembly, 156
GGE, 155, 156
Guomindang and, 180
human rights definition, 106
International Telecommunication Union (ITU), 153
Internet Governance Forum, 152
Law of the Sea Convention (UNLOSC), 138
Responsibility to Protect, 137
Security Council, 64–5, 132
World Summit on the Information Society (WSIS), 152, 153
United States, 217, 244
Afghanistan War (2001–14), 136, 222
Artificial Intelligence in, 211, 213–14
Central Intelligence Agency (CIA), 46, 111, 120, 123, 124
California Gold Rush (1848–1855), 32, 218
China, relations with, see United States–China relations
civil-military integration, 214
Clean Network initiative (2020), 237
Committee on Foreign Investment (CFIUS), 228
COVID-19 pandemic (2019–20), 233–9, 251
Department of Commerce, 151, 168, 169, 170
Department of Defense, 123, 167, 214
Department of Justice, 162, 170, 223
Department of State, 123, 124, 219
dollar, 12, 61, 227, 243–4
drone warfare, 206, 214
education system, 213–14
Entities List, 102, 168
Five-Eyes, 6, 119, 166, 247
freedom of expression in, 156
global financial crisis (2007–8), 135–6, 222
global policeman role, 143
Gulf War I (1990–91), 136, 179
Gulf War II (2003–11), 137, 222

Hainan Island Incident (2001), 125–6, 222
hegemonic model, 143
Hollywood, 94, 132
Homeland Security, 166
Huawei in, 160, 165–6
immigration, 32, 213–14, 218–19
Intermediate-Range Nuclear Forces Treaty (1987), 185
Internet in, 57, 151–4
Korean War (1950–53), 133, 177, 220
Kosovo intervention (1999), 183, 221
mental hygiene in, 95
NASA, 204
National Security Strategy, 226, 228
Office of Personnel Management (OPM), 124
opium trade, 218, 219
Outer Space Treaty (1967), 204
Perry Expedition (1853–54), 253–4
pivot to Asia (2012), 136
Plaza Accord (1985), 227, 243–4
quantum technology in, 209
Red Scare (1947–57), 219
Revolution in Military Affairs, 136, 179
September 11 attacks (2001), 99
Shangri-La Dialogue, 223

Snowden disclosures (2013), 81, 118
Space Force, 205
Stuxnet attack (2010), 123
Surveillance Strike Complex, 183
Taiwan Relations Act (1979), 180–81
Taiwan Strait Crisis (1995–6), 181, 221, 222
telecommunications in, 165
Uighur Human Rights Policy Act (2020), 101
Unit 61398 indictments (2013), 223–4
War on Terror, 100, 136
United States–China relations, 217–39
Belgrade embassy bombing (1999), 221
Chinese Exclusion Act (1882), 32, 219
containment and, 134, 137, 244
COVID-19 pandemic (2019–20), 233–9
currency and, 12, 61, 225, 244
Cyber Agreement (2015), 119
cyberwarfare, 8, 117–27
espionage, 7, 111, 113–14, 115, 117–27, 223–4, 232
fishing vessels incident (2009), 223
global financial crisis (2007–8), 135–6, 222
Hainan Island Incident (2001), 125–6, 222

Hollywood and, 94, 132
Hong Kong and, 149, 237
Huawei and, 9, 160, 165–71,
237
Korean War (1950–53), 133,
177, 220
manufacturing and, 57–8, 188,
194, 225, 233, 246–51
NBA and, 149
Nixon's diplomacy (1969–74),
133, 180, 220
One-China policy, 225
opium trade, 218
Phase One deal (2020), 230
pivot to Asia (2012), 136
Red Scare (1947–57), 219
Shangri-La Dialogue, 223
Sino–American Mutual De-
fense Treaty (1954), 180
South China Sea and, 138–9,
223, 237
space and, 204–5
students and, 232
Sunnylands summit (2013),
66, 224
Taiwan and, 180–82, 221, 222
tech corporations, 57, 83
technology embargoes, 12, 47,
102, 168–70, 220, 221, 231,
237
trade war (2018–), 11, 196–7,
226–33, 248
Unit 61398 indictments (2013),
223–4
World War II (1939–45), 219

Xinjiang and, 101, 237
universalism, 74, 76, 146, 175
universities
China Academic Network, 54
Cultural Revolution (1966–76),
49, 54
data science in, 201
ideology in, 213
PLA and, 177
plagiarism in, 213
Reform and Opening Up
(1978–2005), 52–3
University of Cambridge, 20
University of Science and
Technology of China (USTC),
209
UNIX, 84
Unmanned Aerial Vehicles
(UAVs), 184, 187, 206, 214
Unrestricted Warfare (Qiao and
Wang), 184
Upjohn Institute, 247
urbanisation, 16

vaccination, 18
Venetian Republic (697–1797),
127
Venezuela, 164
Veracruz, Mexico, 132
Versailles Treaty (1919), 40–41,
43, 132
Vietnam, 52, 130, 173, 177,
178–9, 194, 220
Virtual Private Networks (VPNs),
63

Virtual Reality, 207
Vo Nguyen Giap, 177
Voitinsky, Grigori, 43

W88 miniaturised nuclear warhead, 113
Wahhabism, 99
Walia, Apjit, 249
Wall Street Journal, 236
Wanda, 233
wandao chaoche, 207
Wang Anshi, 97
wang ba, 59
Wang Huning, 76
Wang Jisi, 239
Wang Lijun, 71
Wang Pufeng, 183
Wang Shaogang, 75
Wang Xiangsui, 184
Wang Yangming, 28
Wang Yi, 235, 238
Wang Zhen, 70
wangluo kongjian, 55
War on Terror, 100, 136
warfare, 17
warlords, 38, 44
Warring States period (475–221 BCE), 24–7, 130
Washington Post, 147
Water Margin, 88
water stress, 230, 242
WeChat, 61, 237
Weibo, 64
Weimar Republic (1919–33), 75
Wen Jiabao, 60

Wenzhou train collision (2011), 64
Westphalian sovereignty, 130, 137
Whampoa Military Academy, 44
White Lotus Rebellion (1794–1804), 88
white-hat hackers, 83
Windows XP, 57, 83
Wing Loong drones, 206
Winnie the Pooh, 66
Wise, David, 113
wolf culture, 161
wolf warriors, 235, 238
women's rights, 39, 67, 195
World Bank, 234
World Conference on International Telecommunications (2012), 153
World Economic Forum, 2, 79, 227
World Health Organisation (WHO), 181, 234
World Intellectual Property Organisation (WIPO), 196
World Internet Conference (WIC), 79–80
World Summit on the Information Society (2003), 152
World Telecommunications Development Conference, 2
World Trade Organisation (WTO), 60, 134, 197, 222, 224–5, 228, 247

World War I (1914–18), 40, 252
World War II (1939–45), 166, 219
Wu Jingzi, 28
Wuhan, Hubei, 234, 235, 236
wumao dang, 65–6
Wuzhen, Zhejiang, 79

Xi Jinping, 10, 15, 69–75, 91,
  139, 163, 242
  art, views on, 94
  Belt and Road Initiative
    (2013–), 99, 140, 144
  Central Military Commission
    chair, 119, 174
  China Dream, 15, 74, 76, 140,
    193, 243
  civil-military fusion, 188
  community of common des-
    tiny, 140–43
  corruption crackdown, 72–4,
    175, 178
  Cultural Revolution (1966–76),
    50, 69
  Cyber Agreement (2015), 119
  cyber security, views on, 80, 84
  discourse power, 146
  Document Number Nine
    (2013), 74, 83
  'entanglement and struggle',
    243
  'Four Comprehensives' (2014),
    82
  Governance of China, The, 74–5
  Leading Small Groups (LSGs),
    77

Lou Jiwei, relationship with,
  197
  maritime power, views on, 186
  Marxism–Leninism, 72, 82
  Phase One deal (2020), 230
  PLA, reform of, 10, 175, 178,
    188
  Putonghua, use of, 55
  South China Sea policy, 138
  Sunnylands summit (2013),
    66, 224
  term-limits removal (2018), 66
  trade war (2018–), 229
  Trump, relations with, 226,
    229, 230
  Winnie the Pooh memes, 66
  World Economic Forum
    (2018), 227
  World Internet Conference
    (2015), 79–80
xiaokang shehui, 74, 140
Xi You Ji, 130
Xi Zhongxun, 50, 69
Xi'an Incident (1936), 94, 176
Xiamen Tuoke, 105–6
Xiangshan Forum (2018), 205,
  208
xiao fenhong, 65
xiaokang shehui, 74, 140
xinao, 96
Xinhai Revolution (1911–12), 37
Xinhua, 79, 92, 238
Xinjiang, 98–103, 114, 201, 237
xinxihua, 55, 58, 78, 183, 189, 190
Xiong'an, Hebei, 201

Xiongnu, 18, 130
Xu Caihou, 73, 175
Xu Lin, 80
Xuande, Ming Emperor, 20

Yan Fu, 38, 41
Yan Lianke, 93
Yan Xishan, 38
Yan Xuetong, 221
Yan'an Forum on Art and
    Literature, 93
Yan'an, Shaanxi, 45
Yang Jiechi, 142
Yang Shangkun, 70
Yanhuang Chunqiu, 92
Yanyang Tian (Hao), 93
Yao Emperor, 141
Yellow Emperor, 147
*Yellow Emperor's Classic of Internal
    Medicine*, 18
Yellow Turban Rebellion (184–
    205), 88
Yongle, Ming Emperor, 20
Yu Guang, 174
Yuan dynasty (1271–1368), 18,
    22, 23, 88, 130
Yuan Shikai, 37
Yunnan, 34

yuzhou, 23

Zhang Heng, 18
Zhang Qinsheng, 173
Zhang Xueliang, 176
Zhang Yang, 175
Zhang Yimou, 93, 147
Zhang Zhidong, 36
Zhao Lijian, 235
Zhao Ziyang, 53
Zheng He, 19, 131
zheng nengliang, 193–4
zhinenghua, 189
Zhishi Fenzi, 200
Zhongnanhai, Beijing, 89
Zhou dynasty (c. 1046–256 BCE),
    24, 130, 141
Zhou Enlai, 45, 110
Zhou Shuren, 39–40
Zhou Yongkang, 73, 120
Zhu Xi, 28
Zhu Yuanzhang, 20, 88
Zhuangzi, 25
Zimbabwe, 164
Ziye (Mao Dun), 42
ZTE, 58, 124, 145, 159, 161, 164,
    168–9, 170, 231, 237
Zuboff, Shoshana, 4